*Q - Quote
* -R - Research
+ I - Important

# THE
SORITES
PRINCIPLE

## How to harness the power of perseverance

Ian Gibbs

C000165062

The Sorites Principle
©2016, Guid Publications
Bruc, 107, 5-2
08009 Barcelona
España
Email: guid@guid-publications.com

Design: Estudio Hache

ISBN:
978-84-945213-4-8 paperback
978-84-945213-5-5 ebook

This book is dedicated to my father, Llewellyn Gibbs,

for everything he taught me and all the love he gave.

# Content

# Introduction

In my university days at Saint Andrew's, Scotland, I was fortunate enough to be befriended by John Firth, who is cited later in this book as being the originator of the phrase "Isn't it amazing what you can find to do when you don't want to do any work?"

On one such day he decided that one way to distract himself from his work was to distract me from mine and persuade me, without too much effort, to accompany him hill-walking one weekend. And so it came to pass that early one spring morning in 1985, I found myself parked just outside Fort William with the fresh morning sun on my face and a weighty rucksack on my back, admiring my newly acquired walking boots while John frothed about what a good time we were going to have and how much fun it was all going to be.

And so it was... for about the first 50 minutes.

After about an hour, however, I began to realise the new walking boots had been a mistake. They had seemed a fine fit in the shop, but now they were starting to rub in places I really didn't care for too much and even with the help of a cleanish handkerchief and some paper tissues strategically stuffed down my socks, the rubbing didn't seem to be much alleviated. But as I am nothing if not a trooper I decided to keep my complaining to a minimum[1] and we continued on to enjoy the sights, sounds and assorted fragrances the West Coast of Scotland has to offer in spring.

Not much after that, and in spite of the assurances to the contrary from the weatherman the previous night, a huge black cloud appeared out of nowhere and it started to rain. Not your pleasant sprinkle of April showers, but more like a flash flood. A sudden downfall that lasted barely a few minutes but just enough to get us completely soaked. We hadn't brought any waterproofs; we didn't think we were going to need them and we were well out in the open with no shelter. Our clothes were saturated.

But in almost no time the rain-clouds had moved on and the sun was out again. We soldiered on (John at this point had stopped frothing and started squelching) and our spirits were finally raised when we happened

---

1- John's version of this tends to wildly exaggerate the facts at this point

upon a pub. Our spirits were raised even further when we learnt that it was a free-house with four different local brews and two guest brews to sample. It would have been rude to refuse.

It was about four hours later when we, in some ways better and in others much worse, half staggered, half limped out of the pub thoroughly convinced the whole idea of hill-walking had been a huge mistake. We made it back to the car, and back home to St. Andrews and I have never tried to go hill-walking since.

In my later days as a coach, I use this personal anecdote as a metaphor for how we go about trying to do things, especially those things that can be considered an important goal or objective. We all know the expression "The journey of a thousand miles begins with a single step." I believe this sort of talk is not only mistaken but also downright dangerous. It's the sort of idea that brings frustration, disappointment and even depression. There is a tendency to think that as the idea of achieving our goals just one small step at a time is simple then logically it must be easy. I beg to differ. A journey of a thousand miles is littered with potholes and stumbling blocks, with wrong turns and dead-ends, with distractions, temptations and a whole range of unexpected obstacles. We think we can set out with the minimum of preparation but sadly, we are mistaken. How many of us have started a new year's resolution only to give up after just a few days? How many of us have embarked upon some great venture only to find that we don't have what it takes to persevere?

I would like to propose that the journey of a thousand miles does not begin with a single step. Instead, the journey of a thousand miles begins with a lot of planning and preparation, of increasing our awareness of what sort of mental as well as physical obstacles we are likely to come up against. How we can, at best, avoid them and, at worse, deal with them face-to-face when confronted.

And so that is what this book is about. It's a book about thousand mile journeys and how to set about walking them. It's about achieving great big things by doing lots of simple little things. It's about perseverance, progress, positivity and several other important words that begin with 'P', too.

But most importantly it's a book about how you can increase your chances of achieving all those big important things in your life that require effort and dedication that, up until now, you might have thought were beyond you.

In a way, this book is a testament unto itself. If it hadn't been for the ideas, stories, tricks and tips that I have collected and packed together into these pages, I would never have had the courage and perseverance to write it. I don't know whether a book of 77,000 words sounds like a little or a lot to you, but it seemed like a very daunting and formidable task to me especially during those first few months when I'd just started. This book is the fruit of a labour that took me almost a year of constant writing, re-writing and an incessant jotting down of ideas while at the same time fighting off the frequent visits from General Futility and his ugly little friends: Apathy, Distraction, Lethargy and Self-doubt. I'm pleased to say that General Futility and his cronies lost the battle, largely due to the ammunition of ideas and information in this book.

I have enjoyed writing it (mostly) and it contains part of my soul. I find that many self-help books or the like are fairly formal, dare I say, sterile texts that, while full of useful information, tend to lack the personality or individualism of the author. I hope that while you benefit from the information herein you also get to know me a little, what I am about, get to know my sense of humour and enjoy the stories and anecdotes for what they are meant to be: simple means to convey ideas in an easy-to-swallow form. I therefore hope you find this book as enjoyable to read as it has been for me to write and that its 'enjoyableness' is only equalled by how useful it is to help you, the reader, to achieve all those goals that are important to you.

## Stating the Obvious

A fundamental law of coaching is it is confidential. Coaching is based on trust. Everything that a client divulges to their coach is absolutely private. A person has to open up quite a lot in order for their coaching relationship to be successful and this is unlikely to happen if they think that their coach is going to go writing about it afterwards.

For this reason, I would like to state categorically that while many of the examples and anecdotes I have included in these pages are squarely founded on my clients' experiences (as well as my own), their names and specific details have been altered to avoid any undesired attention, embarrassment or lawsuits. So as they say in the cinema, any apparent similarity between the people mentioned in this book and those out there in the real world are entirely coincidental - honestly.

## In Praise of My Wife

While reading this book, you will come across the occasional description (or confession) of my domestic lifestyle. By this I mean details about how I do the housework and suchlike. At first glance I might give you the impression I do most of the housework while my wife does practically nothing. This is not exactly true. We all tend to overestimate our own contribution in such situations. If you ask any husband and wife to each estimate what percentage of the housework they do, more often than not the two figures add up to more than 100%. To be honest, even though I'm aware of this tendency, the same observation about the imbalance of domestic chores occurs to me. Try it for yourself. Now it is true that in my case I do most of the dishes, the laundry and the hoovering (of her own volition, my wife admits that she doesn't even know how the vacuum cleaner works), I do the bulk of the shopping, the D.I.Y., making the fire.[2] It's also my job to get the kids up, dressed and breakfasted, prepare their lunchboxes and take them to school weekdays. But, as my beloved points out this is because she has a 'proper job' where she has to get up at an 'ungodly' hour (referring to 7am) and comes home knackered (from all that sitting she has to do at her desk, I assume). She's also quick to point out that given the horrendous incompatibility the Spanish working timetable has with having kids, that if it weren't for the fact that she took a cut in pay to reduce her working hours, she wouldn't even be able to help pick the kids up from school in the afternoons.

---

2- We don't have central heating, we have a real log-burning fire which I dearly love when it's lit and roaring away - less so when I get up in the grim mid-winter months to discover that the bloody thing's gone out and it's cold, dark and pissing it down outside where the stupid firewood is kept

So, although I do quite a bit around the house, my wife does most of the cooking, tidying, keeping an eye on the accounts, putting away the weekly mountain of washed and dried children's clothes and looking after the kids in general, both in sickness as in health. In fact I would like to state for the record that my wife has the patience of a saint. Not only with the constant demands, tantrums and attention-grabbing tactics of the twins but also with the constant demands, tantrums and attention-grabbing tactics of my own. In her own words, and she has said this on more than one occasion during these last twelve months, "Now I understand why authors so often give thanks to their partners for all their support."

# 1. Sorites? What's Sorites?

Imagine that it's a lovely day and that you're sitting in your garden enjoying a nice quiet cup of tea when there is a huge kerfuffle from somewhere beyond the bottom of your garden and suddenly a large out-of-control yellow dumper truck reverses through the privet and spills its load of sand onto your recently manicured lawn. The driver apologises profusely but as nobody seems to be hurt he gets back in the cab and after assuring you that someone from the council will be round in the morning to 'sort things out' drives off leaving you with a very large heap of sand which reminds you of one of the more decrepit pyramids from the neighbours' holiday photos from last year.

The rest of the day passes uneventfully and sure enough at 9 o'clock the following morning your doorbell rings. You open the front door to discover a little man in a brown jacket accompanied by another little man in blue overalls. The man in brown apologises for all the inconvenience and assures you that the removal of the heap of sand from your garden will begin immediately. This pleases you. Less than 24 hours and something

1

is being done. The council have clearly improved their public services department (getting that hole in the pavement sorted took two years).

"Is it okay if we start now?" says the man.

"Of course" you reply and the three of you go round to the scene of the crime.

"Alright, Bob" says the little man. "You know the procedure. I'll see you in the office later." And with a courteous nod he leaves.

Bob, the man in the overalls, then prepares himself and, just as you're starting to wonder whether he's going to ask the use of your new wheelbarrow, he produces from his pocket a small transparent self-sealing bag the size of a large postage stamp and a pair of tweezers. He then bends down and carefully picks up a single grain of sand from the heap, puts it into the tiny bag, seals it, winks and puts it back in his pocket.

"See you tomorrow!" he says cheerfully and walks away.

"What?" You exclaim as you chase after him. "You've got to be joking"

"Not at all. It's the new Sorites way of working. One grain of sand per day"

"What?!" you exclaim, "One grain of sand per day? It's the stupidest thing I've ever heard. I have a heap of sand in my garden now and I'll still have a heap of sand in my garden tomorrow. What's the point? One grain of sand makes no difference at all!"

As you watch Bob drive off in his little white van you start to get the feeling that this might take a bit longer than you were hoping.

"One grain of sand makes no difference at all": This is one of the two basic ideas (or premises) of the Sorites Paradox. The word 'Sorites' is Ancient Greek for 'heap' and the Sorites Paradox considers how we perceive (or fail to perceive) the erosion of a heap of sand over a period by removing one grain of sand at a time.

When we remove just one grain it makes a small difference but the difference is so microscopically small that it is considered 'insignificant' to the perceiver. If you compare the two photos below I think it's reasonable to say that even though the one on the right has one grain less than the one on the left, the difference is insignificant. They might as well be two photos of the same thing. But in spite of this insignificant removal of a solitary grain, the heap can be gradually reduced slowly over time, grain by grain, until it has paradoxically disappeared completely. Paradoxically because, as we've just established, at no point does the removal of just a single grain change your viewpoint; you never notice the heap getting smaller.

It is the subtleness that is the important factor. If, while you had gone out to do the shopping, someone came and removed a couple of shovels' worth of sand, when you came back you would notice the difference.

But if the same amount of sand is removed grain by grain each time you popped off for lunch or went to the loo, then you would be completely oblivious to the process.

**Figure 1:     Before**                              **After (with one grain less)**

So, using this 'new Sorites way of working', the complete removal of the heap of sand from your garden would be a long and drawn out process. Even if we assumed your heap to be an extremely modest one of just a millions grains, by removing one grain a day it would still take 2,740 years to clear up completely which is quite a long time even for the council.

This means that after 2,739 years your future heirs will have a 'heap made up of just a few hundred grains. In fact, eventually there would be a 'heap' of just one grain and probably quite a large party to celebrate.[3]

---

3- For a more philosophical analysis of the Sorites Paradox as well as paradoxes in general, please see Appendix I.

Leaving the philosophy aside, the Sorites Paradox is an example of how insignificant change leads to surprisingly significant results.

And this is the nub of the matter. Change can and often does happen so slowly and so subtly that we are completely unaware of it. You can test it out for yourself. Look at yourself in the mirror carefully for ten minutes and try to observe your hair grow, or if you don't have much hair watch your stubble. After ten minutes, or as long as you can stand it, you will have noticed no change whatsoever. But in spite of the fact that you can't see it, it is still growing - insignificantly slowly but incessant, relentless and unwavering nonetheless so at some point, but much later on, you will eventually notice that you need a haircut, shave, depilation or whatever method you choose for controlling your hirsuteness. Sometimes insignificant change happens regardless of what we do (like aging) and sometimes we are totally responsible for the change (like slowly gaining weight or emigrating).[4] So at this point I'd like to divide these changes into two kinds: the kind that happens regardless of what we do and the kind that very much depends on our own actions.

The first kind includes gradual changes that you as an individual have no control over whatsoever. These include things like continental drift (the Mediterranean Sea will be squashed out of existence as Europe and Africa slowly but relentlessly collide), evolution of a species (Homo Erectus slowly evolved into Homo Sapiens), coastal erosion (Happisburgh, in Norfolk used to be an inland village. Now it's a coastal village and in a few centuries will likely be a marine curiosity) and the sinking of landmasses (London is sinking by about 1mm per year) which are changes that are

---

4- You might reasonably think that going to live permanently in another country is not a process that happens little by little. But although I have the pleasure of living in the beautifully sunny and vibrantly cosmopolitan city of Barcelona, in all truth, I never intended to do so. I came out here almost by accident. I was unsuccessfully trying to get a job as an English language teacher in Paris. So when I was offered work in Barcelona, I took it. My intention was to stay here for one or maybe two years and then move on - to Paris, Prague or maybe even Saudi Arabia where I could work tax-free for a couple of years, save up and return home with enough money to buy a small castle. But during my first few months here, things began to happen. I made friends. I developed a social life. I learned Spanish. I started dating local girls. I got promoted. Then, after inheriting a modest amount I was able to buy a small flat (3 flights up with no lift and so small that the shower cubicle and toilet occupied the same space which meant you could sit on the loo and have a shower at the same time - useful if you're in a hurry!) Slowly, step by step, I became more attached to the place. I set up my own business here. I got married to a Barcelona girl. My kids were born here and so are half Spanish. And now my publisher is based here in Barcelona, too. So, even though it was never originally my intention, my permanency here in the 'Diamond of the Med', as Barcelona is also known, is yet another example of something that has happened little by little.

so slow they are hard to perceive even when viewed over a lifetime. This category would also include yourself growing wrinklier and/or balder (sorry but it's true).

The second kind of change therefore is that which gradually happens but is entirely due to our own individual actions or lack of action such as keeping fit, learning to speak a new language, developing bad posture, learning to play a musical instrument, losing touch with friends, becoming a leading expert in a given subject, having a clean and tidy house (or allowing it to become a mess) or keeping the garden well-manicured (or allowing it to become overrun with weeds).

Notice that I'm not including here things like getting fired, winning the lottery, breaking your leg or giving birth. These are not gradual changes. They are changes that are so obvious that the way we relate to them is completely different. These changes, like an explosion in the local firework factory, have a large and immediately perceivable effect. There is an awareness of the change and usually an emotional and physical reaction. While such change is intrinsically interesting it is not the type of change that we are interested in here.

The type of change that interests us in this book is that which happens so gradually that we can be completely unaware of it, it seems to have no significant effect what so ever. In a way, it slips under our radar and doesn't cause any reaction. After all, how can you react to something that you don't notice? You might only notice the change after a long period of time and even then only if you could remember what things were like before. It's like Andy Warhol said, "When a situation develops gradually, no matter how weird that situation is, you get used to it." This is why those family photos and videos from our (not so distant) past are in some small way a bit shocking - it makes you aware of all those insignificant changes that have been happening to us below our radar.

So to summarise: Insignificant change comes in two forms.

1. Change that is inevitable regardless of what we choose to do as an individual.

2. Change that only happens because of what we choose (not) to do as an individual.

Although the first kind of gradual change is interesting (at least I find it interesting that Japan and the U.S. will - tectonically speaking - soon become united), we won't be considering it in the rest of this book. There's nothing we can do about it so what's the point of worrying? It is the second kind that is of interest and is what we're going to be looking at from here onward: The slow but steady change we can cause to happen when we apply ourselves over a long period of time and what we can do to keep applying ourselves when the change we want to make is so insignificant it happens without us noticing.

If we can accept that a mountain can be eroded over time, little by little, is it not therefore equally acceptable that we can create a mountain little by little over time also without noticing? Certainly this is true if the number of newspapers in my garage is anything to go by. And what if that metaphorical mountain was something big that we wanted to achieve intentionally?

If the paradox of the forever diminishing heap is called the Sorites Paradox, then it seems only fitting that the principle of achieving great change by the application of insignificant actions be called the Sorites Principle and for a more detailed consideration I suggest starting the next chapter.

## Things to Think About

- The Sorites Paradox, the paradox of the never decreasing heap, is an example of how, when insignificant change happens, we are unable to perceive it.

- Many of the changes we experience in life happen little by little and therefore we are often unaware them, too.

- When we try to change ourselves by learning a new skill, improving our health or our behaviour, progress can happen very slowly - so slowly that we simply don't notice it.

## Questions to Ask Yourself (and Answer)

- How many examples of the Sorites Paradox are you experiencing right now?
- Apart from aging what other slow but steady changes are affecting your life?
- Which of these are happening because of your (lack of) actions and which are happening regardless of them?
- What metaphorical mountains could you move if you had the perseverance to do it little by little every day?

# 2 The Sorites Principle

*"Little by little, one travels far"* - J.R.R. Tolkien

*"The journey of a thousand miles begins with you having to go back to get your passport"*

When I was about eight years old, my mother did a cake-decorating course. One day she produced a lovely creation covered in white icing, lovingly and meticulously decorated with hundreds of tiny blue and white flowery sugar squirls all around the base and all around the rim. Her success was to have produced a masterpiece. Her failure, however, was to leave it in the living-room under a cloth alone with an 8 year-old. My reasoning was simple - there were so many flowery icing-sugar squirls that nobody would notice if one were to 'disappear'. It did. It was deliciously sweet and crumbly in a dusty, crunchy sort of way. Of course the same reasoning followed five minutes later and throughout the rest of the afternoon. Needless to say that there were substantially fewer sugar squirls by the time I went to bed. I wasn't there the following day to see my mother's reaction when she unveiled her creation but I understand that 'disappointed' didn't come anywhere close. We both learnt that day that the consequence of constantly repeating an insignificant action can be quite substantial.

If you put your mind to it, you'd be surprised by what you could achieve by applying yourself every day. According to the experts, if you wanted to become one of the world's top trombonists you would 'only' need to practise for about ten thousand hours which, unless you have a soundproof room, would mean annoying your family and neighbours for four hours a day, every day, for almost seven years. 'But' I hear you say 'surely a large amount depends on talent, doesn't it?' Well, actually the answer is 'no' and 'yes'. It really depends on what you mean by talent.

To start with... no. If by talent you mean a latent ability to play the trombone then no, you don't need talent to become very good at playing the trombone or any other instrument. The human brain is rather more malleable than scientists used to think. The belief was that the human brain developed through childhood and adolescence and then pretty much settled down to relax and enjoy the ride for the rest of it. 'You can't teach an old dog new tricks' is the old adage that reflects this idea - an idea which we now know to be wrong.

Since the end of the twentieth century there have been huge developments in imaging techniques used to investigate the brain and how it does what it does. One of these discoveries is that the brain is, in fact, constantly changing and adapting. The brain cells that are responsible for our thinking (called neurons) are constantly evolving, growing and withering according to our experiences. Every new thought that you have creates new connections between neurons (known as synapses) and the more you have the same thoughts then the stronger those connections become. You might be a bit dubious of this. After all, Granny has had her mobile phone for three years and still doesn't know how to use it. Trust me on this. If it meant getting free food, Granny would learn how to use her mobile phone today. Within reason we now know that anyone can learn anything if they practise enough. The brain is much more adaptive than we used to believe. Award winning soccer coach Dr. Ivan Joseph once had to train a goal keeper who couldn't catch a ball to save his life. The solution? Joseph set him to kick a ball against a wall and catch it 350 times a day for eight months. By the end of the period not only was he able to catch a ball but he went on to be an international goal keeper.

Given the right amount of input the brain never stops learning. It's even possible to get parts of your brain to learn to do the tasks usually done by other parts of your brain. People who, due to accident or illness (such as stroke victims), have lost the use of one part of their brain that did a certain task can, with the right rehabilitation, relearn how to do things by adapting other areas of their brain to do that same task. In a nutshell, with enough time and practice, you can get your brain to learn to do almost anything you want. So this is why my answer to 'Does learning something depend on talent?' is 'no'.[5]

However, learning to do something by practising four hours a day every day for years on end requires perseverance. It requires that you put in the hours which means that you must be willing and able to put in the hours. Even if you are completely useless at playing the trombone, if you love it and relish every minute you spend blasting away on the damn thing then, given seven years in the hands of a good (and very patient) trombone teacher, you will become a proficient trombonist.

And there lies the rub. It is not the initial ability of the student that is important; it is the willingness to learn. There are none so blind as those who will not see and there are none so ignorant as those who don't have the perseverance to learn. Here then is another possible interpretation of talent. Talent could be seen as the ability to want to do something, to stick at it, to go the whole nine yards. So this is why my answer to 'Does learning something depend on talent?' is 'yes'.

---

5- You might be quite rightly tempted to doubt this idea. "What about the outstandingly talented people such as Mozart?" you might ask. It is undeniable that given the same amount of practice, one individual will improve more than another. The issue here, however, is how important that practice and experience is. Mozart, for example, didn't produce anything noteworthy until after he was twenty years old but before then, and almost from the very moment he was born, he was listening to and absorbing music. Mozart's father was a music teacher and his students came to his house to practise. Young Mozart would have been able to hear these students play for hours and hours every day. The question is this: If Mozart's father hadn't been a music teacher, if Mozart hadn't listened to thousands of hours of music during his childhood, if he hadn't had a house with a piano to practise on himself, if he hadn't been raised in a family environment where music was so important and valued, would he still have grown up to be the musical genius he was? For a more profound discussion of Mozart I recommend reading 'Bounce' by Matthew Syed.

But whichever way you look at it, the result is the same: if you want to overcome some great difficulty, if you want to learn something that is hard to learn then you have to put your mind to it; you have to do the time.

Remember the film *The Shawshank Redemption*? Starring Tim Robbins and Morgan Freeman, it tells the story of a banker who is mistakenly given life imprisonment for a murder he didn't commit. It's one of my favourite films - a classic! It has many things going for it. But what makes it stand out for me is not the theme of maintaining dignity and honour in a chaotic environment, nor the ability to achieve happiness where happiness doesn't usually exist. No. What for me stands out the most is that the hero (Robbins) manages to dig, over a period of 17 years, a two-foot diameter tunnel, over ten feet long using a small rock hammer the size of a child's toy. That for me is moving a heap little by little. That is the result of applying the basic principle of this book which for succinctness I will refer to as the Sorites Principle and define as follows:

*The Sorites Principle:*

*The constant application of insignificant actions when coherently focussed will inevitably lead to dramatically significant results.*

It is the idea behind doing the journey one step at a time or eating the cake one mouthful at a time. It is a powerful tool because it doesn't require great intelligence, or strength or any other incredible talent. You don't need to be incredibly wealthy, powerful, beautiful or privileged. All you need is a goal, the time to achieve it and a steady perseverance (so, actually if you're celebrating your 105th birthday this might not be for you although it would make an excellent birthday present for your grandchildren). We can all achieve amazing results by doing little actions over and over again.

## Little Steps Are Easy Steps

A few days ago I arrived home from a frenetic day in the office. I opened the front gate to be greeted by a bouncy and elated young Labrador (called Scottie) and as I made my way to the front door of the house - a journey of some 20 feet, I found in my path a doll, presumably left there by my five-year-old daughter[6] (called Sol). I picked it up absentmindedly and entered my home, where two five-year-olds had spent the day playing.

The day our home is burgled and ransacked, I doubt that we would be able to tell at first glance. 'Ransacked' seems to be the defining adjective of the state of our home. Toys, cushions and assorted detritus are liberally scattered about the place. Just looking at the mess gives me palpitations and my wife a headache. The place has to be tidied but the apparent enormity of the disaster area is immediately off-putting - giving me the knee-jerk reaction of just turning round and heading off down the road to the bar. Yet, tidying up a disaster area is just another example of achieving a big thing by carrying out a lot of little things; I had, without any stress or mental squirming, picked up the aforementioned doll outside. So what's the problem of just repeating an easy action 200 times? The problem is all in our head. It's just the problematic, self-defeatist way we look at 'big' objectives. Instead of simply looking at a big objective as a collection of lots of little easy actions, we naturally look at the task as something that has to be done 'all in one go' and that can appear much more intimidating.

That we can achieve great things by doing lots of little things over and over again is not earth shattering news. We all know the 'Journey of a thousand miles' stuff. Nevertheless, given that so many things that we desire can be achieved little by little, why is it that so often we fail to follow through? You know from the beginning that getting your stomach muscles to look like a six-pack takes perseverance, as does setting up your own business or learning Spanish. And yet even though we start out with enthusiasm, after just a relatively short time we give up. What goes wrong? Why do we give up? How many New Year's resolutions have been broken before the end of January? How many times have we set out to do something but just run out of resolution? What factors do we need to take into account if we find a mountain that we want to move little by little? How can we make the most of the Sorites Principle? This is what we shall consider in the following chapters.

---

6- Scottie seems to find the children's toys of no interest whatsoever. The dog we had before Scottie was a golden retriever called Críspulo (Crispy to his friends) and needless to say for anyone who has had experience of golden retrievers, he found all the kids' toys absolutely irresistible and would proudly strut around with as many of them in his mouth as he could fit as if to say 'Look at me! Look what I've got! Aren't I clever?!'
The kids learned the word for 'dog drool' in three languages at a very early age.

## Things to Think About

✽ Large significant changes can happen because of many, many small insignificant ones.

✽ Small insignificant changes can be the result of the application of lots of small insignificant actions.

✽ Therefore, we can achieve 'large' goals by the constant application of easy insignificant actions providing all the little actions contribute to taking us in the right direction.

✽ Put another way - the constant application of insignificant actions when coherently focussed will inevitably lead to dramatically significant results.

✽ This is the Sorites Principle.

✽ Doing something easy every day is not a question of intelligence, age, wealth, physical strength, beauty or any other privilege; it's a question of just doing it. Everyone can do it. You can do it.

✽ Although the Sorites Principle can't help you achieve everything, it can help you to achieve a surprisingly large number of goals that you might have thought beyond you.

## Questions to Ask Yourself (and Answer)

❤ How many major achievements have you successfully made which were the combination of a series of small actions?

❤ If you had started five years ago, what goals could you have accomplished by now using the little by little process?

❤ What things would you like to achieve in the future if you could improve your perseverance?

# **3** Putting it into Practice

*Bob goes to Barcelona and while he is in the taxi from the airport to the hotel he discovers that the taxi driver is studying English. "Every day..." boasts the taxi driver"...I memorise ten words. That means that in two years I learn seven thousand!" "Seven thousand..." remarks Bob impressed, "...wherever do you store so many words?" The taxi driver winks knowledgeably, taps the side of his head and says "Here... in my bum!"*

At times it seems that the Sorites Principle is the most normal thing in the world. Everything you've learned, you've learned little by little: walking, talking or doing your tax returns. Nobody is born with a 'knowledge chip' in their brains that tells them how to speak a language and no one can take a pill to instantly know how to fly a helicopter (at least not at the moment). None of this is surprising. We accept it because… well, because there's no alternative.

But there are other times when we overlook just how much can be achieved 'little by little' when we think about a task which we perceive as being rather large. Instead of looking at it as a series of lots and lots of tiny little tasks we see it as one great big fat, formidable task.

## A Formidable Task

One trivial example of this was the top draw of my desk. Over many happy years of work, my top drawer had developed into some sort of Black Hole sucking in all sorts of office debris: thousands of things that didn't work, fit or belong. Biros with no ink, staples of bizarre sizes, keys which belonged to no one, bits of printers that no longer existed... you know exactly what I'm talking about, don't you? I knew full well that one day I'd have to clean it out but as it was a rather daunting task (what if the bits started to fight back?) it always seemed to get put off another year. Then one day I remembered the Sorites Principle and I decided that instead of sorting out my top drawer in one go I would remove just one object each day (or maybe more if I were feeling brave). The result? In less than a month I had things under control. Easy! Just by dedicating a few seconds each day I was able to deal with something that had taken me years to get round to.

But is it really that easy? Obviously not, otherwise you wouldn't be reading this book, would you? Why don't all prisoners dig tunnels to freedom or all would-be trombonists become experts? What are the common reasons why we fail to follow things through? And what can we do about it?

The first and simplest reason is that it just doesn't occur to us. A friend of mine decided to redecorate his house using some nice uplifting colours. In each room when he got to the light switches and the electric sockets he painted around them as carefully as he could. Of course as he was only human he occasionally got a bit of paint on the edge of the switch or socket and as they were all white and the paint was of a different colour the overall impression was not of a perfectly professional job. I tend to pride myself on my DIY abilities (maybe a bit too much for my own good at times). I asked him why he hadn't simply unscrewed the casings and then put them back on when he'd finished as it would have saved time and looked much better. "It never occurred to me" was his answer. So often it seems like the obvious eludes us with frustrating or even heart-breaking results.

A tragic accident happened in China while I was writing this book. A mother was 'eaten' by an escalator in a commercial centre. She rode up the escalator with her young son but when she got to the top a metal floor plate that hadn't been screwed down properly collapsed and although she was able to push her little boy to safety she fell into the mechanism and to her demise. Three employees of the centre were standing just a couple of feet from her at the time and witnessed the whole tragic accident. They were also standing just a few feet away from the emergency stop button. Why didn't any of them press the button to save the poor mother's life? In that moment of horror, it just never occurred to them.

Now, I'm sure that in this case the 'non-occurrence' of the idea of hitting the emergency stop button was mostly due to the shock of the moment. But I've come across many examples of people not doing something for years without a simple idea occurring to them. We are creatures of habit. If an idea fails to cross our mind today, then the likelihood of it failing to cross our mind tomorrow is more than likely. Habits, both good and bad, can have a huge effect on our lives and we shall be exploring them later.

Another reason why we don't apply the Sorites Principle is because of our lack of patience. In today's society we are becoming more and more accustomed to the idea that when we want something, it has to be done immediately. Having to wait for a meal to be cooked or a suit to be made is less and less acceptable. We want it now! If we want to improve our waistline we want it by the end of the month. If we want to set up our own business, we want it up and making a profit definitely before our dole runs out at the end of the year. And expecting too much, too soon leads to another reason why we don't use the power of the Sorites Principle - the feeling of futility: that the whole idea of trying to achieve something 'big' is pointless, that we are incapable of achieving 'big' goals and the whole concept would just be one great monumental waste of time. This is due to some naturally occurring internal resistance in our minds. This is entirely due to the way in which we perceive the goal and the task(s) required to achieve it. If we consider the task as a whole (instead of lots of small ones), it can easily dampen our enthusiasm. There's a rebellious little voice inside our head that says "No! It's too big! It's too difficult!" I know of people who are put off reading Lord of the Rings because it's over a thousand pages long which is a pity because it is brilliant and that if you were to just enjoy it chapter by chapter it is no more formidable than any other book. It's just that novels with page counts that run into four digits are quite uncommon and therefore out of our comfort zone. But if we're trying to achieve something substantial then most likely we're trying something out of our comfort zone and our comfort zone can be so very enticing. There is a stubborn inner part of us that doesn't like the 'new' or the 'different'. It likes 'familiar', 'safe' and 'comfortable' - hence the name 'Comfort Zone'. Although we might decide that embarking upon some long-term goal seems like a good thing, the stubborn part of us has some definite opinions on the matter, too, and they are not particularly conducive to our new mission.

Even if we do remember the Sorites Principle, sometimes we fail to recognise that certain tasks that seem quite daunting are just a group of smaller tasks. For instance, spring cleaning the kitchen probably seems like a major task, but if you did just one shelf of each cupboard at a time (starting at the top and working your way down) then suddenly it appears more manageable. What's the most daunting task that you're putting off at the moment? If it's something like telling your parents you're pregnant or gay (or both) then, no, the Sorites Principle is not for you - they are not the sort of tasks that can be broken down into lots of little parts (leaving copies of 'What Pram?' or 'Gay Pride Weekly' about the house doesn't count) but finding a new job, setting up your own band, becoming a successful freelance photographer, learning to control your kids, getting healthier, giving up smoking and sorting your life out, most definitely are.

Yet another reason why we don't use the Sorites Principle is that we don't know what it is that we actually want to do. Let's say that the summer holidays are looming up on the calendar and you've just had one of those experiences with your bathroom scales. Enough is enough! You are going to shed a few excess pounds quick before you get mistaken for a beached whale and a bunch of Greenpeace volunteers try to push you back in the sea. So you skip breakfast and then forego the doughnut that usually accompanies your eleven o'clock coffee (white with one sugar) but by lunchtime you're ravenous. You try your best with a salad and a slice of quiche but already it's becoming unbearable. After lunch you have a meeting with your superior which doesn't go well. You finish the meeting stressed and tired. As if by magic, you find that a chocolate biscuit has miraculously materialised in your hand and, well, you did skip that doughnut so you deserve one…or maybe two as doughnuts have more calories, don't they? At home with the family it's dinner time and everyone is stuffing themselves (everyone except Sally who's decided that today she doesn't like pasta). You're tired, hungry and after all you did skip breakfast and you had a healthy lunch so eating a decent dinner is acceptable. After all, you don't want to overdo it do you? You go to bed with an uneasy feeling about the success of your latest 'lose weight' venture. It doesn't help when you weigh yourself the following morning to discover your weight has actually gone up.

What's missing here is a plan: A clear objective carefully thought out with a few important details included. If you were going to have a new kitchen put in, you wouldn't just get in a few boxes of tiles, a bit of random Formica and the first electrical appliances you came across and hope that somehow they would put themselves together in some miraculous way. No, you would measure what you've got and you'd start looking for what options would fit. You'd take into account colour, style, size and cost. You'd probably discuss the matter with your partner for a second opinion. Then you might ask for quotes from a few places and after selecting the supplier you would probably discuss the issue of time: when can the process start and how long will it take? Only then would you sign on the dotted line and embark upon your 'New Kitchen Project'.

And so it is with the Sorites Principle. You have to have an objective and a plan. You need to know your precise destination and you need to have a map of how to get there. In other words, you have to have a clear idea of what it is you want to achieve and how you intend to achieve it.

If you don't know what it is you're trying to achieve, then you'll probably just plod through the years following the path of least resistance, which unfortunately usually equates to doing what other people want you to do. There is, I admit, a certain life philosophy of just living in the now, mindfully living out one's day with a kind of serene Taoist flow. If you are the sort of person suited for this, then great but it's a choice. For me life is about the thrill and passion of setting yourself a goal and following it through to the end.[7] In fact, there are psychological benefits of having goals in life.[8] One of the key factors to being happy is having a purpose or goal and progressing each day in pursuit of that goal. It gives you a reason for getting up each day and something to look forward to.

Then again if you do know what you want but you're not sure about how to get it then you're just going to wander through life aimlessly and feeling a bit frustrated seeing that what you want never seems to be getting any closer. Therefore, goals are important but only if they are attainable, benevolent and backed up by progress.

Here you might be thinking this all sounds very well but how do we translate it into practical actions? Well, I'm glad you asked because it is exactly what the rest of this book is all about. We will address this issue in a series of steps. The first one is to understand and accept the Sorites Principle: that the constant application of insignificant actions when coherently focussed will inevitably lead to dramatically significant results. Straight away you are acknowledging that, given enough perseverance, you can move mountains. Welcome to the dawn of a new era of your life!

The method to make practical use of this principle can be simplified into three simple steps. Please note that here, 'simple' does not equate with 'easy'. Nevertheless, these three steps, if followed correctly, will inevitably get you to where you want to be. Each step has a chapter dedicated to it. Here I will briefly outline each one so you get a feeling for them, or if you prefer, you can skip straight to the chapter of your choice as they are independent of each other.

---

7- At which point my wife would roll her eyes and point out that the fence I started to mend when we first bought the house in 2006 is still not finished, as is the bracket holding the telly onto the wall (it just needs a lick of paint) and the bedroom ceiling still hasn't been properly repaired three years after promising that I would do it "next weekend". My reply, of course, is that it is a delicate question of balancing time, resources and priorities and, after all, Rome wasn't built in a day! Besides, all my time is taken up with my book. Her reply is to point out that if she had the same lame excuse for not getting dinner ready, I wouldn't be so blasé about the matter. There's no reasoning with some people.

8- These psychological benefits suppose that your goal is the right sort of goal and that means positive, realistic, beneficial and feasible. Having a goal that has one or more of the opposite components (i.e. negative, unrealistic, harmful or impractical) can lead to unwanted stress, frustration, low self-esteem or a sense of failure. The goal of trying to fiddle as much money out of your company as possible is not going to cultivate habits or behaviour that are going to make you happy.

## Figure 2: The Sorites Principle in three steps

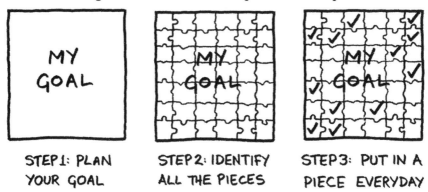

STEP 1: PLAN
YOUR GOAL

STEP 2: IDENTIFY
ALL THE PIECES

STEP 3: PUT IN A
PIECE EVERYDAY

# Step 1. The Plan

Assuming that you have the idea of what you really want[9] (e.g. a new kitchen, a new job or a new life) then you have to decide what tasks you are going to do to achieve it. This requires thought. 'There's more than one way to skin a cat' as they say and identifying which one you are going to opt for and all the tasks it involves (the obvious ones and the less obvious ones) can require clear logical thinking mixed with a creative flair. Here is where we sometimes start to come unstuck straight away, impulsively launching ourselves towards a new goal without really thinking things through. New Year's resolutions are a prime example. It's 11:30pm on New Year's Eve. You're standing with a glass of bubbly in your hand and a paper hat on your head feeling slightly the worse for wear. You've got thirty minutes to go and you still haven't come up with a New Year's resolution yet. Your mind's already a little fuzzy from what you've already consumed during the previous hours of celebration and the apparent conversation you seem to be having with a couple about how they avoided a 'frightful' Christmas by going skiing in the Alps seems to be making it fuzzier. You know it would be a good idea to take the start of a new year as an opportunity for doing something to improve your lot like giving up smoking, getting a steady partner (that new assistant

---

9- When I was researching this book, many people I spoke to already knew what they would like to achieve if they could increase their power of perseverance. But I admit that 'many people' is not everybody. Therefore, I have included a chapter dedicated to choosing your goal just in case you are one of those who'd still like to give it a bit more thought.

in accounts seems nice), getting your finances under control or doing a bit more exercise. But they all seem to blur somewhat. As you sway in the revelry of 'Auld Lang Syne' you plump for the smoking (as it might help with the other options) and now having chosen a resolution you can relax and get on enjoying yourself in the company of another large glass of bubbly.

Twelve hours later you're slumped somewhere in your dressing gown with your second cigarette starting to suspect that it's actually the alcohol rather than the nicotine that is jeopardising your future wellbeing and you are absolutely convinced that you should definitely bear this in mind when it comes to making your New Year's Resolutions next time.

Planning what you want to achieve is something you should not do impulsively nor under duress. You need to do it slowly and carefully in the cold light of day where you can think the whole thing through - preferably with a clear and sober mind, free of distractions. Only then, having established what you want your new life to be and how you expect to achieve it, can you move on to step two.

## Step 2. The Pieces of the Puzzle

The basic idea behind step two is to break down your journey into lots of little steps. This bit seems obvious. But you might be surprised that there are probably quite a lot of steps that you haven't considered so far. Let me explain this by using the analogy of a jigsaw puzzle. If you can imagine your newly intended life as an image, then this image could (just like the picture on the box of a jigsaw puzzle) be broken up into lots of little pieces. In our analogy, each little piece represents one small action, one small achievement that you will have made in order to construct the whole puzzle. Some of these pieces that constitute the main part of the image are obvious. However, there are lots of pieces of blank sky, general foliage or whatever that, while containing none of the important detail, are still needed to support the other pieces and to complete the whole picture.

These parts of our jigsaw we might call peripheral actions because they don't seem to contribute to the main objective directly. Nevertheless, as you will see, although they might seem irrelevant at the moment, they might very well provide important support for the main objective sometime in the future in ways that are completely unpredictable at the moment. I feel that an example would help clarify things.

Let's say that after careful consideration you have decided that it is your mission in life to be one of the world's greatest trombone players. Marvellous for you - not so much for the rest of your family and neighbours! Obvious parts of the puzzle are acquiring a trombone, practising (at least 4 hours a day), getting a good teacher and thinking up a good title for your autobiography (*How I became Supertrombonist*, for example). However, peripheral actions to consider would be such things as attending concerts, getting a business card printed, letting others know of your new career, contacting local press, joining new groups on social media, subscribing to 'What Trombone' or following current famous trombonists on LinkedIn or Twitter, having friends who are musicians, joining a local band, actively searching for opportunities to play in public and to promote yourself in the eye (ear) of the public, get on local radio or T.V., dress like a world famous trombonist, eat like a world famous trombonist, walk and talk like a world famous trombonist, have sex like a world famous trombonist - well, maybe that's taking things a bit too far.

Each one of these is actually formed by the combination of lots of other smaller actions. Individually some of them might seem insignificant. But put together over the years they start to create a powerful force which causes momentum. Momentum that if aimed properly from the start will take you directly and inevitably to where you want to be. The only thing left then is to carry out each one of these actions; to put each piece of the puzzle into place. This means following through with the plan which probably involves doing several of these little actions every day over a period of time which could extend over several years. More consideration of this part is covered in chapter 5.

## Step 3. Perseverance

The first two steps are the 'easy' steps. Admittedly they require a certain amount of mental effort, creativity and concentration but by using the right mental tools for the job, the whole process can be achieved in just a few hours if you have a clear head and a bit of peace and quiet. Often, once you have decided on an Action Plan and then broken it down into hundreds of little actions, you'll get little flashes of inspiration; new ideas will suddenly leap out at you as you are in the middle of something. Great! Make a note of them and add them to your plan. Nothing is set in stone. So as long as you are constantly moving towards your objective, all is well.

The challenging part of applying the Sorites Principle is in step three. It is in the persevering - the doing a little bit every day - where people most often come unstuck. At the beginning of a new goal things are usually quite simple. Starting out on a new project fresh in mind is invigorating. Bright-eyed and bushy-tailed you are off to conquer the world and it feels great. This can last for days, weeks or even months but at some point that fresh flow of optimism begins to fade and the willpower evaporates. The inevitable is going to hit you at some point - the feeling that things are no longer moving forward, that it was a nice idea but it's never going to happen, the seeds of self-doubt start to sprout and it all seems so very, very far away. So perseverance is a challenge in itself. Fortunately, the benefits of perseverance are numerous and powerful, only matched, in fact, by the resistance you will encounter when you do it. The importance of perseverance is covered in general in chapter 6 and more specifically, in chapters 7 to 15 which look at what tools, tricks and techniques you can use to optimise your leverage in the war of perseverance and how to reduce the risk of surrender.

So we can summarise the practical application of the Sorites Principle - using the process of 'little by little' to achieve our long-term goals in three steps:

1. Decide on a comprehensive plan of action for how to achieve your goal.

2. Just like collecting all the pieces of a jigsaw puzzle, identify all the little actions that need to be carried out in order to realize this action plan.

3. No matter how insignificant these actions might seem, carry out one or two of them every day until you reach your goal.

If it sounds simple, then that's because it is. But in spite of its simplicity it is not easy. Not easy but nevertheless inevitably effective. In the following chapters we shall be looking at each of these deceivingly simple steps in more detail, how they work and what we can do to make them work for us.

## Things to Think About

✖ The idea behind the Sorites Principle, namely doing things little by little, step by step, is nothing new and most people are aware of it.

✖ In spite of this most of us fail to use it to our advantage.

✖ This is due to factors such as:

  ✱ Unawareness - Not knowing of the Sorites Principle

  ✱ Lack of recognition - Not seeing the task as one where the Sorites Principle can be applied

  ✱ Lack of patience - Wanting too much, too soon

  ✱ A sense of futility - A voice in our head telling us that it's too big, too difficult. It's all a pointless waste of time.'

  ✱ Confusion - Not having a clear idea of what to achieve

✖ The basic way to apply the Sorites Principle has three parts: The Plan, The Pieces, The Perseverance.

✖ Of the three parts, Perseverance is where most people come unstuck.

✖ Understanding how you manage each of these parts can improve your effectiveness, your productivity and ultimately your whole life.

## Questions to Ask Yourself (and Answer)

- What goals have you failed to achieve in the past? What factors contributed to your failure?
- What daunting tasks are you putting off at the moment?
- What goals would you like to achieve if you could improve your perseverance?

# 4 Planning Your Goal

*"Setting goals is the first step in turning the invisible into the visible."* - Tony Robbins

*"If you fail to plan, you are planning to fail!"* - Benjamin Franklin

This book is about harnessing the power of insignificant change but conscious change requires that you know what the change should be. Thus before you change, you need to choose yourself a goal and it would be irresponsible of me to suggest that choosing your goal is easy.

When I was in secondary school I played chess. I was rather good at it. I won the school chess trophy and represented the school and the city teams. However, as I improved there came a point when in order to stretch myself further, I needed a chess computer. Remember that we're talking about the 1970s here and computers were still in their fledgling state. Steve Jobs' dad was probably just starting to think about building his garage and the Atari (bip...bip...bip...) was the bee's knees in home video gaming. So a chess computer was a big deal. Nevertheless, I wanted one -- badly. If I got one, I'd never ask for anything else ever.

So what happened? I got one and spent two months playing it. I then got bored with it (as far as I know it stayed in the living-room cupboard for about twenty years until my dad took it to a charity shop). The following Christmas I wanted a new racing bike -- badly.

What we want and what we need are not necessarily the same thing.

A friend of mine who shall remain nameless had the idea that owning his dream car would solve all his problems. He'd be more confident and consequently more attractive and therefore more successful with the opposite sex. He saved up and got a second hand Porsche (a flashy red job with a fold down roof). But he quickly learned that owning a Porsche just meant he was still an introvert but £30,000 poorer and with an impractical sports car that got scratched every time he parked it in a public place. After 6 months he sold it at a total loss of £14,000.

So what are your reasons for achieving your goal? Is it for you or is it to satisfy others' expectations? Is it to make you more money or to make you happier? Is it to possess some physical object or to achieve some self-realisation?

If you are considering setting yourself an important goal, it is worth giving it some serious thought -- thinking things through. Identifying and choosing the right goal can make all the difference. Pouring your time, effort, money and future wellbeing into a project that is ill-thought out is just asking for trouble and we can all do without that. But why take the risk? Wouldn't it be better, safer, not to bother and just take things 'steady as she goes'?

## Goals Can Make You Happy

Leaving the obvious football references aside, having the right goal can make a huge difference to how you live your life and how positive you feel about it. Helen ran her own small educational publishing company selling learning resources to schools. The company was small but regularly made a tidy profit. But after fifteen years of doing the same thing, Helen was starting to get a bit lacklustre with the routine of it all. And then the economy went to pot. Schools no longer had so much money to spend and suddenly things started to look bad. But, ironically, this in one way for Helen, was good. Suddenly she had a challenge! She had a clear goal: to figure out a way of getting through the economic slump and saving the company. Instead of crawling out of bed in the morning hobbling off to work, she fairly bounced out of bed and sprinted down the road.

Having a clear and worthy goal gave Helen a challenge, verve, drive, positivity. In fact, having the right sort of goal in life can be very good for us. Firstly, as we saw with Helen above, having a goal can provide you with a challenge. If we didn't have challenges in life, our existence would be boring, tedious and mundane. We are naturally attracted to challenges -- preferably not too easy and not too hard. This is why there are companies that make their fortunes supplying us with crosswords, word-searches, sudokus and the like with varying levels of difficulty.[10]

The second reason why goals are good for us is that they give our life a direction. By 'direction' I mean that they provide you with an answer to the question 'So what am I going to do today?' Without direction you would aimlessly wander through life, or flit from one shiny attraction to the next but without any clear sense of where you are going -- or why. You'd follow the easiest path, that of least resistance, doing all those simple familiar things, day in, day out, until one morning you realise that you've spent the best part of your life accomplishing bugger all and then start acting all indignant and resentful about it. One way to think about it is this: Imagine that you are at the end of your life and you have to write your own epitaph. What would you say about yourself? "Here lies me. I watched a lot of television, played a lot of games and did a lot of puzzles." Inspiring stuff for your grandkids? I think not.

---

10- My niece, Kate, introduced me to sudokus a few days before I got married. I distinctly remember the family huddled around her, sat at the large oak table in the kitchen of the farmhouse that we had rented for the wedding, as she explained what a sudoku was and how it works. Since then me and the missus must have done thousands of sudokus, mostly on sunny Sunday mornings, all thanks to Kate and our natural attraction to a challenge.

Thirdly, if we have a goal then we can get closer to it. This means that we are advancing and making progress. As we shall see later, the sensation of progress is deeply rewarding and satisfying. The opposite is the feeling of monotony and stagnation, which in turn can lead to stress, depression and regular outbursts of profanities - especially if you're stuck in a traffic jam on the M1 due to interminable roadworks which are exacerbated by an accident at Watford Gap.

Finally, having a goal, especially if it is a profound one, can give our lives meaning and a meaningful life is a good life. If you see yourself as having some profound goal, some purpose, some mission then making progress to that end fills us with positivity. It gives us this wonderful sense of fulfilment. Here I'm not talking about having a clean and tidy home although I dare say that there are those who get a deep satisfaction of having a home that could feature on the front cover of 'Home & Garden'. Personally, I feel more empathy for people who want to better themselves or better the lives of others. For those who want to find a cure for cancer, save the whale or eradicate drought, famine or bad punctuation. There's a lot to say about leading an altruistic life, benefiting society and helping others which I'm not going to get side-tracked onto here. Suffice it to say that having one of the more noble goals can give our lives meaning and that is what so many of us are after.

So in short, having the right goal can provide us with a challenge, direction and meaning which all help us live an interesting, rewarding and fulfilling life. This sounds pretty good to me. Of course it's not obligatory and if you prefer to veg out on the sofa, watching the television while your brain rots and seeps out your ears, then that's entirely up to you.

## Planning

I bet the last time you went on holiday you had a pretty good idea of where you were going. You probably looked it up on a map. You might have briefly considered the different ways to get there: car, train, plane, maybe even by bicycle, and you made your choice depending on the resources at your disposal and the other factors that had to be taken into account such as whether you were travelling alone or accompanied, how much time you had available and how much the whole thing was likely to cost.

If you finally managed to have a holiday, then the success was mostly due to having a good plan. Good planning is just one of the many things our brain can do that sets us apart from lesser evolved species like lizards, stick insects or a certain type of civil servant. Our brain excels in planning - it's what it was evolved for. Even with the developments in computing and information technology, your brain is still more powerful than the latest state of the art computer - which is nice to know.[11] So with the reassuring knowledge that you already have the most sophisticated piece of planning equipment known to humankind already set up inside your skull then it would be a good moment to consider what it is that makes a goal plan a good one.

## The Three Golden Rules of Goal Planning

Although you are perfectly entitled to set yourself whatever goal plans you like, there is a wealth of material and advice about what makes a goal a good one. I like to keep it simple and offer you here my three 'golden rules' for goal-planning that you might like to compare with any ideas you already have.

## 1. Keep It Positive

This means focussing on what you want rather than what you don't want. Nobody wants to die in abject poverty, unloved, unwanted and unknown. But stating that you want to avoid such an end isn't being practical. After all, how would you know when you had achieved it? You are only

---

11- In 2013 one of the most powerful computers in the world - the K Computer at the Riken research institute in Kobe, Japan - simulated the activity of just 1% of the human brain. It took the mega-computer which was made up of 82,944 processors (capable of doing about 1016 billion operations per second) 40 minutes to carry out all the operations and calculations that the brain, your brain, does in just a mere second. The process also gobbled up almost 10 megawatts of power, the energy needed to run 10,000 suburban homes. Your brain uses less energy than a standard lightbulb. While computing technology is improving each year, it will be some time yet before they can build an artificial brain that can work as effectively and as efficiently as yours - which I find reassuring.

specifying what you don't want to happen and not specifying what you do. The opposite could be to want to become a universally recognised sex-symbol - not everybody's cup of tea, but if you did, it would certainly comply better with the first golden law.

Also, good goals are constructive goals -- they reinforce themselves. Focussing on the positive helps with this. Some say that we subconsciously dislike negative concepts and that we are therefore uncomfortable with such words as 'loss', 'stop', 'refrain', and 'give up'. For this reason, they believe it is psychologically incorrect to say 'I want to lose weight' and that the positive equivalent of 'improving my BMI (Body Mass Index)' is more preferable. Personally, I'm not entirely convinced but whether you subscribe to this idea or not is not the point. The point is that, as we shall see later, positivity is a key element to perseverance. The more positive your goal, the more likely you will achieve it.

## 2. Keep It Clear

Goals that refer to becoming a 'better', 'happier' or 'healthier' individual might meet the first rule but they don't meet the second. What does 'better' actually mean? What is 'happier' or 'healthier'? The question might seem odd. The answer might appear to be obvious to you but as you begin to scratch the surface these terms are woolly and imprecise. The same problem with negative goals applies here: Again, how would you know when you had achieved your woolly goal? The meaning of 'happier' is not clear in this context. Whereas 'improving your self-confidence so you can ask someone out on a date' or 'earning enough money to be financially independent' are clearer examples of personal goals.

Being clear means that the objective should be clear to you and also to anyone else who you explain it to. The terms should be specific without vagueness or ambiguity. For example, 'I want to be a better parent' is a vague statement in so far as it doesn't say anything about how it is to be achieved. Compare that to 'From today, my goal is to spend at least one hour a day of quality time[12] with my children, reduce the amount of time I'm away from home at the weekends by 50% and attend all of their

---

12- The more critical reader will point out that terms like 'quality time' are also vague statements and they would be perfectly correct. But they are less vague and that's good enough at this stage.

important sporting events for the next twelve months'. Notice that clear goals should also have a time reference for when it starts and when it can end. Having an end date for your goal is important, too. If not, it plods on and on becoming more and more taken for granted. "But..." you might say "...I want my goal of being healthy to last for ever!" That's absolutely fine. Nobody is saying that after your first goal period comes to a successful end you can't renew it. But there's a big psychological difference between saying - "I am going to diet until the end of next month," and "I am going to diet forever."

## 3. Keep It You

Harry snored. It didn't bother him but it bothered Gina, his wife, tremendously. She kept nagging him to sleep on his side. She would nudge him, prod him and even knee him in the back. She tried all sorts of things to reduce his nocturnal raspings but nothing worked. Besides which, Harry wasn't entirely convinced. He wasn't even aware he snored -- especially no more than normal. Eventually, thinking it might be a medical condition, Gina persuaded Harry to accompany her to the doctor where she explained in vivid detail the stress and mental discomfort her husband's snoring was causing her. The doctor listened attentively, asked a few relevant questions and then came to a conclusion.

"I recommend a few sessions of hypnosis. That should help quite a lot." Gina was very pleased - finally, a solution Harry hadn't tried!

"When can you start, dear?" Gina asked. "You're free tomorrow!"

"I don't think you understand" interrupted the doctor, "The treatment isn't for your husband. It's for you."

You can't change other people. Okay, so your boss is incompetent, your neighbour is a moron and you have acquired the in-laws from hell. That's their problem and there's absolutely nothing you can do about it. You can only control yourself: your thoughts, your actions and your behaviour. So do yourself a favour and accept the failings of others and focus on what you can do to improve your lot. As Reinhold Niebuhr said "Grant me the serenity to accept the things I cannot change, the courage to change the things I can, and the wisdom to know the difference."

These three Golden Rules provide the backbone of personal goal planning. They help guide us to formulate and improve our objectives so that we are more likely to achieve them. However, I do know that some people like to have something more detailed and I think that writing anything about goal planning wouldn't be complete without referring to the SMART model for goal planning that is well established in business and coaching and has stood the test of the last forty years.

The model was popularised in 1980 by the management consultant Peter Drucker. SMART[13] is a mnemonic acronym - a helpful way of remembering something by representing each part by its initial letter.[14] There are many, many variations of the SMART model but the overall idea is the same: to give effective guidance in establishing goals. The five criteria I use for my SMART goals are:

- Specific
- Measurable
- Action-oriented (other versions include achievable and agreed)
- Realistic (other versions include relevant and resourced)
- Time-based

Its strength is it gives an almost universal template to check our goals against and to make sure they are well thought out and good enough to put into action. The advantage of this model is that it not only works for personal goals but also works for more complicated goals involving more factors such as other people, departments, organisations and so on. If in a work environment someone comes to you with a new business

13- In his book Coaching for Performance, John Whitmore suggests that goals should not only be SMART (which for him represent Specific, Measurable, Agreed, Realistic and Time-Framed) but also PURE (Positive, Understood, Relevant & Ethical) and CLEAR (Challenging, Legal, Environmental, Appropriate & Recorded). While I applaud his idea in theory, I feel that mnemonic acronyms can be taken too far at times.

14- Richard Of York Gave Battle In Vain is a mnemonic for the colours of the rainbow. My Very Educated Mother Just Served Us Nachos is the mnemonic for the planets of the solar system Mercury, Venus, Earth, Mars, Jupiter, Saturn, Uranus and Neptune. NATO is an acronym as is LASER, GPO, CSI and FUBAR.

idea, to see if it has 'legs strong enough to run with,' then you get out your metaphorical baseball bat and give its legs a good bashing. By this I mean to look at it with a critical eye and to figure out if it has any flaws or weaknesses by asking lots of questions, most of which begin with 'What if...?' If the idea is still standing after this ruthless assault, then it is more likely to be a good one. The SMART model is a way of checking which legs to bash in order to see if it can run.

Let's look at these five SMART points in a little more detail.

## Specific

This first criterion stresses the importance of having a clearly defined objective and corresponds to my second Golden Rule of keeping it clear. The 'Specific' part of your goal plan will answer the questions 'Who?' (e.g. Who is involved?), 'What?' (e.g. What is to be achieved?), 'Why?' (Why should it be achieved?), 'Where?' (e.g. Where will it take place?) as well as any other questions such as 'How much will it cost?', 'How will it be implemented?', 'Who's going to be in charge?', 'What's the point?' 'Do I get my travelling expenses paid?' and so on.

## Measurable

If you can't measure something, then you can't manage it. How do you know if you're making progress or not? How will you know when you have achieved your goal? Whether it's minutes, money or word-count, you really need to have some sort of way of measuring your goal. Sometimes the measuring part goes without saying. If your goal is to save €100 a month towards a new TV, then money so far accumulated in the jar is pretty obvious. If your goal is to squander your savings on a new luxury yacht, then having the thing on a trailer parked outside your home is a clear and measurable indication that progress has been made. But not all goals have 'measurables' that are so easy to measure. Consider things like training to become a better actor, dancer or negotiator. Our tendency is to go on our own opinion -- but as we have seen, when our progress is little by little we simply don't perceive any progress. And our opinion can vary quite a lot depending on our mood and circumstances. So opinions are not at all reliable -- especially our own. If your goal is to become a better partner, you could choose your measurable to be how many days can you go without arguing or insulting them. Or how many hours of quality time you spend together or how many meals you have together, without distractions such as the television, phone conversations, computers or smartphones.

## Action-oriented

In a business setting this is about what is going to be carried out and by whom? But for just one individual it is simply about what you are going to do to achieve your goal. What actions are you going to carry out and in what order? For example, you might want to get a new fridge. So going to the shop to buy one might sound like a good action. But, hold on, there are many different fridges of many different manufactures so maybe before you go to the shop, researching refrigerators would be a good idea. So that would probably mean finding some consumer guides or reviews on the subject. But before you can do that, you need to know what size appliance you're looking for. So you need to measure the space available. But the tape measure is not where it should be and you seem to remember that Freddie was using it recently for some reason. So in practical terms, your first action to getting a new fridge is to ask Freddie where the tape measure is.

## Realistic

Let's suppose that you have decided what your SPECIFIC objective is, you have identified how this will be MEASURED and you have considered all the ACTIONS that you will have to do. Now comes the part when you have to be brutally honest with yourself, look yourself in the mirror and ask yourself how REALISTIC you are being. Some people have eyes bigger than their stomachs and when in a restaurant, order far too much food. They base their expectations on how they feel when ravenous but forget that this sensation fades after the first course. So when we are considering our objective we might be fired up and desperate to go but we do need to remember that we are living in the real world. We have to accept that we have limitations, responsibilities and basic needs to satisfy.

Now don't get me wrong. I'm all in favour of setting our sights high but there are different heights that range from very simple (you've never flown and want to experience your first flight in an aeroplane) through to defying the laws of physics (you've never flown before and you want to have your own spaceship and fly it to the next galaxy and back by next Tuesday). 'Getting fitter' is realistic (although not very clear), winning a gold for running in the next Olympics is not so realistic, especially if you're over 50 with a bit of a dodgy knee.

I personally believe it is far better to have a modest goal and -- once completed -- go for another a bit more ambitious than to go for something too big and then get frustrated and disillusioned about the whole matter.

Another point to take into account is your life environment. You might have other responsibilities or obligations: you might have a partner, children, a pet to look after or a rare tropical pot-plant to nurture. Unless you want to cause yourself immediate stress and external resistance to your new project then your plan must realistically fit into the universe you share with everyone else. Opinions are divided on how much you should take into account the feelings and opinions of those around you. Some point out that we have a moral responsibility towards our nearest and dearest while others point out that succeeding requires sacrifice, after all, where would Barack Obama be if he had to be home by 5pm every evening to be with his family? Therefore, it's important to take into account that although running two hours every evening might be realistic if you were single, is it still realistic given that you have a husband that can't cook and three toddlers to look after?

So make sure your goals are realistic physically, financially and socially - and with the right level of challenge: not too difficult, but not too easy either. 'Completing your first marathon', 'getting your light aircraft pilot's licence' or 'losing 10 lbs in the next five months' are fair goals to aim for. Once achieved, the success factor can provide motivation to go onwards and upwards to the next level. But too much, too soon can only point to disaster as being our final destination.

## Time-based

So you've decided that you're going to become a professional composer or open up the best restaurant in town. Part of being specific is answering the question 'when?' but not just regarding the achievement as a whole. The complete process will be made of smaller tasks that each need their own time frame and remember, when your tasks depend on other people, your sense of urgency is not likely to be shared by them. Establishing a time-frame with deadlines is recommendable because it creates a clear structure to your goal, it gives you something to measure your progress against and can increase your motivation. We shall be looking more about how to get the most out of deadlines in chapter 11.

## One Important Thing

In their bestselling book 'The One Thing' Gary Keller and Jay Papasan give a marvellous explanation of the advantages of limiting the number of your goals to just one. Yes, you want to improve your health, wealth and happiness. You want to climb Everest, see the Northern Lights and Saving Private Ryan. But you can't do it all right now. As the Russian proverb at the start of their book says "If you chase two rabbits, you will not catch either one." Trying to achieve several goals at the same time is like trying to play several musical instruments at the same time. There are those who can manage it, but they are maestros of none of them. If you try to achieve too many goals, you end up with conflict and stress. We aren't very good at multitasking at the best of times and having multiple goals sucks our energy, our ability to concentrate, reduces our efficiency and leaves us feeling overwhelmed -- unable to cope with the demands we have chosen to impose upon ourselves. If you have two burning ambitions (such as writing a book and having the body of Charles Atlas) then the key to success and mental stability is to do the first one and then do the second one after you've finished the first.[15]

---

15- I went for the book first.

# Yolanda

Yolanda was a 37-year-old primary school teacher who had just been through four years of hell. She had been in one of those relationships with her boyfriend Lucas, that plodded on and on but never seemed to progress. She loved Lucas very much. She got on very well with his parents but Lucas always seemed to resist becoming more committed. This had gone on for twelve years. Yolanda wanted to get married. Lucas wanted to wait a bit longer.[16] But then fate took control. In spite of taking 'the necessary precautions', Yolanda got pregnant. Her immediate reaction was joy. Although not planned for, this would mean taking the relationship up a level. But Lucas wasn't of the same opinion. He wanted Yolanda to have an abortion. After much arguing mostly between Lucas on one side and Yolanda backed up by both sets of parents on the other. Lucas finally gave in and they got engaged. Three weeks later, Lucas and Yolanda were involved in a traffic accident. Lucas died in hospital two days later. Yolanda lost her baby.

From there on things went from bad to worse. Although she now had the love and support from four parents (Lucas had been an only child and his parents cared for her as if she were their own daughter) she started to run off the rails. She suffered from depression. She became bitter and angry. She didn't know what to do with her life. It was all pointless. But then it all changed, after reading an article about artificial insemination she got an inspiring idea. "It was like the clouds suddenly opened and a beautiful sunbeam shone down on me." She wanted to be a mother. Seeing all those happy mums bring their happy kids to school every day was like being stabbed in the soul with a thousand tiny knives. If she didn't have a baby soon she would regret it for the rest of her life and in her mid-thirties she felt she didn't have much time left. But she didn't want just any baby.

She wanted to have Lucas's baby -- or the next best thing, which was to have Lucas's father donate his sperm. After talking things through with her parents and then her 'in-laws' it was finally decided. The necessary paperwork and planning was done and three years after losing her first family, Yolanda started her second by giving birth to Lucas Junior -- a beautiful 9 lb. baby boy.

---

16- This is another example of insignificant change: One day you wake up to realise that you've been in a relationship for far, far too long.

Yolanda's story is a clear example of how having a goal transformed her life. She went from a mental and physical wreck to someone who had drive, purpose and a positive outlook on life almost at the flick of a switch. Her life practically changed overnight and all due to having the right objective. At the time of writing, Yolanda is enjoying her maternity leave while Lucas Junior's four grandparents wrestle it out to decide who gets to look after baby when Yolanda goes back to work.

## 10-10-10

While we're on the subject of choosing your one goal, I'd like to mention a very useful tool coined and popularised by the American author and business journalist Suzy Welch in her book of the same name: '10-10-10' which represents 10 minutes, 10 months and 10 years. The idea behind it is that when it comes to choosing our goals in life or any other major decision-making moment, it is very useful to consider how that choice would affect our lives in ten minutes from now, ten months and ten years. As Susy says herself, the '10's here are purely arbitrary; it simply represents the immediate future, the medium future and the far future. The book could be called '2 hours, 9 months and 13 years' but I think we all agree it wouldn't be such a catchy title.

Thus, when considering your one goal from all the possible goals you have on your plate at the moment, think about the short-, medium- and long-term effects of each one. Which one would have the greatest positive impact on your life?

Before I started writing this book I had several options open to me. I could write this book, and I was also in the process of developing a series of workshops to help align our behaviours with our thoughts. I had my steady flow of coaching clients, a company to run and a family to provide for. After careful consideration, writing this book came first. In the short term it meant postponing some clients, putting on hold my workshop project and shortening the time I spent at the office. But, in the medium term, the book would definitely help me in both the coaching and workshop departments. Furthermore, the idea of promoting the book -- travelling around doing book signings and presentations quite appealed to me. I might even get a TED Talk out of it! And, of course, it might help a bit to provide for my family. So the book came top of my 10-10-10 weightings and, Hey-Presto! Here it is.

The truth is that when we are up close and personal with all our projects, they all seem big and important. But with hindsight, attending a distant relative's wedding, organising a school reunion, or redecorating the kitchen is something that, six months after, has paled into insignificance. Postponing, delegating or simply forgetting about certain tasks is not an end-of-the-world scenario. So look at the medium and long-term implications of your possible goals and go for the one that will have the biggest positive effect.

## What's in it for Me?

Once you have decided on your goal, you need to identify all the reasons why this particular goal is The One. What benefits will it bring? What problems will it solve? What negative emotions will it eradicate and what positive emotions will it produce? In what ways will it make your life (and the lives of others) better? What factors exist that make your current circumstances so unbearable that you want to put yourself through such a gruelling ordeal? It is important that you identify each and every reason because later you are going to need them. Later on, much later on, you are going to feel stressed by the pursuit of your dream. You are going to start doubting that it is worth it. Part of your brain will try to convince the rest of you that things weren't so bad; that compared to what you are putting yourself through, your old life was much more bearable. The same part of you will try to ignore all those reasons why your goal was so important in the first place. This feeling will happen. The best way to deal with it and remember just how important your goal is, how bad your old life was and how good your new life will be, is to write it all down, preferably in your new Goal Diary.

## Your Goal Diary

So far, so good. You've got the general idea behind the Sorites Principle -- little by little and slow and steady wins the race. You've considered what major goals you have ahead of you and you've taken time to identify which one will have the greatest positive effect on your future. You've set your goal (maybe to set up your own dating website, run your first marathon or become a professional song writer) and you've identified all the reasons why it's a great idea. What's next?

The next thing is to WRITE IT DOWN. Writing down your goal is really, really important. Why? Well, first of all putting your goal in writing helps you to consolidate your ideas. The very action of setting your ideas out in written words means that you have to mentally process your thoughts in a different way -- a way which helps clarify and understand. It helps you mentally 'absorb' or 'digest' the full weight of your goal. By writing it on paper, you are transferring an idea which up until now has only existed in your imagination and 'giving birth' to it; putting it out there in the outside world. It is your first 'insignificant' step towards converting your goal into a reality and helps you to start shifting your attitude to one more earnest -- taking yourself more seriously. Writing your goal down (preferably in permanent ink) means that there's no turning back. It's fixed. You can't pretend it never happened -- that you didn't mean to set it down on paper. Similarly, the written word is more difficult to distort. An idea is easy to modify or change (consciously or unconsciously) depending on your mood or attitude.

The spoken word is also susceptible to selective memory ("I never said that" or "that's not what I meant!"). So your goal should be clearly, permanently and indisputably written down to avoid back-sliding. These are just a couple of reasons why you should start a Goal Diary. There are many more. I strongly recommend investing in a nice pocket-sized notebook -- the sort with a hardback cover and a little ribbon for marking the page. One that's small enough to comfortably and discretely fit in your pocket or bag so that you can always have it at hand. Let's say the quality of your notebook psychologically influences how serious you are towards your goal. Notice the word 'notebook'. Although I refer to it as a 'diary' I don't recommend getting a real diary. Diaries have spaces for each date and a limited amount of space at that. For your Goal Diary you might need a lot of space to write on some days and next to nothing on others. I find a blank notebook ideal for this; you just go adding the dates as needed.

So get a nice new notebook and start by setting out your goal at the top of the first page and write the date next to it. Under that you set out all the reasons why you are doing this, all of them in graphic emotional detail, to remind you during those difficult times to come. All the following pages will serve to set down all the steps to come that will take you slowly but unwaveringly towards success: the actions that you plan to carry out in the future as well as a record of how you are progressing. You will also keep a record of any new ideas, observations or discoveries you make during your journey as well as how you feel: your moments of jubilation as well as how you feel during those moments of despondency (and you will experience both). Your Goal Diary is to bear witness to your good times and bad times, your wins and losses, your breakthroughs and your setbacks. Its pages, as we shall see later on, will become absolutely invaluable when it comes to dealing with those inevitable problems you are going to run up against: lack of patience, frustration and the feeling of general futility.

## Peter

Peter was one of those larger than life characters - a veritable mountain of a man, extrovert, charismatic and wore his long hair in a ponytail. He was 43, head of project management in a big multinational and he loved his job. He travelled a lot, supervising several teams in several cities and when he wasn't at one meeting he was on his way (sweating and gasping for breath) to another. He worked long hours. His job was demanding, stressful and in 2012 it almost killed him.

In June of that year Peter celebrated his 44th birthday and a week later followed up by celebrating his first heart attack. "Just a mild one - nothing too serious" his doctors had assured him. Nevertheless, it put the fear of God into him.

He'd always been aware that his lifestyle had been unhealthy for as long as he could remember but his efforts to lose weight and get fit had always been half-hearted. Peter loved his job, his food and his computer and that pretty much summed up Peter's life. When he wasn't working, he spent his time at home on social media or playing online games with his online friends. And he loved it. He was one of those rare people who was comfortably single. He was a middle-aged bachelor and now wanted to become an old-aged bachelor. After his scare he decided that staying alive was his one goal and that he was more likely to achieve this by getting fitter: by losing weight, getting more exercise and reducing his blood pressure. This, when converted into his goal statement, was as follows

*I, Peter Hargreaves, hereby promise myself that I shall increase my life expectancy in these three ways:*

*1) I will reduce my weight by 2 pounds per month until I get to 14 st. (on the day he had his heart attack, he weighed 20 st.).*

*2) I will get at least 30 minutes of moderate exercise every day.*

*3) I will learn how to become more aware of my stress level and control it.*

Peter is on the right road. It's long and it's very trying at times as he fights distractions, temptations and his old habits. But he knows where his destination lies and he knows it'll be worth it.

So setting yourself one clear goal and writing it down in a SMART way is the first of the three parts to the Sorites Principle for getting what you want out of life.

## Before You Open Your Mouth

One final note. In a study done a few years ago they tested a group of people regarding their ability to carry out their personal goals and what happened when they told other people about them.

The curious and surprising result was that the volunteers who talked to others about what their goals were and what they intended to achieve progressed slower than those who kept their mouths shut. The conclusion here was that we tend to equate talking about our goals with a false sense of progress, much like the feeling that simply buying a book on yoga makes you healthier. As we shall see later, recruiting the help from others is useful and can be very effective but the statistics suggest you are better off being selective about who you take into your confidence regarding your exciting new life-changing goal.

## Things to Think About

✽ The first part of applying the Sorites Principle is to devise a Goal Plan.

✽ We have a tendency to set ourselves goals that are not properly thought out.

✽ The ideal goal is something which is not too easy but not too difficult -- something that presents us with a challenge that is 'just right'.

✽ A goal that provides us with an optimum challenge can improve our attitude, give us a direction in life and even give our life meaning.

✽ Progressing with such goals can provide us with satisfaction, fulfilment and help us live happier lives.

✽ Goals should be positive, clear and based on what we can achieve -- they should not be negative, vague or depend on others.

✽ Furthermore, according to the SMART model they should be Specific, Measurable, Action-oriented, Realistic and Time-based.

✽ You should only have one goal if you seriously want to achieve it: If you chase two rabbits, you will not catch either one.

✽ When deciding on your one goal, consider how it will affect your immediate, medium- and long-term futures.

✽ Identifying all the reasons WHY your goal is worthwhile is crucial for your future perseverance.

# Top Tips

✤ Take some quality time to think carefully about your life: Your health, your career, your family, your finances, your environment.

✤ Make a list of all your major goals in each area.

✤ Identify the single most important one. The goal that once achieved would have the most positive impact on the others. This should be your main goal.

✤ Get yourself a Goal Diary. Something of quality that reflects the importance of your goal and will do justice to your efforts.

✤ Write down your goal in a form that is clear, positive and solely based on what you can control.

✤ Avoid 'woolly' terms like 'better', 'happier' or 'healthier' and avoid saying what you don't want. Your goal should clearly state what you do want.

✤ You can try writing it out as a SMART Goal Plan. Be as specific as possible what you want to achieve. State what factors you will be able to measure to check progress and to know when you have succeeded. Identify what actions you are going to carry out. Give yourself a reality check to make sure you are being reasonable and always give a time-frame for your plans.

✤ Write down all the reasons why it is worth embarking on this journey in pursuit of your goal. What are the benefits of achieving it and what would happen if you didn't try?

## Questions to Ask Yourself (and Answer)

✹ What are all the important things that you want to experience and accomplish in your life?

✹ Which of these is the most important? Which is going to help most with all the others?

✹ Which one are you going to choose to be your next goal?

✹ How many ways will you be able to measure your progress?

✹ When do you want to achieve your goal?

✹ How are you going to know when you have achieved your goal?

✹ What are the next actions you need to take?

✹ Where can you get a nice new Goal Diary and when will you go there to get it?

✹ Is it worth pursuing your goal? Why?

.

# 5 ▸ The Pieces Of The Puzzle

*"The secret of getting ahead is getting started. The secret of getting started is breaking your complex overwhelming tasks into small manageable tasks, and starting on the first one."*                                        - Mark Twain

*"Nothing is particularly hard if you divide it into small jobs."*     - Henry Ford

Do you like jigsaws? I used to do jigsaws with my big sister Hilary - big ones with several thousand tiny little pieces. The sort that require commandeering the dining room table for two months and have the whole family leaning over it looking for 'that elusive browny-blue piece with the end of a finger' which you discover at the end to be missing and is finally recovered from underneath the sideboard (How on earth did it get there?). In a 1,000-piece jigsaw puzzle, each piece is just 0.1% of the big picture. Individually that's rather insignificant. If you went into a restaurant and complained that your steak was 0.1% too small they'd think you were an escapee from the nearest funny-farm. Although 0.1% may be insignificant I don't think anyone would consider not putting in all 1,000 pieces of the jigsaw or even worse - throwing a piece away (and risk the rest of the family looking under every piece of furniture for eternity). That wouldn't be playing the game, would it? Even the most insignificant of things can have a big effect. One tiny action applied regularly can change your entire future. Just like the domino effect, one thing can lead to another, which leads to another, ad infinitum.

## Un Tout Petit Peu Plus[17]

French. French is great, isn't it? It sounds so smooth and stylish. It has 'panache' as they say. I really enjoyed studying French at school. I wasn't brilliant at it but I wasn't bad either. When I started secondary school we had a great French teacher called Mr. Darwin. He was enthusiastic and funny. He made his lessons interesting and enjoyable. Curiously about that same time, my father introduced one of his many pearls of wisdom into my education: specifically, the idea that 'you don't have to be much better to be better than the rest'. I applied this idea by doing my French homework and then doing a little extra something afterwards of my own design.[18] Drawing a picture and labelling it or writing a few extra sentences or whatever. And just making that extra bit of effort started to pay dividends. Mr. Darwin saw the extra effort and commended it. I got better results for my homework. My attitude towards the subject further improved. I became more receptive and started to learn more which had, in turn, a positive effect on the quality of my homework and my extra input. So much so that I became one of the top of the class. All because of doing a little bit extra twice a week.[19]

17- A little bit more

18- Why I applied it to French instead of maths or physics is beyond my recollection. I have no idea. The rationale of a young adolescent sometimes leaves much to be desired.

19- Unfortunately, fate has a perverted sense of humour at times. In his ultimate wisdom the head of languages at the school decided that as there was a shortage of French teachers, the top ten percent of our year would drop French and learn Spanish. Spanish?!? Suddenly I found myself in a new class with a new (and decidedly unfunny) teacher. All the extra work I had done was for nothing. Wasted! I was so pissed off. I was there back at the bottom, learning from scratch again. I didn't want to be there; I didn't want a different teacher. I didn't like Spanish and I didn't want to learn it. What was the point? I was never going

When putting the pieces together, doesn't each one understand was a part to play?

Important goals can be truly life changing. After all, that's why we want to achieve them - to change our lives. Visualise how your life would be once you've made it, once you've achieved your goal. Now imagine that if this new life were represented by a jigsaw it would be made up of hundreds if not thousands of little parts. Each part is important. It's not just your current life with a little bit photoshopped into it. It would be different - influenced and affected in lots of ways. Just as the mountain is made of many small stones, your new life would be made of many small achievements. Each of these small achievements would have been the result of your actions. So when you're considering your actions you need to consider the big picture - you need to consider everything. If you don't, it could cause problems.

Why?

I'm sure you've heard of Pavlov and his dogs. Those of you who are familiar with dogs know that the moment that the dog knows you are preparing their food they start to get excited. They anticipate their forthcoming arrival of a bowlful of Doggie Chow and either sit there staring at you while dribbling at the chops or alternatively (like mine) start bouncing around the kitchen in uncontrollable joy. (I'm sure my dog has some kangaroo in him). Well, what Pavlov did was to ring a bell just before the arrival of the Doggie Chow and after only a few repetitions of this routine the dogs 'got it'. They cottoned on to the idea that the bell was the prompt that meant lunchtime. It was the bell that became the prompt that caused the dogs to start bouncing and salivating. Even though the bell had nothing intrinsically to do with food, the dogs had learned to associate one with the other and had incorporated it into their behaviour as a prompt for a certain type of routine. What Pavlov showed was that the behaviour of his dogs - and later that of human beings - could therefore be conditioned, controlled, primed. This is very important because we have a great many prompts in our lives, each one with an associated routine.

---

to need it, never going to visit Spain, never going to use it at all. What a pointless waste of all my previous French dedication and all my future time wasted on Spanish. Was it any surprise that I failed Spanish with one of the worst grades in the school? Things might have been slightly different if somebody had told me that twenty-five years later I would be living in Spain with a Spanish wife and two Spanish speaking kids, running my own Spanish company and coaching and training Spanish people in Spanish. But I don't think at 14 years of age I would have ever believed them.

A great many things that you do are habit - the way you get up, your morning routine, your commute to work etc. Some you might be aware of, others less so.

For example, I have a routine when I arrive home. The way I park the car, the way I hold my keys to open the door, the way I greet the dog, hang my coat up, fix myself a snack, get the dog's lead, smile as I watch the dog jumping for joy at seeing his lead, the way I leave the house to take the dog for his walk. You get the idea, don't you?

Our routines are many. They are powerful things that can be difficult to resist as we are unaware of most of them. Think about it for a moment. What is your routine for starting the day? For arriving at work? What is your routine when you are bored or stressed? What is your routine when you finish work? Or when you go to visit your family? Or have a meal? Or wash? Routines are a combination of habits and a habit is something that we do when given a particular stimulus. Just like Pavlov's dogs who drooled when they heard a bell so do we react a certain way with the same series of actions when we hear (or see, smell, feel or taste) something familiar. These routines are very powerful because they happen regularly and as the Sorites Principle states, any simple action when carried out regularly can have a large effect. So our old environment along with our old routines were prompts for our old behaviour. And our old behaviour was what produced our old results - the results that we used to get before we decided we wanted to change. As Henry Ford once said, 'if you always do what you've always done you'll always get what you've always got'. So if we want new results, we need to change our behaviour which means changing our routines which means changing all the little prompts that cause them and this means changing lots of other little things.

Developing a new routine can be challenging. We can easily slip back into the old routine without realising it. So in order to follow a set of new routines which take us along a new road towards a new life we need to change quite a lot. Some people are instinctively aware of this - this is why people ending a relationship need to move house - too many prompts, too many routines, too many memories which lead to too much heartache. We will be considering the power of routines later in chapter 12.

There is a certain world view that all things are interconnected. The late great Douglas Adams wrote a novel entitled 'Dirk Gently's Holistic Detective Agency'. Dirk Gently is a "holistic detective" who works using "the fundamental interconnectedness of all things" to solve the 'whole' crime and thus find the 'whole' person which involves running up large expense accounts and then claiming that every item (such as needing to go to a tropical beach in the Bahamas for three weeks) was, as a consequence of this 'fundamental interconnectedness', actually a vital part of the investigation. Regarding our own behaviour, I think it's fairly accurate to say that in our world (the world we experience directly) all things are 'interconnected' because our routines and prompts overlap each other.

The effects of one set of routines become the prompt for another just like the falling dominos, one thing leads to another one. You wake up in a bad mood (produced by some previous prompt) and this causes you to carry out your 'I'm in a bad mood' routine. This in turn is the prompt for you (and for others) to start carrying out other routines and so on. Our everyday experiences, along with our existing routines, blend together to shape our daily actions that wear out a very predictable rut in our behaviour patterns.

If we want to apply the Sorites Principle to maximum effect, we need to change as many of our behaviour patterns as possible. It doesn't matter how insignificant each one of these changes might seem. Over the course of time each one will have a compound effect. Slowly but surely these tiny changes will become more established through repetition. Their influence on your daily life will grow and develop and even more powerfully, they will start to become interconnected: each one will support the others until a powerful set of new thoughts, attitudes, behaviours and routines have established themselves that were intentionally selected by you to point you towards the goal of your choice. The combined momentum of all these new routines together will inevitably take you to your new destination. This is not a question of faith or spirituality or asking the universe to help you. It is simple mathematics. Just like a tiny tugboat can alter the course of a huge ocean liner coming into dock, so can a coherent combination of small periodic actions, habits and routines alter the course of your life.

# Douglas

Douglas was fifty and had spent most of his life working in a small company that made handmade carved wooden picture-frames with the added treatment to make them look like an antique. However, the pictures he was really interested in were the moving ones. The ones you see on the big screen while eating popcorn. He was a big film fan and his dream had always been to be a film director. When I asked him why he'd never tried to nurture this dream into reality his reaction was "How could I be a film director? I'd love to but I don't know anything about it!"

Do you see Douglas's error?

Douglas was looking at going from 0 to 60 mph in four seconds. He was comparing his current situation with his desired goal without considering all the steps necessary in between. He had completely overlooked the fundamental principle of Sorites, the idea of achieving great things, little step by little step. For those of you who have started to get the idea, you might like to think about and maybe write down what some of these small steps would be (see the end of this chapter for some suggestions).

In the previous section we looked at choosing a SMART objective. So let's assume that you have decided what great thing it is that you have set your sights on and that you are going to achieve step by step, little by little using the Sorites Principle. This idea of the interconnectedness of our behavioural prompts and routines means that if we were to try to change just one habit among a whole sea of daily routines then we are fighting against the tide. What is more effective here is to start a whole set of small actions, thoughts and behaviours that over time will become mutually supporting and 'interconnected'. Each one helping to prompt another. This brings us back to the metaphor of the jigsaw puzzle; that our life can be considered a jigsaw puzzle made up of hundreds of pieces. Each one connected to others, supporting them and holding them in place.

Later on we shall be returning to the power of periodic actions, habits and routines but for the moment we are going to focus on the individual pieces of the puzzle: the small individual actions that are going to combine to pave the way to your future objective.

The salient point from the example of my 'O' level French classes is that the insignificant action of doing an extra five minutes' homework increased my overall grades. One small detail compounding over time to have a big effect. So if we introduce a whole set of small actions then the combined result will be rather powerful. Let's say that for some pleasantly unexpected reason you have just discovered that you have to learn French and soon (let's say within a year). What, according to the Sorites Principle should you do?

Well, following the three steps, the first step has already been taken: that you are going to learn French within one year. To be more specific I would suggest rephrasing this to 'Twelve months from today I will be able to understand normal French conversation, verbally I will be able to converse at a reasonably fluent level, I will be able to read French newspapers and magazine articles and I will be able to write reasonably fluently.

So far, so good. Now, what are the pieces of your puzzle?

The answers to this question are to be found in the following chapters but to give you a general idea let's first consider how I managed to learn Spanish in just six months without even studying that hard.

In 1990 I got a job as an English language teacher in Barcelona (Spain). As you might remember from before, my previous Spanish studies were negligible and had long since been forgotten. When I moved there I was fortunate enough to find accommodation in a shared flat with three Spanish girls Maria, Cristina and Núria. Between the three of them they hardly spoke any English at all. So everything I heard, everything I saw was in Spanish. If I wanted to know where the nearest supermarket was I had to ask in Spanish and if I wanted to find out what the news was I had to read a Spanish newspaper (note: this was pre-internet, pre-wifi, pre-satellite TV). In addition, I had invested in a 'Teach Yourself Spanish' course (okay, I did study a bit) that included cassettes (yes, pre-mp3 as well!) that I could listen to on my Sony Walkman (pre-iPod, too) as I drifted off to sleep. After one month I'd learnt the basic vocabulary needed to survive (the words for beer, toilet and party - just kidding!) along with common expressions like greeting people and asking for things, after two months I'd probably learnt several hundred words and started to conjugate common and regular verbs. After four months I was able to engage in simple and sometimes even intelligent conversation. The learning curve just continued up and up and I enthusiastically absorbed all of it.

In linguistic circles, this way of learning is called 'immersion learning'. But I'd like to consider what is actually happening here. 'Immersion learning' is just having a whole load of separate experiences that are mutually supporting (or interconnected) that when combined have a powerful effect on one's knowledge, thoughts and behaviour. It's not so much to do with being surrounded by Spanish (I know several people who have come to live in Spain but hide themselves away in a little Anglophonic cocoon and so have hardly learnt anything) it's to do with having lots of new prompts, new stimuli that each lead to a new thought process or routine that are all interconnected: they are all pieces of the puzzle that link together to form one coherent picture.

Now for most people who want to learn a foreign language, moving to a different country, France for example, is not feasible. But establishing a whole new set of prompts is, especially in this new information technology era of internet, smart phones and the like.

Starting with the obvious, the first piece of the puzzle is to acquire a copy of Teach Yourself French or to enrol in an evening course at your local college (or why not do both?). Unfortunately, many people leave it at that and then get all upset when after twelve months they still struggle with asking for a decent cup of tea. 'One little piece does not a puzzle make'.

So, let's add a few more pieces and see how it goes. A few other 'easy' pieces to add would be to listen to French music. Forget what you've experienced watching Eurovision, there does actually exist a wide range of excellent French music which is extremely pleasant on the ear such as Jean-Jacques Goldman, Noir Désir, Charles Aznavour, Vanessa Paradis or Edith Piaf. So acquire a few albums of French music and make sure they have lyrics, (Jean Michel Jarre isn't going to do anything for you linguistically), read them and learn them - get a few that are relaxing; something that you can listen to while you're having that little lie down after work, Carla Bruni for example. Commuting time is also an excellent opportunity to subliminally absorb knowledge, so getting a few albums of more lively music to buoy you along during your regular commutes to work and back is another piece to add. In fact, listening to anything in French would be a good idea whether it be music, audiobooks, podcasts or French radio. Whatever tickles your fancy even if it's the shipping forecast, it's still another piece of the puzzle.

Read. Get hold of some books in French. I'm not talking about *Ulysses* or *Wuthering Heights*. They are great books in their own right but unless you have a burning desire to read Joyce or Brontë in French then go for something easier and more fun. Via the glorious internet (how did we cope without it?) you can get virtually any French literature you fancy. Children's books,[20] Mills and Boon, whatever. Buy a book that you've already got in English that you really like. That way you've already got a translation for when you get stuck. It doesn't even have to be in book format. Comics, magazines, newspapers, online articles, blogs, the list goes on. Find them, get them, read them and above all, enjoy them. They are each another piece.

As French is a dynamic, interpersonal skill then talking in French is another useful piece. Join the local French society if you have one available to you. Seek out and make contact with French people in your area. Find people with whom you can talk in French at work or in your neighbourhood - even if it's just in a light-hearted way. Let people know that you're learning French and see if anyone can support your venture. Get a language exchange partner: someone in your area, ideally French, who will help you practise your French in exchange for you helping them practise their English. Get a French au pair, although most au pairs come to practise their English. Date somebody French or even marry one (why not? It worked for me!)

Use what you learn. Label things in the house or at work. Put Post-its up by the bathroom mirror or on the fridge. Make yourself a set of little flashcards with new and useful words or phrases to go through when you have a quiet five minutes. Learn French songs and sing them when you're alone in the house or recite French poetry or nursery rhymes. Watch

---

20- A friend of mine learnt English by, amongst other methods, reading, memorising, and writing out the entire collection of the Mr. Men books that he got for a pound in a charity shop in St. Albans.

French films in French with the French subtitles on. Watch French TV or surf YouTube for whatever it is you find interesting and funny.

Go to France. Not to live there but for a weekend away or a summer holiday. Intentionally choose somewhere where you'll be mixing with native French speakers rather than lots of English speaking tourists. Pay an interest in French news, French politics, French history.

Learn about French food and French cooking. Get a cook book (in French) and start writing out your shopping lists in French. Follow famous French chefs on twitter and YouTube. Follow anybody French on twitter and YouTube. Connect with French people on Facebook and LinkedIn. Start chatting or texting in French. Follow French fashion, wear French style clothes. Download a few of the hundreds of Apps to help you learn French. Memorise useful phrases or structures and repeat them while showering, cleaning your teeth, preparing dinner, queuing, waiting for appointments, or just lying in your hospital bed waiting for them to take your ingrowing toe-nail out. Learn how to say "I speak French really well" or "Every day, in every way, I improve my French a little bit more" and repeat it to yourself frequently. Remember your goal diary, written in French of course, and keep an account of all the progress you've made so far. (We'll be looking at Progress later on).

But whatever you do, do something: something simple, something easy, something fun. Because all of these little insignificant somethings build up little by little and interconnect to form something powerful. This not only applies to learning a foreign language, it applies to changing your life in almost any way you want.

If you want to achieve something substantial, something that's worth doing then you have to begin with one step after another to develop new ideas, new habits, new routines, new behaviours, new feelings, new friends, new contacts, all of which combine to inevitably take you to a new destiny.

The beauty of it is that none of these steps have to be particularly difficult or arduous. If you do them regularly over and over again these insignificant actions will have a surprisingly profound effect. A river cuts through a mountain not because it is strong but because it perseveres and effortlessly achieves a little every day.

# Douglas's Pieces

Earlier in this chapter I mentioned Douglas who'd always wanted to be a film director. Having several good friends who work in the entertainment industry, here is a list of 'puzzle-pieces' that anyone who has a dream to become a film director can apply.

* Get a copy of *Filmmaking for Dummies* or similar.

* Do a course on filmmaking (or several).

* Acquire films that have won 'best film' awards - or any films that inspire you and study them. Watch them with a critical eye. How are they put together?

* Read as many books about filmmaking as you can.

* Start small - focus attention on 'shorts' (films not long enough to be a feature film).

* Start making your own mini-shorts with your smartphone.

* Get a decent affordable camera or make friends with someone who has one.

* Join a club of would-be filmmakers or form your own.

* Talk to other people about filmmaking. Get involved.

* Get a video editing programme and learn how to use it.

* Make friends with would-be actors, technicians, makeup artists (they need to start small, too!).

* Offer your services for free.

* Get relevant experience, any relevant experience.

* Work or volunteer as part of the crew on a film production.

* Network with people in the business.

* Look at smaller more attainable projects like making adverts for local companies, music videos for local bands, a lip dub with your friends, family or co-workers, documentaries for local associations, video books for your new actor-friends' web-pages, interior-guide videos

for the web-pages of local establishments (bars, restaurants, estate agents, etc.), wedding videos for friends.

* Get a script for your first 'serious' short film project.

* Get a team of people together and make your first 'serious' short. Then make your second one.

* Start entering short film competitions.

* Promote yourself - get yourself known - get a business card stating your title as 'film director'.

* Present yourself as a film director on social media.

* Tell people what you're doing/will be doing soon.

* Get a webpage and put your creations on it.

* Go to film festivals.

* Get yourself interviewed on local media.

No doubt you'll have a few of your own suggestions, too. The important idea is to realise that doing any one of these is relatively easy and within your abilities but doing just one is not enough - they are all single steps that take you in the right direction.

All of these together might take you between five to ten years, but each one is a small realistically attainable step. Nevertheless, by the end you would find yourself on the top of your mountain. (Douglas, it's not too late!)

## Things to Think About

♣ Small actions are relatively easy.

♣ Like the 10,000 pieces of a large jigsaw puzzle, each one helps to create the final 'big' picture.

♣ Your goal plan will be carried out by lots and lots of little actions.

♣ Many of these little actions might not be obvious nor seem important.

♣ The second part of applying the Sorites Principle is to create a list of every little action you can carry out in order to create that big picture.

♣ All of these things are interconnected and each will give support to others.

♣ As soon as you start carrying out the small actions each of which will fill in one tiny part of your big picture then the big picture will start to take form.

## Top Tips

♯ Investigate what there is available to listen to such as audio books, motivational songs and podcasts (e.g. while you commute).

♯ Whatever you're interested in, there is probably a website or forum set up by people who've already done it.

♯ There are lots of really great support videos on YouTube and Vimeo.

♯ Join a group in your area where you can get support and ideas from likeminded people.

♯ Write down in your Goal Diary all the little pieces you are going to do.

♯ Even little details like a new business card, door sign or desk plates can be a little piece of your goal-puzzle.

## Questions to Ask Yourself (and Answer)

❇ How many different little actions can you think of?

❇ Where could you get more ideas and suggestions?

❇ What new useful habits could you start to cultivate?

❇ What could you do to improve your attitude to your goal?

❇ What organisations exist that could help? How can you contact them?

❇ Where can you find a few spare minutes during your day? What little pieces can you put in during that time?

# 6  Perseverance

*"Nothing else matters except sitting down every day and trying. Why is this so important? Because when we sit down day after day and keep grinding, something mysterious starts to happen. A process is set into motion by which, inevitably and infallibly, heaven comes to our aid."*

- Steven Pressfield, *The War of Art*

If you Google 'characteristics for success' you'll get a wide variety of answers ranging from 'power-dressing' to 'public speaking'. But on most of the lists that come up, one of the more consistent candidates for 'top characteristic for success' is perseverance. Not necessarily using this exact word but whether it's listed as tenacity, dedication, grit, stamina, determination, persistence, drive, endurance, relentlessness or even stickability, for me, it is referring to the same thing: Perseverance - the ability to keep going and never give in.

Over the years of observing the successful people around me I have my own top seven candidates for characteristics for success. They are...

1. Perseverance

2. Initiative - the ability to think for yourself

3. Emotional Intelligence - the ability to empathise and get on with others

4. Concentration - the ability for deep uninterrupted thought

5. Patience - the ability to postpone gratification

6. Creativity - the ability to make new associations and think out of the box

7. Optimism - the ability to maintain a positive attitude[21]

If we could cultivate these seven skills in our children, if we could promote and develop these ideas in our schools,[22] then the world would be their oyster.

But of these seven characteristics, I put perseverance at the top. Look for yourself at people like J. K. Rowling, Mahatma Ghandi, Thomas Edison, David Beckham, Steve Jobs, Albert Einstein, Muhammad Ali, Richard Branson, Nelson Mandela or even The Beatles. None of them would have made it if after the first sign of difficulty they had given up and thrown in the towel.

These people achieved what they wanted by having a goal and doggedly sticking to it through thick and thin. They had 'Grit'. If you need any more convincing about the power of perseverance I recommend spending six minutes watching the TED Talk by psychologist Angela Lee Duckworth who spent her time studying people in challenging environments such as

---

21- Close runners-up are 'Invisibility', 'Mind Control' and 'The Ability To Find Things That You Put Down Just Five Minutes Ago But Are No Longer Where You Are Sure You Had Put Them' (such as your car keys, the remote control for the telly and bits of paper with important information scribbled on the back).

22- Don't get me wrong. I don't want to start a polemic discussion here. Teachers are already overworked and underpaid - I know; I started my professional career in education as a secondary school maths teacher. I think it is important that we parents should also take our fair share of bringing up our offspring. Let's just take it as a hypothetical suggestion such as 'Hypothetically, if our children were taught perseverance, initiative, emotional intelligence, concentration, patience, creativity and optimism early in life they would greatly benefit from it. If you want to take the idea and run with it then that is your choice - and the subject for an entirely different book.

rookie teachers in tough neighbourhoods, cadets going through military school, trainee sales people and children in spelling bee competitions. In each group she looked at who was succeeding in each environment and why. What she found was that there was one factor that came up as the significant indicator that predicted if a person was going to succeed. It wasn't I.Q., it wasn't emotional intelligence or being rich or good-looking. It was having the ability to persevere or, as Angela puts it, having 'grit': working really hard to make your future a reality, not just for weeks or months but for years.

Perseverance is a fundamental characteristic because when applied it generates three important results: talent, progress and power.

## Perseverance Produces Talent

In his wonderful book *Bounce*, the UK table tennis Olympic champion Matthew Syed points out that what people see as talent is really just thousands of hours of relentless practice. He uses his own experience as an example of this and points out that during his heyday the majority of table tennis champions came from the same town: Reading, in England. Not only that, but they all lived on the same road. If we were to accept the idea of natural talent, then the chances of several table tennis champions being born around the same time to independent families living on the same street is bizarrely improbable (unless the milkman also happened to be a table-tennis champion - which he wasn't). Syed points out two factors that were influential. The first was that one of UK's best table tennis coaches taught at the local school and the second was Syed and his colleagues had the keys to the local table tennis club (a shed with a table-tennis table in it). This meant that Syed and his friends could pop in and practise whenever they wanted (which was often) and which in turn meant that they were clocking up many hours of experience beyond what was 'normal' for other budding table-tennis players. They persevered with their practice which meant they improved their reactions, their experience and their feel for the sport. In short, they became more 'talented'.

Closer to home I can see something similar occurring with my five-year-old children, Sol and Alex. I'm a snooker fan and I follow the Championships whenever I can on the telly. This means that Postman Pat goes off and the BBC Sports coverage goes on and it's green baize and brightly coloured balls for the next few hours. You would think that my kids would protest but they sense my enthusiasm and a chance to sit with daddy and can actually spend hours following the sport assisted by my own passionate style of politically-incorrect commentary. This means that by the age of three they had already experienced more snooker than the average child their age and "Good shot!" became part of their everyday vocabulary. This in turn meant that whenever we were out somewhere where there was a snooker or pool table their little eyes would light up and they would be drawn to it like a moth to a bright light. By the age of four they had already had dozens of 'games' played to their own rules which included both players playing at the table at the same time and putting the other player off by poking them with a cue just as they are about to take their shot (most professional snooker player don't do this). For their fourth Christmas they got their very own little snooker table which became a permanent feature on the coffee table and the main source of entertainment for the next few months. Not surprisingly then on the few occasions when Alex and Sol are in public with other children of similar age or even a bit older, they are proud to show off their ability to hold a cue and pot a few balls. The on-looking parents of other children usually comment about how talented they both are and how naturally they play compared to the other kids who struggle just to hold a cue correctly. Of course, they are completely unaware of how many hundreds of hours of practice the little rascals have already racked up.

## Perseverance Produces Progress

Here's a little experiment you can do at home. Get a chess or draughts set. Put one piece in any one of the four centre squares and then find a dice[23] from somewhere. Shake the dice and move the piece according to the following instructions:

---

23- A note for grammatical perfectionists: I am well aware that technically, 'die' is the singular of the plural 'dice'. But I was brought up, like so many, using dice as a singular. It's yet another example of how the Sorites Principle applies to language and how 'incorrect' usage slowly becomes considered 'correct', so please don't write in. 'Never say die' - is one of my mottos.

1 = Move one square forwards

2 = Move one square right

3 = Move one square backwards

4 = Move one square left

5&6 = Don't move

Keep going and only stop when your piece moves off the board.

The objective of this experiment is to see what happens when you keep shaking the dice and moving the piece to create what hopefully should be a purely random movement.

What you should find is that it takes you somewhere between 15 to 75 shakes until your piece breaks the perimeter of the board. If you do this repeatedly, it will prove two things:

1. Random motion is not the same as no motion.

2. You have more time on your hands than is healthy for you.

If you live your life without direction, without a definite goal just like in this experiment, you will make some sort of apparent progress, but the progress happens more by luck than by judgement. The progress is slow and without structure. Now try this second set of instructions:

1 = Move one square forwards

2 = Move one square forwards

3 = Move one square forwards

4 = Move one square forwards

5&6 = Don't move

In this second example, you could expect to get off the board with far fewer shakes. You get there sooner by progressing faster but at the same time using less effort.

Among the many definitions of perseverance is that it is the art of keeping yourself moving forwards by overcoming obstacles, distractions and temptations that would otherwise impede your journey or lead you astray. Having perseverance guarantees that you will progress by having a fixed destination and relentlessly moving towards it. Maybe a little today, maybe a bit more tomorrow, maybe hardly any the day after that. But if you keep at it and align all your actions towards that one goal then your progress is guaranteed.

## Perseverance Produces Power

If you keep working on some field of interest for any length of time, interesting things start to happen. You start accumulating experience. You gain specialist knowledge. As we have seen, you improve your 'talent' and you make progress. Unless you are living in isolation, your knowledge, experience and talent will draw the attention of others. You will get recognition. Your achievements will be valued by those who haven't been so persevering. Your work will be valued by others in your field and you will be given status.

Being viewed by others in this way gives you power. It means that you are in an advantageous position because you are seen to be more experienced, wiser, more knowledgeable and more skilled. This means that you can do things or get people to do things for you that others who have persevered less could not. You will acquire prestige, privileges, preferential treatment and doors that previously had been barred will be opened for you to freely pass. This, in turn, will allow you to progress and develop even further. It is a virtuous circle. Constant perseverance pays dividends. You get further and further and further until one day you get an invite from the Queen to go and collect your MBE for your constant and incredibly devoted work to whatever it was that got you there in the first place.

## Perseverance Is Not Just Repetition

Perseverance is not just repetition. Perseverance is an iterative process, each small success is fed back into your subsequent actions to make them bigger, better or more effective. Each day you should be capable of achieving a tiny bit more, a tiny bit better with a tiny bit less effort. You should constantly strive for this to happen. You need to constantly push yourself, constantly stretch yourself to your limit. Because if you don't, your progress can become less and less and eventually grinds to a halt as the level of difficulty and resistance rise to meet your level of ability.

Take my typing for instance. I type quite a lot but I've never learned to type the way typist do with two hands. I'm definitely a one-handed typist and to be frank, I just type using my index and middle finger and use my thumb for the space bar. I'm nowhere near as fast as the trained typist but it is adequate for my needs. The point here is that although I've spent thousands of hours typing, I've never tried to stretch myself. So although my hand can flit lightly over the keyboard while I pay minimal attention to where each letter is, I never get any better at typing because I don't make any effort to do it any differently. I don't challenge myself about that part of my writing - my concentration is on what I am typing rather than how I am typing it.

So with every step forward there should come a corresponding increase in the challenge we set ourselves. If you continue to set yourself simple challenges your improvement will be much limited.

## Davy

A friend of mine has an 8-year-old son called Davy. Davy was frustrated because (in his own words) he was 'rubbish' at football. When this subject came up I asked his father how much time Davy had spent playing the game. 'Very little' said his dad 'we live in an apartment, so there isn't a garden to go and play in. Sometimes we go to the local park but there aren't any kids his age to play with so he just kicks the ball against the wall'. Following what we've considered above, is it any surprise that Davy's football ability is a bit below par with his classmates? Not only is he not getting in much time kicking a ball but also when he does he's not stretching himself much. If Davy wants to improve his ball skills then he needs to practise certain parts of the game such as ball control, dribbling and shooting accuracy (as well as spitting a lot and making lurid gestures to the crowd) in a structured and measurable way so that he can see he is improving. For example, instead of just kicking the ball against the wall, he would be more challenged to put a tin-can on a couple of bricks and try to hit it from a distance. He could improve ball control by trying to keep the ball off the ground while kicking it from foot to foot. He could set a course around the trees, lamp-posts and litter bins and get his dad to time him dribbling around the circuit.

Perseverance, constantly applying our experience, knowledge and skills to progress further in the direction we have chosen will inevitably achieve success. Perseverance moves mountains bigger than you ever dreamt of moving. But whether you are trying to write your first film-script or win the local tennis championship you are not going to achieve it overnight. It's going to need effort and we often associate effort with willpower. By far the commonest mistake is to assume the willpower you'll have tomorrow to help you persevere is going to be the same as the willpower you have today.

## The Problem with Willpower

Goals take time. They also require a considerable effort over that time. The most common mistake we make regarding our decision to persevere towards achieving our goals is that we can do it through sheer willpower. We genuinely believe that if we have solemnly decided to do something challenging that requires effort and persistence then we can do it simply using our self-control.

This is an overly optimistic and naïve approach to perseverance. We are staggeringly bad at predicting our emotional future and how we will feel in just a week from now. We inevitably believe that our feelings and emotions we experience today will be what we will experience in the next few months. If you are deeply in love with someone it is almost inconceivable to imagine that in only two years from now you're going to be screaming at each other over a solitary dirty coffee cup. If you are depressed, then to think of your life in the future as being anything other than depressing is almost impossible. (If someone discovered a technique that were to make it possible then I'm sure the suicide rate would plummet overnight.) As we will see, willpower, just like our feelings and emotions, is not to be relied upon in the long term. When we initially set off to achieve our new goal we are convinced it's a good idea and our willpower is enough to get us through. But it's simply not true. Our state of mind is a fickle thing and to think that we will feel the same tomorrow as we do today is a fantasy.

As well as being fickle, our willpower requires a huge mental effort and the strength of our willpower varies from hour to hour. The part of your brain responsible for controlling your willpower is called the prefrontal cortex (PFC). It's the front part of your brain, the bit just behind your forehead. Your PFC has many jobs to do and one of them is to reject other undesirable forms of behaviour that other parts of your brain keep suggesting. These suggestions would be for behaviours which would be considered more primitive, more visceral, more instinctive. Your 'instinctive' behaviour is to reach for that second helping of chocolate gateaux but it is your prefrontal cortex that rejects this suggestion and gets you to say 'no thank you. I've had enough'. This is what willpower is.

However, one important characteristic of your PFC is just like an overworked housewife,[24] it does several jobs at once. It is responsible for decision-making, for comparing concepts, setting objectives, planning, short-term memory and evaluating. This unfortunately means that just like the housewife who has to look after the baby and toddler, do the cleaning, cooking, shopping, tidy the house, answer the door and phone to wanted and unwanted callers, the amount of energy is finite and exhaustion can soon set in and when it does our willpower begins to disappear. The toddler already has started to learn that if he badgers his mummy when she is on the phone while feeding the baby and trying to cook then mummy is more likely to give in to his request for a biscuit or seven. The reality is that, unlike other parts of your brain that can keep going like one of those toy rabbits out of a certain battery advert,[25] your

---

24- ...or househusband. Of course, as I'm frequently reminded, househusbands are crap at multitasking. My standard reply is that's because we just organise our time better.

25- For example, you never get too tired to be afraid of snakes, or too tired to forget how to ride a bicycle. You don't get too tired to stop hearing - though you might get too tired to consciously concentrate on what you are trying to listen to (another job done by your PFC). You don't get too tired to recognise people's faces or voices and you don't get too tired to forget to breathe, dilate your pupils or control your body temperature.

PFC gets very tired very quickly, it consumes a lot of energy and needs to rest regularly in order to function properly.

So if you are well-rested, calm and focussed then your chances of inhibiting the desire to snack (or stay in bed or light up a cigarette) is good. However, in moments of mental exhaustion, periods of high stress or cerebral incapacitation (e.g. being drunk) your PFC simply doesn't have any energy to divert to inhibiting our more natural instincts. This is why we do things when we are stressed, tired or drunk that we wouldn't dream of doing in other circumstances such as violently trashing your computer or telling your boss to do certain physical actions that he/she would not normally find compelling. I'm as guilty as the next person. I once got so angry while I was tired and stressed I kicked one of our armchairs so hard I fractured my toe. It was very painful and I was hobbling around for days afterwards and got no sympathy whatsoever from the wife. Where was the sense in that?

Willpower is fine when we are calm and can think straight but as soon as we become stressed (and stress can often creep up on you when you're not looking) then the beast takes over and one of the first things it throws out the window is willpower.

So willpower is an admirable characteristic and some people are able to force themselves to do some phenomenal things but for most of us mere mortals, after a few days (or even just after a few hours) we need another strategy if we want to continue persevering. We need to find a way of controlling our behaviour that doesn't rely on willpower.

Fortunately, there are eight.

## 1. Prizes and Punishments

The simplest kind of motivation that we have available to us when willpower cannot be relied on comes in the form of the 'Carrot and Stick'. The carrot represents the prize; some enticing reward like a slice of cake for doing good. The stick represents the punishment; some unpleasant forfeit like having to empty the bin for doing something bad. This is one of the basic methods that the powers that be use to get you to do what they want you to do. It can be very effective in the short term. ⌐ℛ

## 2. Progress

The feeling that you are 'getting there' is a great motivator that doesn't involve giving any external prizes or punishments. The sensation of progress - of seeing your project come together is rewarding in its own right. But when the changes we are living are too small to notice, just the opposite happens - we feel frustrated and demotivated. So it is crucial we find some way to objectively monitor and acknowledge these small steps forward and to celebrate them regardless of their size. Each one is important.

Even when we are aware of our 'insignificant' progress - when our goal is intimidatingly large and our progress seems demoralizingly small, the feeling of futility is common. This is why it is extremely important to focus on the smaller activities where our progress involved will be comparatively much larger and to put our final goal out of our mind for the moment. This can be put to greater effect by dividing each little action into even smaller pieces. If we do this, then accomplishing each of these little sub-actions is even more noticeable. And, of course, the completion of each sub-action is motivating in itself.

## 3. Passion

Some people naturally have a burning desire to press on and persevere with their plans. They fervidly live for their goals. They are deeply emotionally involved in what they do. In short, they have passion.

Persevering via passion in all its forms is just having our natural feelings and emotions aligned with our rationally chosen behaviour. It might sound like 'the chicken and the egg' dilemma: did these people choose their goal because they were passionate about it? Or did they become passionate about something they rationally chose to do? Maybe it's a bit of both. Passion can drive us when our willpower has dried up, we have taken our prizes for granted and our apparent progress seems frustratingly small. If we can find a way of fixing our feelings and emotions onto our destination, then we are sorted.

## 4. Peer Pressure

The problem with passion is it comes and it goes. One day you're in love with your goal - the next day you wake up to find you're not so sure. While our own emotional drive might wax and wane, the social pressure exerted upon us from our friends, family and idols is as enduring and constant as our own emotions aren't. Finding and cultivating a benevolent peer pressure is our fourth 'P'.

## 5. Pointers

The time will come when you are so worn out you will be too numb from the neck upward to think or care what anybody else says about your goal. For these moments you need something that works even when your brain doesn't. The first of these I call Pointers: signs in one form or another that guide you in the desired direction. By restructuring our surroundings when we are in a calm and rational state we can control our behaviour for when we aren't. The easiest way to stop 'sneaking a biscuit from the biscuit barrel is to not have any tempting bikkies in there in the first place. Similarly, decorating your world with 'signs' that tell you what to do can work very well. Clocks are a great example of this: they eradicate the need for you to 'decide' to carry out an action - the clock says it's time to get up so you get up. Sign posts are the same. They guide you along, pointing out which way to go and how best to travel along each road. Today it has never been easier to set alarms, reminders and pop-up notes that can help us to persevere along the road to success.

## 6. Periodic Actions, Habits and Routines

We are all creatures of habit. In fact, we have so many of them that you could say that the person you are is really just a collection of learned habits and routines. The way we get dressed, the way we eat, the way we greet someone, how we behave when we're bored, stressed or tired are all actions that we tend to do so often that we do them without much thought at all. And quite rightly so. If you had to think of how to do every single thing, then you'd start to go a bit mad. It would be like learning to ride the bicycle all over again. There is part of our brain whose job it is to take familiar series of actions (like riding a bike, folding your arms or going to the loo) and store them deep down so that they become fixed, automatic. This is very good news for things we want to do regularly - not so good for those 'bad' habits like biting your nails.

## 7. Patience

The next factor is Patience: Not expecting to achieve too much too soon. Here I'm talking about the ability to wait - the ability to delay gratification. There is another type of patience which is the ability to not go ballistic when your five-year-old is making too much noise in spite of being told to be quiet for the umpteenth time. This has to do with positive karma, counting to ten and going for calming walks around the garden. However, desirable this kind of patience is, it is not the kind that I'm interested in. The patience I'm referring to here is the ability to postpone gratification to optimise results. It's about not expecting too much, too soon. It's about focussing on the small wins rather than on that big and distant objective. If we fail to control our patience we can become dissatisfied with our agonisingly slow progress (even if it is steady). We will want to have too much, too soon and that is the recipe for disaster. The greasy slope of negativity starts where our patience ends. Regardless of what passion drives you, if you can't learn to wait for the good things in life, then the bad ones are ready waiting to be served.

## 8. Positivity

In *The Lord of the Rings*, Tolkien wrote as part of the epigraph "One Ring to rule them all, one Ring to find them. One Ring to bring them all and in the darkness bind them." which refers to the power the One Ring has over all the other nineteen created by Sauron and given out as Christmas presents to the other unsuspecting rulers of Middle-earth.

Just like the nineteen rings, the previous seven factors all depend upon the last one. They all depend on your ability to keep a positive mental attitude. When you start applying the Sorites Principle all will go very well for a while but one day you'll find yourself feeling a bit down, you'll feel that it's all a bit too much and 'It's all for nought'. In that moment you aren't going to pay much attention to the other factors. You'll want to give up and head off back to your comfort zone.

Keeping a positive mental attitude is not easy at times but there are lots of things that you can do during those 'dark' moments when the Lord of Pessimism and General Futility pop round to see if you want to stop with all that perseverance nonsense and come out to play.

So if the question is 'What can we do to increase our perseverance?" the answer is to stop relying on willpower and start using the eight great P's of perseverance: Prizes, Progress, Passion, Peer pressure, Pointers, Periodic actions, Patience and Positivity. We will consider each of these eight P's one by one in the following eight chapters.

## Things to Think About

✦ Of the three parts to applying the Sorites Principle, it is the third part, the part of perseverance, which is undoubtedly the most challenging: Persistently putting in the pieces of the puzzle every day for months or even years.

✦ Perseverance is one of the top characteristics required for success. If we can master the art of perseverance we can do almost anything.

✦ Perseverance begets talent, progress and power which in turn all strengthen your ability to persevere more.

✦ It's a common mistake to believe we can rely on willpower to guarantee our perseverance. But willpower is a limited resource and runs out much sooner than we expect.

✦ The good news is that in addition to willpower there are eight factors we can use to improve your perseverance.

✦ They are the eight P's of Perseverance: Prizes, Progress, Passion, Peer Pressure, Pointers, Periodic Actions, Patience and Positivity

## Top Tips

✦ Don't rely on willpower to do anything that requires long-term dedication.

✦ Concentrate on improving your powers of perseverance. Whichever way you do it will pay dividends.

✦ Use the eight great P's of perseverance to maintain your drive and momentum to keep you going and on track.

## Questions to Ask Yourself (and Answer)

❈ How many cases do you know of where someone tried to achieve some important long-term goal just by using willpower and failed?

❈ Who do you know who is good at persevering? How do they do it?

❈ Does it sound like any of their methods coincide with the eight great P's of perseverance?

# 7 Prizes And Punishments

In one sense at least, the way we live our lives, the things we do and say, is fairly logical in the sense that there is a reason behind most of it. The reason might not be clear at times, but nevertheless it is still there. You hit the snooze button seven times in the morning not because of some random occurrence but because some part of your brain responsible for actions tells you to do so (we will be learning the name of this part of your brain later). It's simple cause and effect. The bat hits the ball and the ball is 'stimulated' to move. The stimuli that we receive come in the form of motivation. As we are sitting at our desk we see the wall in front of us. This is incoming data in the form of visual information but there is no stimulus to action because of it. If, however, we were hurtling towards it at 100 mph in our newly acquired Lamborghini our attitude to the aforementioned wall would stimulate us in a different way and our motivation to act would be very different. It is only when we want something that we choose to act to get what we want or to avoid getting what we don't want. It is the carrot and stick analogy of human behaviour. The carrot represents the reward;

the stick represents the punishment. Either there is something that we want to get (like an extra half hour in a nice warm and snuggly bed) or there is something we want to avoid (like becoming the owner of one and a half tons of scrap metal along with spending two months in intensive care). Everything we do is to achieve something or avoid something else. A baby cries because it wants to feed, a child stops being naughty to avoid going on the naughty step. But the world is a complex place and there are so many carrots and sticks lying around that it is not obvious which ones our subconscious are thinking of when we decide to do certain things. For example, when you feel like going to the pub it could be due to one of several reasons such as…

* You're thirsty

* You're bored

* You want distraction from your current task

* You want a shot of alcohol

* You want social interaction

* You want to stretch your legs

* You always go the pub at this time

* You will be chastised if you don't

* You want to avoid missing out

* You want to find a potential mate

Whether we are conscious of it or not, everything we do has its reason. If we want to control better our behaviour, then we need to identify what drives us and use it to our advantage.

Introspection is a powerful and unique ability that we have: to be able to observe and consider our own thoughts and feelings. You can look under the bonnet of a car and see that the dirty air-filter is causing a certain 'behaviour' of the car. Without getting too psychoanalytical, it is interesting (and sometimes surprising) to investigate why we behave the way we do.

# Jenny

Jenny had recently got a good job in a large company with about two hundred other people. But after just a couple of months she had a behavioural problem. She found she would often get up and go to the office canteen where she would get a coffee and a snack and chat to her new colleges. This would have been fine but she was getting to the stage where she was almost spending as much time in the canteen as she did working. "It just sort of happens" she said, "I find myself standing up and walking out of my office." After ruling out the need for coffee, the social factors, claustrophobia and any negative associations to her work, Jenny considered the physical factor. She was a young urban professional person who was slim, healthy and fit. At least for the moment. But it turned out that she had changed her lifestyle quite a lot after starting her new job. Firstly, she now drove to work. She'd just bought her first car which she was very proud about. Her previous job had involved a 70-minute commute by train and metro. At her new place of work there was no convenient public transport. Secondly, Jenny had been regularly going to a gym which was next to her old workplace. There was no gym near her new place of work. What Jenny was surprised to discover was that her body was craving exercise. Sitting at a desk didn't come naturally to her and she needed to stretch her legs. So, armed with this new-found discovery, instead of going to the canteen she decided to go for a swift walk round the park (there was a green area with a few trees and a kiddies' play area next door to the office buildings. She also discovered that one of the neighbouring companies had a morning yoga club that she was able to join. She had been misinterpreting her desire to move as a desire to go to the canteen. Once identified and correctly addressed, her time-wasting behaviour stopped.

So our actions are driven by certain needs or motivators. Satisfying these needs gives us a little biochemical reward: the prize of a small dose of dopamine (or similar feel-good molecules such as serotonin, oxytocin or endorphins). This is a very good thing because if not, you'd spend your days loafing around feeling completely unmotivated. You'd feel like there wasn't much point in doing anything. The world would seem grey and unappetising. You would feel apathetic, moody and unable to concentrate since nothing would interest you very much. We know this because it happens. Chronic depression can be caused by unhealthily low levels of dopamine and the drugs that are used to combat depression, such as Prozac, increase its production.

So if the production of dopamine is associated with motivation and getting-up-off-your-arse-and-doing-things then one key factor to persevering is to increase dopamine production. Right? Yes. I'm glad you're paying attention. You won't have to browse the internet for long before you find that apart from stuffing yourself with Prozac (not recommended) there are general factors that can affect dopamine production such as a healthy diet, exercise and meditation. I completely support and recommend each of these activities but in my experience they are the result of the Sorites Principle not the cause. What I mean by this is that to change your diet permanently, to get out of the house and go jogging regularly or to adjust your lifestyle to incorporate meditation every day in itself requires a vast amount of perseverance. It's the chicken and the egg dilemma: do you need to eat, exercise and meditate to be able to persevere more or do you persevere more to be able to eat, exercise and meditate. I believe it's the latter. Voluntarily changing any important life routine requires persistence and, coincidentally, some of these are beneficial for increasing your ability to persevere. It's a virtuous circle. But for some reason I don't think the news that we should eat healthily, get regular exercise and learn to chill out is going to come as a great surprise to anyone. If in your case, you would like to learn more about these subjects then I have included a few recommended reads at the back of this book.

## Rewarding the Right Actions

Let's say you want to run your first marathon. Using the observation that rewarding yourself can increase your motivation then it might seem common sense to assign yourself a nice big reward for achieving your goal. You might decide that after you have crossed that marathon finishing line you'll go out and get yourself a nice new laptop. Lovely! That should increase the likelihood of your success, shouldn't it? You might be surprised and a bit confused to learn that the answer is no.

If you're starting from scratch, running your first marathon is rather a big and daunting challenge. And big challenges have a nasty habit of appearing too big, too challenging and too difficult. By adding a big prize to your big challenge you are increasing your focus on the end goal and in doing so you make its ominous presence felt even more. This is a bad thing. As we shall see in the chapter on patience, a key factor to perseverance is to focus on the little things that you can do today. Successfully achieving your goal is not the REASON why you persevere; successfully achieving your goal is the RESULT of your perseverance. It is a question of cause and effect. Successfully running a marathon is caused by training every day. So it is the training you need to focus on. Therefore, whereas putting a reward on the end goal draws our attention to the big result (which is undesirable and counterproductive), putting a reward on doing the activity that will lead to the end result (in this case training) draws our attention to the easier actions which are also easier to mentally cope with and carry out which in turn leads to an increased sense of progress....

What I'm interested in here, as I hope you are, too, is what processes we can incorporate into our lives today that will improve our perseverance straight away. What is it that motivates us? What carrots do we have at our disposal to dangle in front of us? And in front of what actions do we need to dangle them?

## Green Shields

Of course, if anyone knows anything about carrot-dangling, I would suggest looking at the world of marketing. Do you remember Green Shield Stamps? Green Shield Stamps were a way of rewarding you for shopping at certain retailers. Little squares of green printed perforated paper you had to lick on the back (like the old postage stamps) and stick them into a little Green Shield Stamp book. This book could then be exchanged for more goods. Everyone collected them. I remember my mum having loads of them stuffed in the kitchen drawer. The stamps became so popular and pervasive that they became part of British culture and even referred to in the song lyrics of groups such as Genesis and Jethro Tull. Sadly, they passed their heyday and in 1991 disappeared altogether when the whole business was rebranded and successfully remarketed as Argos.

The Green Shield Stamp was an example of a token prize. Not a prize in itself, but a token or symbol that represents something else. And it only seems like human nature to want to collect such things.

## Gold Stars

Did your teacher give out gold stars at school? Mine did. I remember glowing with pride when I saw a little gold star stuck next to something that I'd written or drawn.[26] There's something intrinsically satisfying about getting gold stars or anything similar for that matter.

For a period, I used them with my kids to persuade them to follow their bedtime routine. Each had their own sheet with a grid of twenty-five boxes. Each time they succumbed to my pleas of getting into their pyjamas, cleaning their teeth and getting into bed (as opposed to running around upstairs starkers, chucking stuff about and bouncing themselves off the furniture: their default bedtime behaviour) they got a star, lovingly drawn by daddy. With hindsight, and for anyone out there thinking of trying the same with their own offspring I recommend putting the star-grid NEXT to the bed where they can see it easily because mine had to get out of bed to check that I was keeping to my end of the bargain which was, admittedly, somewhat self-defeating.

Since then, it's a system I've used on other occasions, including myself, as well as other people and which I very much recommend. The Star Chart as I refer to it (as it sounds good), is as simple as it is effective. You can make your own or you can download and print a copy from www.guid-publications.com/soritesworksheets/.

Then go to your local stationery shop (or order from amazon) a pack of self-adhesive gold merit stars. They don't have to be gold, you can get any colour or shape you like, the important thing is that it is something

---

26- Most likely drawn, actually, as my drawing ability far superseded my writing ability - to be honest I reckon I was well behind in the literacy department through most of my school life. In fact, even at secondary school my English was so far behind that my teacher refused to let me sit my 'O' level English saying it was pointless. My father got really angry as 'O' level English was a basic requirement to get into any university. He went to see the headmaster but it was a waste of time. In the end my father had to pay for me to sit my English 'O' level which I'm happy to say I passed or at least scraped through, much to my teacher's embarrassment.

## Figure 3: Star Chart with specified prize

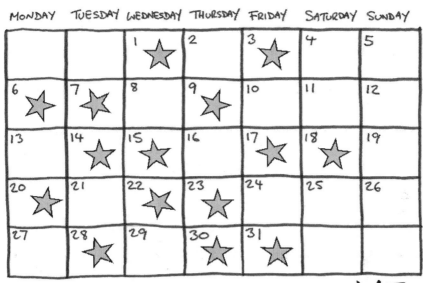

15 STARS = HAVING CAR PROPERLY CLEANED **YES!!!**

that works for you. At the bottom of the paper, underneath the grid write down how many stars you want to collect and what you are going to reward yourself with once you have collected them. It doesn't have to be anything impressive. In fact, for some people, including myself, just seeing the stars build up is satisfying in itself. But just like the Green Shield Stamps, it helps if there is some sort of prize, some sort of treat that you get (and ONLY get) when you get the specified number of stars. I prefer the word 'treat' because is best summarises the idea behind the technique: a little something exceptional that will give you great pleasure. But it's your choice. The more it is something that you emotionally look forward to the better. A few good examples of personal treats for completing your Star Chart are:

* Watch your favourite film or TV series

* An extra hour in bed on Sunday morning

* An extra-long luxurious soak in the bath

* A massage / facial / manicure / pedicure, etc.

* Getting someone to make you a nice breakfast in bed

* Visiting a local place of interest that you've never seen

* Sitting in the park for an hour with a flask of tea and bread for feeding the birds

* Doing something culturally uplifting like going to the theatre, cinema, opera, ballet, a sports event, a concert or poetry recital

* Go to a bar, restaurant or other establishment that is usually out of your price range

* Subscribe for a year's supply of an interesting magazine

The Star Chart works on a number of levels. Firstly, you're getting a little prize at the end of each day and we like getting prizes.

Secondly, it works using our emotions. There's something to be proud of in getting a gold star which goes back all the way to our childhood. Getting a gold star made us feel good. At least it made me feel good. It is a way of getting deserved recognition for our efforts and that is truly motivating.

Thirdly, the Star Chart itself serves as a pointer; something to remind us that there is something to do that we shouldn't forget about.

Finally, if you do it regularly, you should find that it starts to become a constructive habit. The more days you do it, the easier the action will be and at some point you'll find yourself doing the desired activity automatically. Once you get to that point then progress will become almost inevitable.

So as you can see, the Daily Star Chart is a useful little tool that you can adapt to meet your own preferences. Obviously you don't have to use gold stars if you don't think they're 'you'. Just drawing yourself a star or simply ticking off the successful days is fine.

It just has to be something that you enjoy; something that gives you pleasure just by thinking about it. Your prize doesn't have to be impressive, expensive or gift-wrapped. Even the simplest of pleasures can be rewarding, like the simple satisfaction of completing a task and ticking it off.

## Tom

Tom spends most of his working day behind his laptop. He is a freelance translator. He does company brochures, product instructions and press releases, he's also translating his first novel which he finds really challenging.

He works using his own rewards system.

It works in two parts. The first part is that before he goes to sleep he prepares a list of all the things he has to do the following day. Not general things. Specific jobs and tasks that can be easily executed. He puts them all down in an Excel sheet along with times, resources required, notes etc. His 'reward' is then to go through the day crossing each one off. Not by deleting the task but by changing the background of the row to a different colour. Each coloured row is a little reward that says 'I've been done!' This alone is sufficiently motivating for him to get as many things done as possible.

The second part is to break his working day up unto chunks. He knows that if he's not careful he can become tired, groggy and stale at his computer so to avoid this, he times himself in hourly chunks. He sets his alarm on his iPhone to go off after 55 minutes. When it sounds, Tom gets up, does a bit of stretching, a few press-ups, walks about outside which gets a bit of fresh air into his lungs and the cobwebs out of his brain. After that he goes back to his laptop, resets his alarm and starts working again. The simple activity of ticking off another hour, getting up and walking around the garden is a reward sufficient to keep Tom contentedly chugging away at his work. On the days when he is struggling, he has an extra bonus up his sleeve. When he feels he needs an extra push, he packs up his laptop and notes and takes himself and his work (by foot) to the local library. It's quiet, there are fewer distractions and there's a lovely bar in the same building that serves homemade carrot cake and fresh coffee. There is also a large DVD library, so after doing a few hours there he treats himself with a slice of cake, a coffee and whatever film tickles his fancy. It's simple but it works.[27]

So prizes don't have to be big important things they can be ridiculously simple. In fact, the they don't even have to be real at all in order for this technique to work. You can even use abstract prizes such as a personal points system.

## Judith

If ever they make a film about Barbie using real people, then they couldn't do much better than cast Judith for the lead part. Judith is Barbie. She has long blond hair which she keeps in a long flowing pony tail. She is tall and energetic. She bounces with positive energy. She has a lively walk, a positive attitude and two young children. And as you might have already suspected, she is slim. Which you might not find all that surprising until you learn that Judith spent most of her early life verging on the obese.

Up until about fifteen, Judith was, using her own words, "on the wrong side of chubby". She got bullied at school. She had a low self-esteem. She tended to lead a withdrawn, solitary life as a teenager, throwing herself into her studies. As a consequence, she got great grades (which only seemed to exacerbate the bullying) but seeing her marks each week was one of the few things that seemed to be a reward for her efforts.

It was just before her sixteenth birthday that Judith had an epiphany. Her reasoning was this. She knew that she enjoyed studying partly because she got good marks and that motivated her, so why not try using the same idea to lose weight. That evening she drew up a points system. It was something like this:

---

27- I can't help but add here that I have a similar system myself regarding the use of an alarm. In my case, my alarm is white, weighs about 80kgs and is called a 'washing machine' which, even as I type these words, I can see from my desk, churning a warm soup of children's clothes and towels around and around and around. The cycle is 72 minutes. When it beeps that's my 'alarm' to get up and do a bit of 'stretching' next to the washing line in the garden while the kettle boils for another nice refreshing cup of tea.

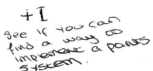

| | |
|---|---|
| Not snacking between breakfast and lunch | 1 point |
| Not snacking between lunch and dinner | 1 point |
| Not snacking between dinner and breakfast | 2 points |
| Drinking water instead of fizzy drinks with each meal | 1 point |
| Each piece of fruit eaten | 1 point |
| 10 minutes on the family's exercise bike | 1 point |

For Judith, it was a simple idea that made a huge difference. 'Before, when I tried not to snack, it just made me think about snacking even more. I got really stressed and just ended up stuffing myself. But with my points list I was thinking about what I could do to get more points. I started thinking in a different way. It was suddenly a bonus not to snack. I know that sounds stupid because not snacking should have been a bonus in itself, shouldn't it? But I couldn't see the bonus before. With my points system, I could see the bonus straight away. It was immediate.' She moved the exercise bike into her bedroom and started burning off the calories while watching TV.

In her first month, she lost over 4 lbs. The most she could ever remember losing. But for her, the breakthrough was not that she'd lost a bit of weight. It was that the whole process had been relatively easy compared to the agony of trying to limit her snacking by sheer willpower.

For her sixteenth birthday, she got a membership to the local gym where she immediately established her own points system again: 1 point for every ten lengths of the swimming pool, 5 points for an aerobics session etc. She would add her points up each day, add her daily points up each week and add those up for the month. Each month she tried (and usually succeeded) to beat the previous month's score. Judith is both proud and slightly ashamed to confess to the fact that by her seventeenth birthday she had lost over 5 st. She has kept to her points system ever since (even on her honeymoon). Her husband is called Ken.

A word of caution. It is best not to reward yourself with something that is counterproductive to your intended goal. It might seem sort of 'logical' that if you've been 'restraining' yourself for so long that letting go and cutting yourself a bit of slack for just one tiny moment might seem only fair. If you're on the road to getting into shape, then a reward of a teeny tiny box of choccies might be very tempting. This idea has one important flaw. If your objective is to get up two hours early every day to write your novel, then having a lie-in till noon is not a good idea. This is partly because the treat in itself is not conducive to your momentum of progress but more importantly it has an important adverse psychological effect. As, hopefully, you're going to be looking at your Star Chart every day as you start loading it with shiny stars, then seeing a counterproductive prize at the end will seed a tiny piece of emotional resistance against what it is that you're doing and, as we have already established, a tiny thing applied every day can steadily build up into something quite formidable. So one day you would wake up and find that the yearning for your ill-chosen prize is so great that it scuppers your steady progress. The whole plan goes pear-shaped and it's back to square one. No. It's better to choose something that has nothing to do with your new goal: something different, something virtuous, something extracurricular.

So, giving yourself points and prizes is one way of motivation. But wait! There is more…

## The Power of Praise

Do you remember the last time you were with a group of friends or at a party and someone said something complimentary about you? Someone commented that you were an amazing cook, or an organizational wizard or whatever. That compliment gave you a little glow of pride, a tiny tingle of pleasure. That is another example of dopamine being produced. We all like receiving praise for our efforts so long as it is sincere, genuine and without ulterior motive. I have a colleague whose universe is rather more egocentric than what most people consider healthy. Every time he comes to me and says the likes of "Hey, Ian, what you did last week was really great, wasn't it? You were great! Really great!" I know he's after something. It's not so much praise I'm experiencing but blatant manipulation and blatant manipulation doesn't get my dopamine flowing. In fact, it does just the opposite, it increases my adrenaline level as I have to fight off the urge to throw my waste paper bin at him and shove him out the door.

There is a certain type of person to whom giving praise comes naturally. These people are more emotionally stable, positive, and have a higher-than average emotional intelligence. Such people are worth their weight in gold especially when it comes to your perseverance.

If you don't have at least one person like this in your life, then I suggest you get yourself one. It is really important to get encouragement, praise and positive feedback. Yes, it is possible to walk that long and lonely road to your goal alone, without any kind of support but it sure as hell makes a difference if you don't have to.

One way to get encouragement, praise and positive feedback is to ask for it. No one is going to praise you if you make your new goal a secret. How can people encourage you about something they are unaware of? So I recommend that you confide in someone who can be supportive and give you that all-important positive encouragement, praise and feedback that, little by little, contribute to your steady progress and perseverance. This, in fact, is one of the major roles of a coach. Channelling positive energy in this way not only provides that all important dose of dopamine but also reduces your self-doubt, reinforces your self-esteem and strengthens resolution to keep going.

## Ivan

Ivan is a personal coach at a local gym. He knows all about the importance of praise and encouragement. In fact, if you look up 'encouragement' in the dictionary you'll probably find his photo next to the definition. Everything he says, everything he does is done to spur his coachees onwards and upwards.

Ivan, in his early thirties, is a natural sports coach. Lean, keen, he bristles with a natural positive energy that is contagious. He naturally takes a vested interest and responsibility in his coachees - who they are, what they want to achieve, where they are coming from, what they are trying to escape. Once he understands what it is that makes each person tick, he verbally probes them to find out what it is that gets the best reaction and from then on it's a constant flow of motivation in the form of praise, encouragement and feedback.

"It's really important," Ivan explains, "to first make a social link with the people I coach. I have to get on their wavelength, connect with them mentally. This way they feel comfortable having me as their coach. They can 'open up' and explain what it is they're trying to do, how they feel about it, what it is they want to get out of their time with me. Once they start doing that, I get to learn what buttons I have to press that will get them fired up and pushing themselves all the way. Sometimes it's just imagining themselves on the beach next summer showing off their bodies. Sometimes it's about how much weight they're losing by burning off all that fat. Sometimes it's about getting back into shape for their boyfriend or girlfriend or getting fitter to live long enough to be at their kid's wedding, that sort of thing."

He gives the example of one of the more challenging people he worked with, Sara. When Sara first came to the gym, she was in a bad way. She had an unstable relationship with her unstable boyfriend. She was vastly overweight, had a pitifully low self-esteem and just felt her life was in an irresolvable mess. Ivan dealt with this by overflowing with praise, encouragement and positive feedback.

"I started off by pointing out that she'd made a really good move by deciding to come to the gym. That if she felt unhappy about her size which was affecting her health, mentally as well as physically, then this was a great way to do something about it. At the start she needed constant support, constant encouragement. She felt well out of her comfort zone, that the gym was a place for slim people. So I ended up doing a 'deal' with her. That it wasn't just her, it was the two of us. We were a team of two. She had to do something for me and I'd have to do something for her. That reinforced her obligation for showing up the next day. So each day I'd praise her for showing up and keeping to her side of the bargain. We'd go over what she'd had to eat and I'd let her know how great I thought she'd done. It was tough, really tough. When things were okay between her and her boyfriend then she'd be alright. But when they were having trouble, when he had left her (he left her frequently) then she'd lose it. She'd binge on junk food and stuff and put on overnight what it had taken her a month to lose."

What Sara needed was all about praise. Not unconditional praise. Not praise without a valid reason. But Ivan used praise with Sara all the time. Every tiny effort that she made was recognised and approved whether it was for having eaten responsibly since her last visit, doing an extra set of repetitions on a machine or just showing up at the gym when she was having a bad day. Every step forward was celebrated and every setback was shared by Sara and Ivan. Slowly but surely, Sara's progress became steadier, and her relapses became fewer and she began to see the light at the end of the tunnel. After two years she got herself on track, fuelled by Ivan's prizes of praise and encouragement. At the time of writing, Sara is currently the size she wants to be, has an improved self-image, a new boyfriend and still goes regularly to the gym with her favourite coach, Ivan.

## Certify Yourself

When we bought our house in 2006, it came with a garden, and the garden came with a set of swings. Not your cheap-n-nasty-fall-to-pieces-after-a-few-years type of swing but the solid, enduring, galvanised-iron type with thick metal chains supporting metal slatted seats that will last multiple generations. And as far as we know, these swings already have lasted several generations as we are sure they are at least 50 years old if not more, originally installed for a little girl who grew up to be the nice retired lady, from whom we bought the house.

Of course, this means two things. The first is that the 'terrible twins' love playing on them, not just swinging but climbing, pushing, twisting and other rough-and-tumble activities. The second is that the swings were made before the health and safety regs became so omnipresent regarding design specifications for children's outdoor play products. If you put these two factors together, you get the inevitable: Little Alex, who was about three at the time got struck in the face by a heavy iron-slatted swing-seat. He caught the full force on his right eyebrow which was neatly split in two down to the bone. There was blood everywhere. It was all very dramatic. Fortunately, one of the advantages to living where we do is that we live within spitting distance of Sant Joan de Déu Children's Hospital - one of the best hospitals in Europe, specialising in paediatrics, gynaecology and obstetrics, to which he was swiftly taken. When the little soldier came out he was the proud brandisher of four stitches and an official certificate of extreme bravery which he was extremely chuffed about. He proudly showed it off to anyone he could and since then it has remained stuck on his bedroom wall in recognition of that eventful day.

**Figure 4: Certificate of a brave little boy**

We all like to get recognition for our efforts. There's nothing more disheartening than spending the weekend cleaning the place from top to bottom - hoovering, scrubbing, dusting, wiping, tidying in preparation for your parent's weekly visit, only to have your mother ask upon their arrival whether you have thought about getting in a home-helper as clearly you are struggling to look after yourself.[28]

Certificates are another example of how having something written down can resonate with our feelings of pride and our need for recognition. I confess to having my certificates framed and hanging on the wall of my office: my degree certificate, my postgraduate certificate of education, my M.B.A., my advanced driving certificate, various public speaking

---

28- While your father surreptitiously investigates the contents of the cupboard where you keep the booze

certificates and my best daddy-in-the-world certificate.[29] And why not? Better than rotting away in the darker recesses of some cupboard, isn't it?

To some of us, a certificate, especially a homemade one, might seem trivial, an insignificant sheet of paper, but remember the whole foundation of the Sorites Principle is based on the importance and strength of accumulated insignificance. Even if the certificates are homemade, they still bear testimony to achievements that are both very real and very significant.

In the company where I work, the rookies, the employees completing their first year got their own personalised 'Certificate of Extreme Excellence' in recognition of having survived their first year. These were awarded during a tongue-in-cheek presentation ceremony at the end-of-year party which was originally intended as more of a form of entertainment than anything serious. But as the tradition continued people started to take the whole thing quite seriously with senior employees pointing out that they never got their certificate. Little by little, the Certificate became an important part of the company's culture.

So if you're the sort of person who appreciates recognition for what you do (and to be honest I think we all do) why not try motivating yourself by creating your own certificate in recognition of some of the landmark stages of the progress achieved towards your goal: for the first stone lost, the first nicotine-free month, your first paying client or for your first 10,000 words written. If you're the creative sort, then you can design and create your own. But you don't have to reinvent the wheel; there are several websites such as www.certificatemagic.com that allow you to produce your own personalised certificates almost effortlessly in just a few minutes. Check them out. Find the one that most catches your imagination and lovingly prepare a certificate for each landmark stage of your goal journey. Keep them stored away ready for each of those important days when you make the mark. Then you can have your own private ceremony of Extreme Excellence and proudly pin up your certificate in recognition of the fact that your insignificant actions are starting to achieve a lot.

---

29- Written in crayon

## Figure 5: A personal progress certificate

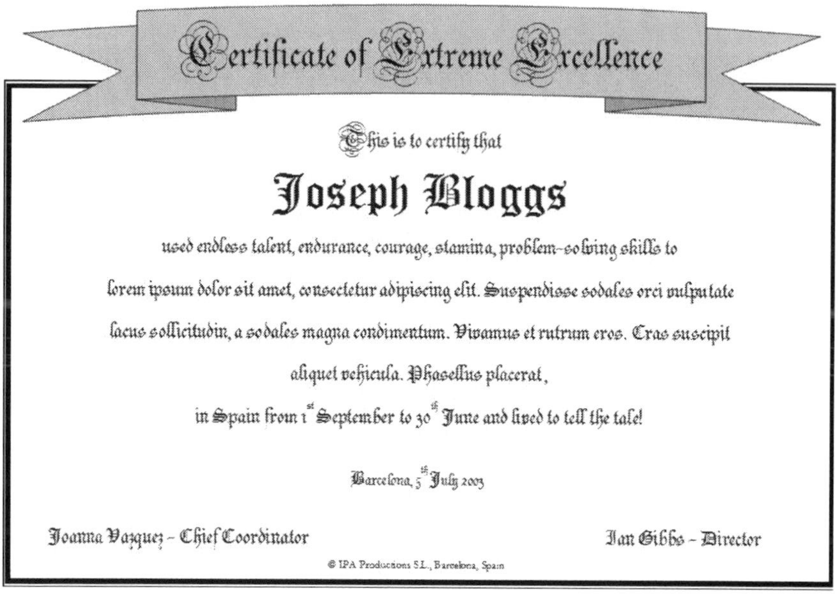

**Certificate of Extreme Excellence**

This is to certify that

# Joseph Bloggs

used endless talent, endurance, courage, stamina, problem-solving skills to

lorem ipsum dolor sit amet, consectetur adipiscing elit. Suspendisse sodales orci vulputate

lacus sollicitudin, a sodales magna condimentum. Vivamus et rutrum eros. Cras suscipit

aliquet vehicula. Phasellus placerat,

in Spain from 1ˢᵗ September to 30ᵗʰ June and lived to tell the tale!

Barcelona, 5ᵗʰ July 2003

Joanna Vazquez - Chief Coordinator                Ian Gibbs - Director

© IPA Producions S.L., Barcelona, Spain

## Punishment

While the right rewards are a very good way to motivate yourself to action, it is not the only way to motivate. As the title of this chapter suggests, there is the flip side of the motivational record: punishment. Although it is a negative concept, I assure you, punishments or the threat of punishment, can be very effective. Think of a job that you would really prefer not to do like thoroughly cleaning the cupboard under the kitchen sink, hoovering your car, giving your mother-in-law a foot massage, getting the first round in after work, polishing the family silver or spending a whole day without your mobile phone. Make a pledge and solemnly promise yourself that if you fail to carry out today's task you shall pay your forfeit.

## Nyr

Nyr Eyal is an American author who used the threat of punishment to maintain his perseverance in going to the gym. He called his method

'Burn or burn'. He got a calendar, a hundred-dollar note and a cigarette lighter. He hung the calendar somewhere where he'd see it clearly every day (in this case on his wardrobe door) and leave the lighter next to it. Every morning he'd stick the hundred-dollar note to that day's date on the calendar. The deal was this: he gave himself two options. Either he would go to bed that night having been to the gym or he would burn the money. Using this method, he managed to keep himself going to the gym every day for six months. That for me is pretty effective.

This method obviously works because we don't like the idea of seeing our money go up in smoke. But there's actually a bit more to it than that. The way we relate to losing something is rather different to the way we relate to gaining something. It's called 'loss aversion'. Some psychologists reckon that the way we relate to losing something is about four times as strong as the way we relate to gaining it. Thus our indignation in having to pay a surcharge of five pounds is much stronger than being given a discount of five pounds. People simply don't like losing stuff.

I did a similar thing to Nyr's 'Burn or burn' method when I was trying to explain the importance of getting an invoice to my working colleagues a few years ago. Team leaders would be going out in their company vans, filling up with petrol and bringing back receipts. The problem with this was that although a receipt justified their expenses, the company couldn't reclaim the tax on the payment and at 21% that was more than €10 for every €50 spent. The problem was that asking for an invoice at the petrol station took extra time and so was often considered inconvenient. So at one staff meeting I asked someone for a €5 note. I put it on a plate in the middle of the floor and set fire to it. The look of shock/horror on their faces said it all and it wasn't more than a few seconds when the unfortunate owner of the €5 leapt up and tried to save what was left of her money.[30] I then explained that each time they filled up a van with €50 of petrol and didn't get an invoice they were effectively burning two €5 notes. The shock tactic worked and since then the Teams remembered to get their paperwork done correctly.

So the avoidance of 'burning up' your money clearly has a powerful effect on our behaviour. But there are other options to burning the stuff. You

---

30- Don't worry, I exchanged her burned note for a good one afterwards.

could also promise yourself to give the money away if you don't follow through on your goal. There are certain 'Personal Commitment Contract' websites that offer a service designed to get you motivated such as StickK. com. The method here is to choose yourself a goal, a referee, an amount of money and a charity. If you keep going and reach your goal then good for you, nothing happens. But if you don't, then the aforesaid money is sent to the charity. The motivation is even stronger if you choose what the site refers to as an anti-charity. For example, if you hate a certain pop group or singer then you could pledge the money to their fan club. Beeminder. com offers a similar service but just pocket the money for themselves if you fail.

If you like this sort of idea but the business with cash is a stumbling block for you, there are various websites that do similar things without the money-losing factor. There's even a site called aherk.com. where you set yourself a commitment contract where the punishment is the posting of an embarrassing photo of yourself onto Facebook for all the world to see.

There is one more factor that I'd like to mention and that is another dopamine producing concept that doesn't involve any physical reward, it's not about interacting with other people. Nevertheless, it is something that is so important and fundamental that without it, any attempt at perseverance is futile and doomed from the very beginning. That factor is the sense of progress and it is so important that I've decided to dedicate the next chapter to it.

## Things to Think About

- All of us are driven by the idea of some sort of prize or by the avoidance of some sort of punishment.
- It is important to assign a prize to the behaviour that will achieve your goal rather that to the goal itself, which can be counterproductive.
- The prize doesn't need to be big, expensive or even particularly special. It just needs to be enjoyable. Something that gives you that tiny dose of dopamine like standing up and having a bit of a stretch.
- Prizes don't even have to be real. You can give yourself a symbolic prize such as points, or your own 'well-done' certificate.
- Prizes depend very much on the individual. What works for one person doesn't necessarily mean it will work for you.
- Some people respond better to punishments.
- Our brains are much more sensitive to negative concepts such as criticism, penalties and loss.
- Similar to prizes, finding the right punishment can be the key to motivating yourself onwards towards your goal.

## Top Tips

✚ Motivate yourself to do some task you find hard to get round to by promising yourself a 'treat', such as watching your favourite film or having an extra-long bath with no interruptions.

✚ Get yourself a Star Chart and some gold merit stars and reward yourself every successful day by giving yourself a nice shiny gold star.

✚ Notice what other little things give you that little dose of dopamine and incorporate them into your work plan.

✚ Draw up a points system and give yourself a daily 'perseverance' score.

✚ Get a praise sponsor who can say 'Well done!' when appropriate.

✚ Promise yourself to do some undesirable activity if you fail to do your daily task such as taking out the rubbish, cleaning the oven or doing the ironing.

✚ Prepare yourself a personal progress certificate for reaching the next stage of your goal. Award it to yourself when you get there.

✚ Bet on yourself. If you don't do your daily task, then it is going to cost you money. Pledge to give money to a charity you disagree with.

✚ Promise yourself your lack of motivation will cost you. Promise yourself you will burn a £20 note if you don't follow through.

## Questions to Ask Yourself (and Answer)

❋ Which of these techniques are you already using? Which could you start to using to strengthen your perseverance?

❋ What are the key actions you need to carry out regularly where a bit of carrot-dangling could help you persevere?

❋ What prizes could you give yourself that would motivate you to do a task you need to complete?

❋ Who could be your Praise Sponsor?

❋ Would giving yourself points for completing desirable actions help you recognise and value your perseverance? If so, what would your points system be? What format would you use to keep score? A simple tally system? A score board? A graph? A bar-chart? Is there some app that could help? Where would you keep the record of your score so it would most motivate you when you see it?

❋ Are you the sort of person who responds more to punishment avoidance? If so, which punishments or forfeits would get you going?

# 8 Progress

*"Every day in every way I get better and better and better."* - Émile Coué de la Châtaigneraie

I live in a metropolitan park and it's beautiful. It's called the Natural Park of Collserola, 20,000 acres of Oak, Holly Oak and Mediterranean Pine which borders Barcelona on its northern side. There's only one main road, lovingly called the C-16, which cuts straight through the middle along its North-South axis. So to get home after a hard day's slog at the office I have two choices - the short way or the long way. The short way is to take a one-and-a-half-mile stretch of the city's ring road which takes me straight to the southern entrance of the park. The alternative is you can take a 20-mile detour going all the way round the eastern side of the park to enter from the north. This route is obviously longer in distance and time and uses more fuel but there are the occasional evenings when I take it. Not because it's more scenic or more interesting. It's because the usual alternative - the city's outer ring road gets so overloaded with heavy traffic, so chock-a-block that just the thought of grinding forward at a snail's pace in first gear is so unacceptably unbearable that almost any alternative is preferable. Even if it requires travelling a further distance, consuming more fuel and ultimately takes a longer time door to door, the fact that it doesn't involve sitting in an agonisingly slow-moving traffic jam is reason enough for me to take the long way home. I can zip along the relatively fluid route unhindered at a more dignified and liberating speed. Here it is not the time or the cost that influences my choice of action. It is the visceral need for a sensation of progress and my corresponding lack of patience with rush-hour[31] and it is a problem that anyone who has spent time in a theme park or at airport security during peak season knows all too well. A lack of perceived progress is a major problem.

As we have already seen, one of the problems of imperceptible change is it's imperceptible, that is to say, imperceptible on a daily basis. Even if something you have done has caused a perceivable change that change might be so small compared to your final objective you might view it negatively, considering the whole thing futile.

The sense of futility is a great demotivator. The feeling that you're wasting your time and effort, that it's all for nought is one of, if not the main reason why many people just give up.

This is a bad thing. What can you do to stop it?

The first thing is that if you're going to measure your progress then you need to have progress that is measurable. Measurable things are important as they are an objective assessment of your progress. If it depends on someone's opinion, then you can't really be sure. Your mum might assure you that you're looking 'much thinner' these days but how much is 'much thinner' and is it true? Is she just trying to be nice or has senility already started to set in and is she confusing you with someone else? To be objective you need some irrefutable truth, something that has a numerical value that can be taken down and used against you in times of despondency.

---

31- Rush-hour: A total misnomer if ever there was one given that no-one is rushing anywhere and that it lasts from 4:30pm (when everyone sets off to collect their kids from school) to 8pm. I think there should be a world-wide petition to ditch the expression completely and replace it with 'the four-hour crawl'.

At times this is easy. Losing weight is, by definition, a process of weighing yourself; a precise no-nonsense numerical which can't be changed even by standing on one leg and breathing in. If you're writing a book, then checking your word count is one way to measure progress, even if quantity and quality are not the same thing. If you're training for a marathon, then you can either measure the time it takes you to run your training route. Furthermore, if you're just starting, you can measure how far you managed to run before you collapsed from exhaustion and even then after that you can measure your heart rate over time to see how long it takes to come out of the 'danger: heart attack imminent!' zone.

You can divide your task up into smaller parts and cross each part off as you finish it. Whenever it falls upon me to do a bit of home decorating and repaint a room in the house I have two techniques that help me. The first is to put my iPod onto random Rock. I find that the energy that listening to Led Zeppelin, Blue Oyster Cult and the Arctic Monkeys (to name but a few) really do put me in the mood. The second is to roughly mark out a square metre of the wall. I then focus on this area. It takes just a minute to paint and it gives an immediate sense of achievement.

The same thing applies to weeding the garden or sweeping the yard. If you have a large area to do, then the overall task can be demoralising. But dividing it up into smaller plots makes each one much less arduous. If you divide the garden into quarters and then each quarter into a quarter, then you're working on just one sixteen of the space. So you go through each sixteenth with the motivation of having made the progress of completing yet another section buoying you along.

## Your Progress Calendar

But at other times it's not so straight forward. What about becoming a proficient public speaker? Or becoming a more patient parent? A better trombone player or a better boss? These things, although very real, are not so easy to measure. Here is where you need to be a bit more creative. One option is to recognise experience. According to the people who claim to know about this sort of thing, if we want to become really good at something we need to practice for between 5,000 to 10,000 hours. So notching up your hours of practice is certainly one thing to count. Here

I would recommend using a 'Progress Calendar'. You take a monthly calendar, preferably a big one, the sort of calendar that has a large agreeable picture on the top half and the dates of the month printed in large, easy-to-see numbers printed underneath on the bottom half. They're the sort of calendars that you come across in gift shops or hung on the wall of teenagers' bedrooms or car mechanics' workshops. If you don't have the time or motivation to get yourself such a calendar, then an easy alternative is just to draw up your own monthly calendar (minus the agreeable photo). Just draw up a grid of 5 rows by seven columns. Label each column with the days of the week and then put the appropriate date in each of the boxes (see figure 6) or if that's too much trouble just go to www.guid-publications.com/soritesworksheets/ and print off a few copies. (and if you can't even find the motivation to do that I suggest you put this book down, watch a bit of telly and forget about trying to succeed in any of the long-term objectives that you might have). The final step, if you'd like to do this seriously is to get hold of a big thick marker pen.

**Figure 6: A progress calendar**

Once you've got your Progress Calendar, you stick it somewhere where you are going to easily and frequently see it (next to your bed, desk, computer or similar) with blu-tack (did I mention you'll need blu-tack, too?). From then on it's simple. Each day that you work on your objective, doing those 20 push-ups, doing those three hours' practice, writing your 500 words or whatever, you cross off the corresponding date with a gratifyingly great big black cross. Over the following days you'll see your calendar disappearing under a forest of thick black crosses which is motivating in itself. This powerful little tool, similar to the Star Chart works because it operates using several factors at the same time.

Just like getting gold stars, crossing off the successfully completed date with a thick black marker feels good. It's a little dose of dopamine. Another tiny prize that makes us feel good about ourselves.

Again, the existence of the Progress Calendar serves as a reminder to carry out your daily task (as well as an annoying reminder that you failed to do a day if such a day happens).

But the main objective and strength of the Progress Chart is the pressure to cross off ALL the dates: to leave no date uncrossed, to never break the chain. This helps your desired activity to become a daily habit and once you get to the point where you have gone for twenty or thirty or a hundred days without leaving a gap then the pressure to keep going becomes stronger and stronger.

I'm told that the American comedian Jerry Seinfeld used a variation of this technique to develop his comedy writing skills. In his case he used a yearly calendar, a big sheet with all the 365 days to view. He crossed off each day that he worked on his comedy writing. For him, it was extremely important that once he had started crossing off the days, he never left a single day blank, never to break the momentum of his work. Trying to measure your ability to write funny jokes is tricky, but counting the days that you've worked on it is simple and it certainly seemed to work for Mr. Seinfeld.

Another variation is to count the number of times you don't do something. At one point, and I'm ashamed to admit this, I was struggling to be a good dad. By this I mean that I was finding it increasingly difficult to keep control of my temper with my two young children (about 4 years old at the time) and I started to regularly shout at them and lose my temper with increasing frequency. This started to worry me especially when my outbursts of anger started to get physical (remember my fractured toe and the armchair?). What was worse was I learned venting off anger and stress in aggressive outbursts actually increases the likelihood of such behaviour in the future: it becomes habit forming. So it had to stop.

One way to deal with anger management is just to try and go as many days as you can without having an outburst. I'm pleased to say that it worked for me and that even though the twins are always thinking up new and original ways to try daddy's patience, daddy is able to remain comparatively calm, count to ten (or a hundred) and deal with the situation without going ballistic, which I think is for the good of everybody. In this case, I didn't use my Progress Calendar (it was already being used to track my writing progress) but I did keep mental track of it and once I'd reached a week of not 'losing it' I started to feel much better about myself and found it much easier to keep myself under control. Very satisfactory progress as far as my family is concerned.

So if you find it challenging to measure your progress by what you are doing, then how about measuring what you're not doing? How long are you able to do something before it goes wrong? How long can you juggle before you drop a ball? How many pieces of music can you play without making a mistake? As you get better, the frequency of undesirable events should also slowly come down. These can also be measured. How many days can you go without upsetting an employee? How long are you able to go before you lose your temper? How long can you go before one of your patients sues for malpractice? Sometimes what you're doing wrong is much more obvious than what you're doing right.

Pick it, track it, reduce it. It's all progress little by little.

Sometimes there's no other choice but to go on opinion. If you want to become a great dancer or synchronised swimmer, then here progress is very much based on opinion. But make sure it's somebody else's opinion and not your own. On the days that you're feeling down, your opinion of what you're doing and the progress you are making will be down, too. You'll change your opinion to justify your frustration and lack of motivation. This negative opinion of yourself will then fuel your negative thoughts to increase your frustration. That's one reason why top sportspeople and artists have coaches: someone who can give an objective evaluation of how they are doing free from self-criticism and self-doubt.

So once you've got one or two things to measure, the next step is to measure them in a realistic way and not to overdo it which can be counterproductive. As we have already said, over a short period of time such as just one day, progress can appear negligible. Of course we are going to remember that although on a daily basis progress may seem negligible, these small steps are real and each one counts. Added together they won't seem quite so insignificant. So forget about trying to measure any progress on a daily basis. Depending on what you're aiming for, do a progress check once a week, once a fortnight or once a month.

For example: If your target is to get your weight under control and down by 10 lbs, then your weight can fluctuate quite a lot from day to day. But over the period of just one week these fluctuations can even themselves out so that you can get a clear idea of how you are really doing.[32] However, if you're training to be a public speaker, then a week is too short a period; you need to monitor your progress on a monthly basis using the evaluation of your objective assessor.

## The Progress Plotter

Of all the tips, tricks and techniques for making the most of the Sorites Principle, this one, The Progress Plotter, is the one that has helped me the most. While other people I have met have used and recommended others, this is the one that I would stick with if I had to rely on just one of them and it has helped me immensely.

One of the wonderful features of writing on the computer is the word count button. In order to write this book, I decided to write at least five hundred words per day. I don't know if you consider five hundred a little or a lot but again it gives me a sense of achievement, a sense of progress at the end of each day to see that I've met my objective. Of course, I'm free to write more if I wish - if I find the creative juices flowing so to speak. But so long as I do my five hundred a day I know I'll have my first manuscript within six months.

One way to keep the sense of progress going is to set up flag points. That

---

32- There is a counter-argument in favour of weighing yourself every day which tackles the risk of over-eating on any one day. While losing weight happens gradually - putting it on doesn't happen by the same process. On those days when we have broken our diet, we have a tendency to say 'Sod it - I've blown my diet for today so I might as well eat what I want until tomorrow' and proceed to stuff ourselves stupid. This of course is wrong: every chocolate biscuit carries its own calories. Knowing you're going to be weighing yourself at the end of the day helps reduce the likelihood of this happening.

is to say to establish markers in some way to identify how far along the

road to success you are. This is why it's important to have goals that can be measured. If it can be measured, then each small progress can be measured. And these anticipated points can be put on the calendar or marked on a graph against time. Plotting these off each week can help to keep the sense of progress working and helps as motivation.

Doing this gives us another simple tool - the Progress Plotter. I can honestly say that this tool has been the single most useful and effective method to keep up motivation and perseverance not just for writing this book but also for keeping my weight under control (more or less) and for paying off the seemingly endless mortgage repayments. Unlike the Progress Calendar which works on counting the days of your past performance, the Progress Plotter works by showing what progress you expect to make in the future and comparing that to reality. This is very useful for a number of reasons.

Firstly, it clarifies (and reminds you if you need reminding) your long-term goal such as writing 75,000 words, getting down to 15 st. or giving the bloody bank all their bloody money back.

Secondly, it lets you see clearly that not only is your long-term goal achievable but also when you are expected to achieve it. Just knowing this provides us with a certainty which can in itself be very reassuring. It gives us a clear idea of time and is a tremendous help in controlling our patience (see chapter on Patience).

Thirdly, it gives you an immediate, short-term target of what you need to be focussing on today, which inevitably is something much more modest and realistic than what you might feel if you dwelt on your final objective for too long.

Finally, it gives you a clear idea of whether your current actions are keeping you on schedule. You can see if you need to pull your socks up a bit and press forwards before pressing forwards becomes such a gargantuan task that you'd need to pull your socks up over your ears.

Here's how it works (if you find working with graphs and numbers easy and you aren't phased by expressions such as 'Y-axis' and 'intersection' then you might want to skip this bit).

**Figure 7: A Progress Plotter**

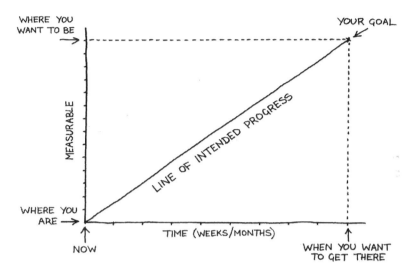

Get a sheet of paper and draw a simple graph. This means drawing a vertical line down the left-hand side and a horizontal line along the bottom in such a way that the two lines meet (intersect) in the bottom left-hand part of the sheet. On the vertical line (see figure 7) you mark the value of what you want to achieve at one end (top or bottom, it's your choice) and at the other end you mark zero or whatever is the current value of what you have achieved so far. So the one for writing this book had 75,000 at the top. Then I wrote the date my publisher wanted the first draft ready on her desk (1st June) at the far right end of the bottom line and the starting date on the bottom left corner. Then you divide the lines into regular steps marking the days, weeks or months. You then mark (or plot) two points. The first represents where you are now with your project and will be either in the bottom or top left hand corner. You then mark the second point which is represents when you want to reach your goal.

Now get a ruler and draw a straight line from the first point to the second. This line represents the future progress you have to make if you want to reach your goal on time. It is your anticipated progress. It shows for any given date what value you are expected to have reached in order to keep up with your anticipated progress. You can then mark each day (week, month or whatever) with the progress you have made and see how that compares to your intended progress.

**Figure 8: My Progress Plotter**

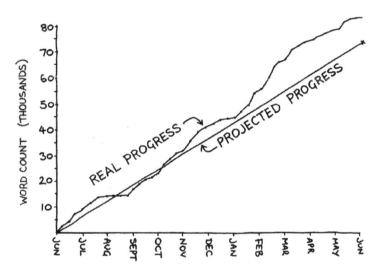

I'm very pleased to say that, as you can see from the diagram, my word count progressed steadily ahead of schedule and my publisher was very happy. Sadly, I can't say the same about my weight or my mortgage repayments. Nevertheless, at least I could see what was going wrong and allowed me to make the effort to make the necessary adjustments to get myself back on track or to readjust my goal.

Again, if you find the idea of drawing up your own graph gives you the heebie-jeebies then you can find a user-friendly version here www.guid-publications.com/soritesworksheets/.

Going back to the weight loss example, if you want to shed a few pounds then, remembering to be realistic, you will no doubt have already decided how much your target weight is. Let's say your target weight is 12 st., and at the moment you're just tipping the scales at 13 st. So that's a stone you are planning to lose. If you feel that losing just over a pound per week is realistic then that equates to about 5 lbs per month. So your markers could be 12 st. 9 lbs at the end of this month, 12 st. 4 lbs at the end of the following, and 11 st. 13 lbs at the end of the 3-month period.

**Figure 9: Progress Plotter for losing weight**

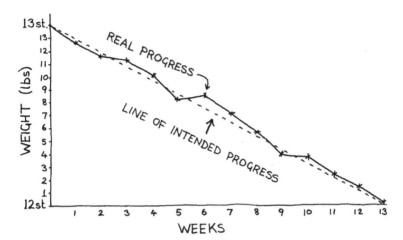

## Your Goal Diary Is Your Progress Diary

As I mentioned in chapter 4 on goal planning, your Goal Diary is for recording all the little successful steps you achieve during your journey towards your long-term objective. Each of these steps represents a tiny piece of progress. They may seem small but over time they become substantial - a force that has to be reckoned with. Each new habit incorporated into your daily routine, each new contact, each deadline met, each weekly target reached are all steps forward. Every new experience, every useful discovery, every pearl of wisdom represents progress in one way or another.

If you are serious about applying the Sorites Principle to maximum effect you must record all of these steps forward because the memory of them will start to fade. You will take your current situation for granted, finding it difficult to recall what it was like just a few months ago. So by writing them all down, you have them fixed in a place where you can easily find them during those dark moments when you feel that you are wasting your time and you're not getting anywhere. Going over your notes is like standing on the hillside and looking back to see how far you've come, which is often much further than you have given yourself credit for.

In my Goal Diary, I not only wrote down my word counts, I wrote down new ideas when they came to me. I wrote down useful contacts I made, meetings and interviews I had. Being interviewed on the local T.V. station was a really motivating step forward. I kept note of new useful contacts I made in the publishing world, my applications and submissions, and the day I signed my contract. I kept a record of feedback from people who'd read my manuscript samples and of workshops and meetings I attended. I also kept a record of when a client was making useful progress persevering and what techniques they had used. Steadily over time, this diary became solidly reassuring proof that things were unmistakeably progressing in the right direction.

Such reassuring proof is uplifting. It increases our positivity and inspires us to go onwards and upwards. We need to have this because when our willpower has evaporated and the prizes and punishments are no longer having the effect they once used to, we need inspiration to kick-start us back into action. Having a clear feeling of progress is one such way to do this but inspiration takes us into the realms of your emotional brain and if you are going to venture down that road, there is someone you need to know about. Some call him the Prince of Passion; some call him the Instant Gratification Monkey. I just call him Grog and you'll be meeting him in the next chapter.

## Things to Think About

✤ In addition to prizes and punishments, the sensation of progress is a motivator in itself.

✤ Similarly, a lack of perceived progress can be demotivating.

✤ When considering a big objective, our progress can seem relatively negligible. This is bad.

✤ If we break down our objectives into smaller pieces, our daily or weekly progress is much more significant.

✤ It is important that progress is detectable and measurable.

✤ Keeping a progress record helps maintain motivation.

✤ Consulting your progress record can also help buoy you up when you're feeling a bit down by seeing how much you have achieved so far.

## Top Tips

✛ Start measuring and recording your actions and activities.

✛ Record only measurable data, don't rely on opinions unless absolutely necessary.

✛ You can use the Star Chart or Progress Calendar as a way of measuring the days successfully worked.

✛ Make a Progress Plotter by drawing a graph and plotting your progress regularly.

✛ Keep a record of your progress in your Goal Diary.

✛ Remember the mathematics of the Sorites Principle: It's just a question of simple addition.

## Questions to Ask Yourself (and Answer)

❈ What are the measurables for your goal?

❈ Which would best suit you - A Star Chart, Progress Calendar or Progress Plotter? Are there any other ways of tracking your progress?

❈ When are you going to make it? Where is the best place to put it?

❈ What different ways could you record your progress in your Goal Diary? Which would best work for you?

❈ What Apps are there that could help you track your progress?

 **9 ▶ Passion**

*"You can do anything as long as you have the passion, the drive, the focus, and the support"* - Sabrina Bryan

Once upon a time there was a Hare and a Tortoise. They were neighbours and tried to get along with each other the best they could. You might have heard of them before. Tortoise liked the simple life, steadily going about his daily business. But hare was busy, busy, busy. She was always doing things. She loved attending meetings, replying to e-mails, starting new projects, texting, rushing from one place to another. Tortoise observed that although Hare was 'busy', she didn't actually 'do' anything.

"What do you mean?" replied hare, "I do lots of things."

"You keep yourself very busy," agreed Tortoise "but you don't really achieve anything, do you?"

Hare felt quite affronted by Tortoise's words. She liked to think of herself as an industrious bunny and she felt her reputation was at stake. After a brief and emotional conversation, where Tortoise tried to underline the importance of steady perseverance, they agreed to have a race, to see just exactly who was right.

The day of the race arrived and the whole town turned out to witness the 'event of the year': A one-mile race cross-country.

Bang! The starting pistol went off and so did Hare, off over the horizon in a cloud of dust leaving the Tortoise and the crowd behind. But it was a hot day and about halfway along the course Hare spotted a nice shady patch with lots of juicy foliage. So she decided to stop for a little snack and maybe a short rest, while she was relaxing she checked her new smartphone and answered a few messages from well-wishers. She took a couple of selfies and posted them on Facebook. She then did a bit of Tweeting. She checked the latest value of carrots on the stock exchange and checked the news headlines. She then got up, stretched, scratched her back, picked a bit of leaf from between her teeth and set off running again. The finishing line was now within sight along with the awaiting crowd. But as she got close, she felt something was wrong. It was too easy. Tortoise was still nowhere to be seen. Just a few feet away from the white tape and with the crowd staring with bated breath, Hare stopped in a moment of concerned thought. "Where's Tortoise? Is he alright? Has he had a heart attack from all the exertion?" To the crowd's astonishment, she turned round and started running back towards where she thought Tortoise would be, lying prostrate on the ground, gasping for breath. It wasn't long before she found him. But he was fine, steadily plodding along.

"Are you alright?" asked Hare

"I'm fine," replied Tortoise, "Have you won yet?"

"No," said Hare, "I was worried about you."

"Ha! See what I mean? Excuses, excuses, excuses! You'll never change. Always doing things but never getting anywhere. You're just a useless busybody who'll never achieve anything!"

Hare was incensed! Here she was, trying to be nice only to be openly insulted and ridiculed! Well, she wasn't going to stand for it. She would show this retarded reptile what she could do. Trying to hold back the tears and with a pain in her soul, she set off at full pelt. In a few minutes she could see the finish again. With the crowd cheering, flags flying and the local press taking photos, Hare burst through the white tape and won the race.

The moral of this story? Even the least persistent are capable of great achievements when emotionally motivated.

## An Introduction to Grog

Whether you like it or not there is a part of your mind that you cannot control. There is an inner part of your brain that is strong and powerful. It is a more primitive, dare I say 'caveman' part of your brain. In his book The Happiness Hypothesis, Jonathan Haidt refers to it as your 'elephant', in his book The Chimp Paradox, Steve Peters calls it your 'Inner Chimp' and

**Figure 10: Grog**

Tim Urban named it his 'Instant Gratification Monkey' but in this book I am going to simply refer to it as 'Grog', partly in reverence to the lovable caveman's caveman character of Johnny Hart's wonderful comic strip B.C. and partly because I think it is funnier.[33]

---

33- In my case, Grog is definitely male. But depending on your gender and persuasion your Grog might be male, female, straight, gay, bi-sexual or asexual. In an attempt to be fair while avoiding all the 'he or she, his or he' references I shall refer to Grog as male and female alternatingly in the following chapters.

Grog the caveman-monkey-elephant, represents the deep-rooted primate part of our brain that governs our emotions, feelings and values,[34] and thus has a very strong influence on our actions, even when we don't like to admit it. It's Grog that makes us terrified of harmless creepy-crawlies, even when we can logically explain to ourselves that there is no need to be frightened. It is Grog that causes us to do the most amazingly irrational and counterproductive acts such as stuffing our faces with chocolate, hurling abuse at our loved ones and trying to have sex with drunken strangers at parties. Grog controls our likes and dislikes, our loves and hates, our envy, pride and fears. And Grog is strong - very strong. At times, trying to stop Grog can feel as futile as trying to stop the tide from coming in. One of the major tasks of the rational part of our brain, the prefrontal cortex, is to try to inhibit Grog's impulses; to keep him under control. This requires a great deal of energy. As Jonathan Haidt puts it - trying to steer Grog in the direction you want is like "a rider sitting on top of an elephant and trying to get it to go somewhere it doesn't want to go." You can shout at it, tug its ears, slap its head, poke it with a stick, bribe it with peanuts or threaten it with taxidermy but it will have precious little effect, if any. We spend an awful lot of energy just trying to stop Grog from getting angry and whacking someone in the face. It takes even more to overcome Grog's natural reluctance and persuade him to do something he's not at all interested in.

If you want to get to know your Grog a little better just quickly knock back half a bottle of whisky (or whatever your favourite tipple might be) and then sit back and enjoy the ride. Alcohol is a relaxant and one of the things it relaxes is the grip your prefrontal cortex has on Grog's reins. By relaxing your PFC, you are relaxing the control you have on the caveman part of your thinking process. So after a few Bacardi and Cokes, regardless of whether you become aggressive, excited, randy, depressed, abusive or just plain giggly, they are all the emotional manifestations of your Grog.[35]

---

34- Grog deals in things like joy, embarrassment and sadness but also in visceral values such as justice, recognition, freedom and social values such as the need for being accepted and fitting in. It is Grog who makes us fall victim so often to peer pressure - a subject that we shall be exploring later.

35- Personally speaking, I inevitably become sleepy. I can only therefore conclude that my caveman lives in perpetual hibernation.

When you start to investigate it, and contrary to what you might think, it is our emotions that mostly govern our life rather than our logical thought. This is not necessarily such a bad thing. Some might be of the opinion that if we didn't have emotions, then we would be calm, serene, logical and clean-living, a bit like Mr. Spock the Vulcan (actually half-Vulcan) from the American sci-fi series Star Trek. Sadly, this is not quite true. If we stopped having emotions, we would simply stop functioning. Without our emotions we would be unable to perform the simplest of tasks, such as getting up in the morning. We would wake up and consider the day before us, should we get up now or have an extra half an hour in bed? Should we go to work or not? Should we get dressed or not? Should we have a shower or not? And if so, with what temperature water? And for how long?

Without our feelings and emotions, without our likes and dislikes, we have no preferences, no fears and absolutely no motivation to do anything. We'd stay in bed unable to make any decision. Without emotions our world would be a monotone grey. Nothing would seem important. Everything would seem pointless and we would be bewildered by a vast expanse of irrelevant choices none of which held any interest for us. We would become completely dysfunctional. We would quite literally curl up and die.

So if we agree that curling up and dying is bad, then having feelings and emotions is not only a good thing but also vital for leading any sort of day-to-day life. It is our emotions that give us the motivation to get out of bed, eat, drink and be merry, as well as nobler actions like striving for world peace and saving the whales.

But our emotions don't work by choice. Grog has his own agenda. He has his own reasons for feeling the way he does. Some of these we are aware of and others we are not (and some we try to convince ourselves that we are aware of when really we aren't and vice versa - it all gets horribly complicated at times).

## Grog's Agenda

So Grog has his own reasons for feeling what he feels, whether it supports your intended behaviour or not, it makes little difference. Grog doesn't do logic. Grog doesn't speak English for that matter or any other recognised language. Grog likes what Grog likes, hates what Grog hates, fears what Grog fears and doesn't give a flying fig about what your prefrontal cortex has to say about the matter.

You can try reasoning with Grog until the proverbial cows come home but Grog doesn't do reason either. No amount of explaining, arguing, persuading or pleading is going to work. You might just as well try whistling out of your arse. Grog is not listening.

For example: You have resolved to embark on a get fit programme. This is a good idea because it will help you lose weight, reduce your blood pressure and risks of cardiovascular disease. It will help you build up your muscle tone, increase stamina and etc. Getting up a couple of hours early and doing a solid hour in the gym before starting work is clearly the logical thing to do. It all seems so obvious. Any idiot could see that it's a great idea.

Unfortunately, Grog is not just 'any idiot'. Grog didn't get the memo. Even if someone stapled the memo to his receding forehead it wouldn't make any difference. Grog can't read. On your third day of your great project, it's therefore no surprise that you find yourself lying in your wonderfully warm and cosy bed feeling how nice it would be to give gym a miss for just this one day. It's Grog that presses the snooze alarm (six times). It's Grog that makes you desire that chocolate biscuit for breakfast. It's Grog that gets you to take the lift instead of the stairs. And the amazing thing is how often we just give in and go with the flow, deftly flexing and twisting our rational thinking to self-justify our behaviour: "One day off won't hurt", "I've been good, I deserve a rest", "It's just a teeny weeny chocolate doughnut." So who is running the show here? You or your Grog? (We both know the answer, don't we?).

## Grogarian

You cannot run from Grog, you cannot hide. You have to accept that you have a strong and over-emotional caveman pushing most of the buttons of your behaviour control centre and the sooner you start learning to deal with this concept, the better.

This, of course, is easier said than done. How do you control someone who is ten times stronger than you? How do you communicate with someone who doesn't speak your language?

The answer is simple: You have to learn theirs.

When I said that Grog doesn't speak your language, it doesn't mean that you can't communicate with Grog. It's just that Grog only speaks 'Grogarian'. And Grogarian is a form of communication entirely based on emotions and feelings. It can be impressively efficient and is. In fact, it may be much more abundant than you might at first think. Consider its use in films for example. Scenes are set, characters are established and plots developed not by someone explaining things to us rationally, but by the emotional content of what we see. Consider the opening scene in the first Star Wars film (Episode IV A New Hope). The good guys in the cute little rebel space craft are pursued, attacked and finally captured by the bad guys in a humongously ominous Star Destroyer. No explanation of what's happening is given, no dialogue is spoken but we get it - which means Grog gets it. The images, lighting, camera position and soundtrack music all communicate to us a clear emotional content. Not only do we understand what is happening, we also know how we feel about it, too.

## How to Persuade Someone to Become Vegetarian

I was once accosted by two very nice young ladies in the town centre. They were out crusading in the name of vegetarianism and were explaining why eating meat is wrong and how there is a more noble and moral route to our nutritional input via a path based on lentils, nuts and tofu. While their logic might have been infallible, their words fell on deaf ears. Not mine, but Grog's. My Grog loves chicken tikka masala, bacon sandwiches and the occasional good steak, not to mention a full English breakfast, a nice 'tapa' of cured ham (with a nice reserve wine) and even the occasional visit to Macdonald's (I have kid's. That's my excuse). If you are serious about getting someone to go vegetarian, then there is a method that is much more effective: take them to an abattoir. The stench of death, the sound and smell of warm furry animals being automatedly slaughtered, the look of the fear and panic in their eyes as these living, breathing, warm-blooded creatures are converted into carcasses at the flick of a switch and the thrust of a bolt is enough to communicate directly with most Grogs. You stagger out of there into the fresh, clean air with a mixture of nausea, repugnance and disgust unable to look at a Big Mac in the same way ever again. There's no logical reasoning, no structured argument of facts. Yet the result is that you have been emotionally dissuaded from eating meat and even if someone now tried to logically persuade you to go back to your carnivorous diet, they would have little success.[36]

So here is the key to this chapter. If you want your Grog to get in line with your intended plan, you have to learn to cultivate the corresponding emotional attitude. You have to learn to subtly point your Grog in the direction you want to go. Not by force. Not by reason. But by the use of emotional influencers and once you learn to do this, then the whole thing suddenly becomes a whole different ball game.

It is the stronger emotions and feelings which get us moving - fervently felt visceral stuff such as love, injustice, pride, desire and the burning need for recognition. Grog provides you with hundreds of feelings and emotions each day but you need to identify the ones that work for you. Unless you have a very specialised outlook on life, feelings such as glumness, bemusement or ambivalence are not going to do much for you at all. You must pick out those that are capable of inspiring you to greater heights than ever - to move mountains by passion alone and if you can channel just one or two of them towards supporting your desired goal, if you can get your Grog to sing from the same hymn sheet as your PFC, then you will find that your thoughts and behaviour become aligned in perfect harmony.

---

36- I speak from experience. Something very similar happened to me. I was invited to a wine tasting evening (for free!) and not wishing to let anyone down I embraced the opportunity with gusto. The evening started well, not only were there several excellent wines to quaff but also a nice selection of cheeses and pâtés. But after half an hour, the guest speaker started to give a presentation about pâté and how it is made. To be perfectly frank, I would have preferred not to know. For me the evening would have gone much better if he would've stayed at home with his wife and kids. But he didn't. He came eager to share his knowledge. He had a projector with photos and diagrams of what they do to the poor creatures and then to top it all he handed out a set of raw livers on little plates which we were then instructed to cut up and 'taste'. Now I admit that in my experience, the British are more squeamish than the Spanish - many of whom still find the public goading, torture and execution of warm-blooded animals to be entertaining. But I also confess to being in the 'more squeamish' half of the British population. Suffice it to say that I found the whole experience absolutely gross and halfway through the presentation I had to invent a polite excuse to go outside, get some fresh air and put my head between my knees. After that I was unable to bring myself to eat pâté for years. Even though the effect gradually wears off and I do have the occasional bit of pâté every now and again, I am unable to enjoy pâté in the same way as I did before that day.

# Lewis

Lewis was an oboist. He played the oboe and he was rather good at it. So good in fact that he played professionally in the OBC (that's the Barcelona Symphony and Catalonia National Orchestra). Now, even professional musicians have to practise (or rehearse as they call it). So Lewis, like all the rest of the OBC had to practice a lot. The OBC's programme changes each week, so this meant that during the week, all the musicians rehearsed together in the concert hall and performed Friday to Sunday. But they were also expected to practise at home alone for three to five hours a day. Now if you've been playing the same instrument in the same orchestra for as long as Lewis had, you'd get some pieces of music that you really love playing, others that you quite like, and others, a bit less than that. There are even some pieces you really don't care much for at all. In fact, as Lewis said, some of the more contemporary pieces sounded like "a bunch of angry musicians having a fight with a pack of demented farm animals." As you might imagine, Lewis's passion for practising such pieces was below average. But Lewis had a trick he used that I feel is a good example of what this chapter is about.

Lewis lived in an apartment in the posh part of the city. With five storeys and two apartments to each floor that was ten apartments in total. Every one of the families was nice except for one: An old couple that were the terror of the community: Mr. and Mrs. Grump. They were the sort of retired couple who thought that everyone else was stupid, irresponsible or mad (or all three). They both wore thick 1950's style glasses and neither of them smiled - at least not in public. They never had a good word to say about anyone and several thousand bad ones which they would use regularly to anyone who they came across in the communal passageways of the building. When they weren't telling someone off for not using the lift properly, or for having a dog that behaved like a dog, or having children that behaved like children, they were complaining, ridiculing and malevolently gossiping about one of the other neighbours. Unfortunately for Lewis, Mr. and Mrs. Grump lived next-door to him. They did, however, tend to respect him a bit more than the others, partly because he didn't have a dog, partly because he didn't have children, but mostly because being an orchestral musician carried a bit of kudos and maybe the Grumps felt it raised the status of the building. Nevertheless, Lewis didn't like them very much at all. So whenever he had to practise a piece of music that for him sounded like "an angry duck having a tantrum" he thought about how much he was annoying The Grumps next-door. It was his way of getting revenge on behalf of the rest of the neighbours and this, he felt, brought a little bit of social justice to the community and helped him through some of the more 'challenging' parts of the pieces that he had to perform.

## Framing

Lewis used a way of looking at the situation to bring into play the two strong feelings of injustice and revenge, which helped him persevere with his goal: to practise a piece of music he didn't like. This technique of finding a way to think of something from a useful emotional perspective is called 'framing' and, believe me, it is really useful. Framing or 'reframing' as it is sometimes referred to is the skill of taking a concept and then looking at it from a different point of view. We change the way that we look at it. A painting can be improved by literally changing the frame that surrounds it and a scene from a film can be improved by changing the position of the camera to enhance the suspense. In the opening shots from Larry and Andy Wachowski's multi-award-winning film 'The Matrix' the suspense is generated straight away as we look at a retro-feel (black background with low-resolution green digits) computer screen while overhearing an enigmatic phone conversation. We don't know whose computer we are looking at. We don't know where it is. We don't know who we are listening to or what exactly they are talking about. The whole 'frame' of the shot communicates with our Grog to generate the feeling of intrigue. The scene then changes to that of a pure bright white light which sharply contrasts with the dim green light of the previous screen shot. Again, we don't know what the light is - the intrigue is maintained. The camera pans backwards to reveal that we are looking into the torch of a modern day American cop who has pistol at the ready and looks like he is expecting trouble. Both of these shots would give a very different emotion if the camera position were different. And so framing is the art of finding the right way to look at something in order to get the optimum benefit.

# Four Little Words

I use my own framing technique for getting myself up early every morning to write this book. I think of my father. My father left this mortal world (of natural causes) several years ago and even though he lived 2000 miles away from me I felt his loss very much. I wasn't aware of it until after his death that the relationship he had had with his father had been quite difficult. His father, my granddad, was a South Yorkshire working man in the Sheffield steel industry and that, as far as my granddad was concerned, was good enough for anybody. So it must have been a bit of a shock for my poor granddad when it turned out that his son had done so well at school that he had the chance of going on to university. I am told that my granddad didn't like the idea of his son becoming all 'educated'. He felt that his son should leave school as early as possible to go and get a proper job like any decent man should. In spite of the pleas of my dad's headmaster, my granddad refused to pay for his son to go on to higher education. I'm pleased to say that in spite of a complete lack of paternal support, once he could afford it, he managed to put himself through night school and got qualified as a charted accountant. Because of this, he went on to become financial director of several companies in the steel industry (one after another, not all at the same time) as well as setting up his own small company on the side.

I'm now absolutely sure that it was this lack of paternal support that caused my father to give me all the moral support he could. He encouraged me to go to university, he encouraged me to go abroad to discover the world for myself, he was there for me when I set up my first business and was my own personal coach when I was having problems with staff, finances or whatever. He never told me what to do. He just listened well and gave me his opinion, a few suggestions and lots of moral support. Sadly, he was no longer around when I decided to write this book, in the physical sense at least. But often I think of what he would have thought and what he would have said and how proud he would have felt to hold a copy of this book in his hands with his son's name on it. So every day when I'm struggling with my Grog to get up early, to sit down and start writing I just imagine what my father would have said to me at the end of the week when we would briefly update each other on the phone. He wasn't a man of many words. If I had told him that once again I had written my quota for week all he would have said were four words "Well done, my son!" But more often than not those four words are the only words I need to get myself going.

## Back in Control

Framing can be very effective because it is a way for the rational thinking part of our brain to influence and 'guide' our emotions to get them to go in the direction we want. We can look at our circumstances and explore them, discovering which aspects stir up our emotions in a constructive way. For example, we can think of a sausage as a popular source of traditional tasty nourishment or we can think of a transparent piece of intestine stuffed with fat, scrotum, intestines, stomach, lungs and other organs, as well as blood and 'head meat' which is a more diplomatic way of referring to brains, face, eyeballs, tongue. Both are equally valid ways of thinking of the same thing. But they probably produce two very different emotional reactions for you, don't they?

You don't even have to stick to the facts. You can change your emotional attitude to something by using your imagination. If you're trying to cut down on your pizza intake, then you could curb Grog's enthusiasm by thinking of pizza in a way similar to the aforementioned sausage. Since pizza isn't made from offal, you could employ your imagination to visualise it riddled with lots of nasty creepy crawlies: maggots, cockroaches and millions of tiny tapeworm eggs. There is absolutely no logical reason why this should be; we live in an age where health and safety standards are higher than ever. But as I pointed out before, Grog doesn't do logic and he struggles very much with trying to distinguish between what we imagine and what is real. So if you imagine the food in front of you to be bug-infested then that's good enough for Grog.

I know of one woman who successfully reframed herself out of a chocolate addiction partly by imagining that each chocolate had been dipped into raw sewage. She suffered a chocolate craving that was starting to ruin her life. But when she made the effort to consciously imagine her irresistible temptations smothered in liquid faeces, her cravings diminished considerably.

Imagining something that encourages or deters your desired behaviour is therefore one very effective way to reframe the way you consider your circumstances. The main disadvantage of this kind of framing is it requires conscious mental effort. It is a form of mentally lying to our Grog and this requires willpower, which can be in very short supply in times of tiredness and stress. In the long run it is therefore better to find a way to reframe our perspective on the world in a way that doesn't require so much willpower - a way that doesn't require us to invent stuff but still provides us with a positive emotional urge to do what we want by taking a point of view that we might not have been aware of or by taking something into account that we had previously overlooked.

## Benjamin

Benjamin recently got his TEFL (Teaching English as a Foreign Language) certificate a few months ago and, after dozens of job applications and unsuccessful interviews, finally found himself gainful employment in a small private language academy teaching English to adults. However, although he was elated when he first got the job, he quickly went off the boil when his dream started to turn into a nightmare.

He promptly learned that his pay was disappointingly well below the average for English language teachers in the city. Furthermore, his classes were each of a different level. This meant that where his colleagues were preparing lessons that could then be repeated with two or three classes, he had to prepare each one separately which he felt wasn't fair. This meant him having to work harder than anyone else. And as if to add insult to injury, he also had the worst timetable. While other teachers had all-morning or all-evening timetables, his timetable was split which meant starting classes at 8am and finishing at 10pm with frustratingly "useless" gaps in between.

Disappointment, unfairness and frustration. These are all negative feelings and all are created by Grog. Demoralised and demotivated, Benjamin was finding it difficult to persevere with his goal of establishing himself as an English teacher. Part of him was thinking of chucking it all in but another part was telling him that if he could just find a way to stick it out then things would start to get better.

In order to solve this problem, he used a combination of reframes, looking at the same situation from an alternative viewpoint.

Firstly, Benjamin considered the fact that he was not being held at gunpoint here. He was free to hand in his notice if he felt the conditions were unacceptable. He wasn't being forced to do anything, it had been his choice to accept the job and he knew what the pay was going to be, the school had been perfectly clear. This helped rebalance the unfairness issue. He had not been tricked. He also considered that for some professions there is a period of induction included in getting their qualification; a training period where they work as an apprentice, sometimes for free or for a reduced rate. Benjamin recognised that all the different levels he was having to prepare was giving him a solid experience to build on. He could view his first year of teaching as a practical continuation of training for which he was also getting paid. This didn't seem like such a bad deal.

His timetable was also a point of frustration for him. Again, this was tempered by looking at the situation from a different point of view: Benjamin lived in a four-bedroomed shared flat and had one of the better rooms as he had been there two years and worked his way up. A new flatmate was now in the fourth bedroom or "cupboard" as he referred to it. This, he pointed out was fair because everyone who came into the flat started off in the smallest bedroom and then moved up as other flatmates moved out. When he realised this was the same sort of thing that was happening to him at work, his level of frustration dropped. Reframed in this way, having the crappiest timetable due to being the newest recruit didn't seem quite so unfair. Furthermore, after consideration of the pros and cons, he realised that having the big gaps between classes gave him the opportunity to prepare well for the next lesson and to write up his notes about the classes he'd just done. Correctly written out and filed, these would prove a valuable resource the next time he had to give the class - an advantage that the other teachers didn't have. With these new viewpoints he was able to see his position in a more positive light; as a year of extra training through which he would get valuable work experience of all levels backed up by a well-organised set of notes, materials and activities. His Grog was convinced. Benjamin found that going to work was much easier. He stopped feeling so abused and was able to persevere with his 'training' until the end of the year by which time he had got a job offer from another language school with better conditions.

Of course, trying to look at your situation from a more beneficial point of view is not that easy when you already have your own point of view well established. This is one of the reasons why coaching is so useful; it is your coach's job to identify and cultivate more productive ways of looking at your circumstances so that your Grog will be more cooperative with your 'Grand Plan'.

Sometimes, you can get other points of view by listening to other people, but they have to be the right kind of people. If Benjamin had explained his frustration to someone whose response was "Yes, mate. They're really exploiting you, aren't they? I wouldn't stand for it myself. Why don't you tell your boss what he can do with his job and set fire to the place?" it would have given him an alternative viewpoint but not a beneficial one.

So talking to positive people and listening to them can be useful if you haven't got your own coach. But there are also other ways of getting your Grog on board.

## Positive Emotional Images

Carrie Green is founder of the Female Entrepreneur Association. When she first started trying to get her project off the ground, she noticed she was being held back by negative feelings of doubt, lack of self-confidence and the fear of failure. She realised that if she wanted to live an incredible life and achieve amazing things, she was going to have to find a way of convincing her Grog to feel differently. In her own words, "I had to find a way to programme my mind for success." She started by noticing all the negative feelings she had and observing them for what they were: irrational feelings that could be changed and she realised it was her job to change them. She started to use the advertiser's trick of positively visualising what it would be like to set up and run her own female entrepreneur's association. As clearly as possible, she imagined all the good things about getting there: what it would look like, what it would sound like, what it would feel like. When she had the idea of starting her online magazine, she imagined what sort of women she wanted on the front cover and photoshopped images of them to make mock-ups of covers which she then printed off and stuck to her wall.

A strong positive image can convince our Grog to do something just as a negative one can turn him away. So what are the positive images associated with your goal? Is it being your own boss, looking like Shakira, sailing your yacht around the world or just being able to make it to the Post Office without assistance? All of these have images associated with them, images that can get Grog back on your side. Of course, there are other ways to experience positive images without having to come up with them yourself.

The road where I grew up was a quiet cul-de-sac. This was an ideal environment for the kids who lived there - Robert, Mark and Nial - to play football, bomb around on our bikes and play hide and seek. But one day we did something different. Robert's parents took us all to the cinema - to the Gaumont in Sheffield's town centre to see *James Bond: The Spy Who Loved Me* (It's the one where Roger Moore drives the white Lotus Esprit that goes underwater). We all loved it and when we came out of the cinema I remember us all hurtling off down the Fargate pedestrian precinct, jumping over benches and shooting make-believe villains. We felt invincible - we all felt like we were James Bond!

Films move us. They connect with us on an emotional level. If they didn't, we wouldn't find them so gripping. We would have a passive attitude to the film, not caring what happened. The feelings of suspense, surprise, tension, joy, relief and elation would not exist. Thus films are another way that we can influence our Grog. I don't profess to be a film buff. But I do pay attention to how films affect us at an emotional level. They can inspire us, make us feel more optimistic, give us hope or conversely, they can affect us negatively. I was so affected after watching *Schindler's List* that five minutes after leaving the cinema I found myself uncontrollably crying for no readily apparent reason, which I think totally failed to impress the girl I was trying to date at the time. It even took myself by surprise, as I couldn't really explain why I had tears pouring down my face, either. A friend of mine (a big muscular fellow whom you wouldn't want to mess with) went to see the horror film *The Blair Witch Project* and was so emotionally affected he couldn't sleep properly for several nights. The film emotionally resonated with him, whereas other people I know who have seen the film just think it's a bit silly. What is clear is that each of us are affected in our own way. What for one of us is an inspiring story about persevering through adversity to finally come out on top, for another is a complete trouser-filler.

Just to prove the matter, here are my top inspirational films about perseverance:

1. *The Shawshank Redemption*
2. *The Matrix*
3. *How to Train Your Dragon*
4. *The Lord of the Rings Trilogy*
5. *The Pursuit of Happiness*
6. *Babe*
7. *The Secret Life of Walter Mitty (2013)*
8. *Groundhog Day*
9. *My Cousin Vinny*
10. *Zulu*

These are my personal films. After I watch them I feel 'empowered'. I feel 'inspired'. I feel that striving for something that you believe in is worth it. And this is what we want, isn't it? To point our Grog in the direction we want? To motivate ourselves on an emotional level?

The next time you watch a film, notice how it communicates to you emotionally. How does it affect the way you feel? Which films have the greatest positive effect on you? Which films inspire, motivate and get you back on track? Find them, collect them and keep them as part of your arsenal to use in your defence when general futility comes knocking on your door.

*"The wind was against them now, and Piglet's ears streamed behind him like banners as he fought his way along, and it seemed hours before he got them into the shelter of the Hundred Acre Wood and they stood up straight again, to listen, a little nervously, to the roaring of the gale among the treetops. 'Supposing a tree fell down, Pooh, when we were underneath it?' asked Piglet. 'Supposing it didn't,' said Pooh after careful thought."*

- A.A. Milne, *The House at Pooh Corner*

Of course, you don't have to limit yourself to cinematography to stir up your desired emotions. Books, plays, music, blogs, poetry, YouTube - there is a wealth of useful material out there. I find the written word an excellent source of emotional inspiration. The above quote is one of my favourites which I often use when pessimism seems to have the upper hand. Printed literature has the advantage that you can underline the important bits (in pencil of course) or make notes in the margin for later reference.[37]

You can take your time with a book. You can read and reread the parts that you wish, which is not something other media lend themselves to.[38] There is something about the written word that you can't get from video or audio. The fact it is written down makes it more powerful[39], more permanent, more real.

Biographies are an excellent source of inspiration such as Richard Branson's *Losing My Virginity* which makes you realise just what can be achieved with dogged perseverance. If you want an inspirational story you can't get much better than looking at the example of Albert Casals.

---

37- There are those who think it is sacrilege to write in books; that 'defacing the written page is fundamentally wrong. This, I believe, is a remnant of what we had drilled into us at school. But I strongly support it. Carefully underlining those important parts of text is good practice as it increases the attention we pay by turning 'reading' into an active exercise rather than a passive one. Marking the text also makes finding those nuggets of information easier to find afterwards when you want to come back to them. I often buy second-hand books through Amazon (they're cheaper and have already developed a personality) and I'm delighted when I find that the previous owner has taken the liberty and done me the favour of already underlining the important bits. It saves me time and it's always interesting to see what the previous owner thought of the matter - giving me a second opinion, as it were.

38- I know you can rewind a film to go over the juicy bits - but it's not the same and often pisses off the rest of the family.

39- When I say 'more powerful' I'm referring to the curious but self-evident fact that our brains are more likely to absorb and believe things when they are written down. If you hear something, it's just 'hearsay', but if it's written down then it must be true, even if it was in the sensationalist newspaper and clearly impossible such as the 'double-decker bus found on the moon' sort of thing.

Albert, who had always enjoyed travelling, was twenty years old when he decided to journey to a lighthouse found in East Cape, New Zealand on the exact opposite side of the world to his home town of Barcelona. A trip he would do without money, luggage or companions. This was an adventure that would be daunting for most people of his age, in fact daunting to most people of any age. But what makes his case so uniquely inspiring is that Albert has been in a wheelchair since suffering leukaemia when he was five. He got the travel bug when he was 14 and by twenty had already hitchhiked his way through more countries than most of us see in a lifetime. His story clearly demonstrates how our lives are far more restricted by our own self-limiting ideas than by our reality. His experiences, already made into two books and a film[40] are truly inspiring for anyone who dreams of achieving more with their life.

But inspiration really depends on what works for you. Biographies, novels, non-fiction, self-help, poetry or even quotations. Quotations are really useful because they are tiny 'text bites' of passion packaged into easily manageable chunks. The list of motivational quotes is almost endless but I have included my own favourites that support the Sorites Principle at the back of this book. If they move your emotions in the right direction, quotations are small enough to pin to your wall, carry around in your pocket or tattoo onto whichever part of your body is most effective. There is a wealth of quote images on the internet. If you can't find one that works for you why not make up your own? There are loads of websites such as quotepixel.com that allow you to quickly print off your own inspirational quotes or save it as an image. Check them out.

**Figure 11: A homemade inspirational quote**

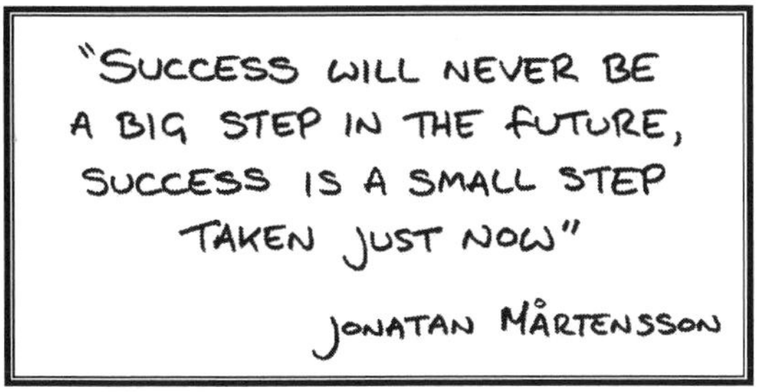

> "SUCCESS WILL NEVER BE A BIG STEP IN THE FUTURE, SUCCESS IS A SMALL STEP TAKEN JUST NOW"
>
> JONATAN MÅRTENSSON

---

40- Books: El Mundo Sobre Ruedas (The World On Wheels), 2010, and Sin Fronteras (Without Borders), 2011; Film: Little World, 2013.

If you're feeling a bit more ambitious, you can even have your favourite quote made into a nice professionally printed full-colour poster and conveniently mailed to your front door. Check out postermywall.com, art. co.uk, createyourmessage.com.

## Michelle

You probably see such inspirational quotes or posters as trivial, as something insignificant like a fridge magnet that your sister gave you. Michelle's sister gave her a fridge magnet with the caption, "The best time to plant a tree was 20 years ago. The second best time is now." It was a little square thing with (unsurprisingly) a picture of a tree on it. "I must have looked at that thing every day for years" explained Michelle, "but there was this day when I'd had yet another really rough day at work and I was like, 'how long am I going to stick this? When is it going to start getting better?' and I went to the fridge to get some juice. I saw the magnet and suddenly - bam! It was like an epiphany. Suddenly, I got it. I understood what it really meant. It was as if that message had finally found a way into my head after all those years of trying. Suddenly it all fitted into place - I had to do something now."

These messages are trivial and insignificant until the moment they have a life-changing result. Maybe it will be next month, maybe it will be never, but if you don't give it a chance then it's an absolute certainty that it's going to be the latter.

## Music

Bono is quoted as saying "Music can change the world because it can change people." How exactly, is up to you. If you find a certain piece of music which lifts you up and gets you going, use it. If you need a few songs with the right lyrics to get you working on your goal, find them, make yourself a playlist and listen to them so many times that it becomes ingrained in you.

Music is not everyone's cup of tea as far as motivation is concerned. I'm aware that there are reasons against as well as for it. But I think they are often based on choosing the wrong sort of lyrics. Listening to songs like 'We are the Champions' by Queen might make you feel good while you're listening to it but can actually make you feel more frustrated and negative afterwards - the message in reality underlines your lack of success, especially if your football team is at the bottom of the division and looking at imminent demotion.

The music you choose has to have the beat that works for you and lyrics that give a reasonably realistic and positive approach to your goal. I find I write best when I listen to calm instrumental music. About 95% of this book has been written while listening to the Scottish group 'Boards of Canada'.[41] I'm not a great believer in all that right brain/left brain stuff, but I do know just listening to BoC gets me mentally set for writing.

I was once asked at one of my productivity workshops what would be my motivational top 10 and I pathetically pleaded a momentary lapse of memory. To rectify that situation for all-time, here is my top 10 playlist for becoming more passionate about perseverance.

1. Big Change Coming - The Stranglers
2. Life's What You Make It - Talk Talk
3. Dark Side of the Moon - Pink Floyd (the whole album)
4. Tubthumping - Chumbawamba
5. With a Little Help from My Friends - The Beatles
6. New Year's Day - U2
7. Something for Nothing - Rush
8. Don't Give Up - Peter Gabriel and Kate Bush
9. Major Tom - David Bowie[42]
10. Runnin' Down a Dream - Tom Petty

---

41- Thanks Michael and Marcus for all your brilliant work. If you're measuring in listening-hours, then I must be your biggest fan!

42- This is included entirely due to the way Kristen Wiig sings it in the film The Secret Life of Walter Mitty. It's one of my favourite moments of the film. I loved the film so much I went out and bought it on DVD and was SO pissed off when I discovered there was a manufacturing defect just at that very moment when she appears with her guitar which caused it to skip. I was even more pissed off when I discovered I'd already thrown the receipt away.

## TED

Finally, I can't end this section on inspiring your motivation without mentioning those brilliant and wonderful people who organise the TED Talks. TED stands for Technology, Entertainment and Design and was set up in 1984 by Richard Saul Wurman who had a vision of what could be achieved by putting together these three fields. Since then the TED conference is held annually in Vancouver, Canada (since 2014, previously in California) where leading experts are invited to give amazingly inspiring and informative talks that last only a few minutes (at most 18 minutes). There are also a series of independent TEDx events organised around the world so that North America doesn't get all the fun. These events are very popular and well-attended. The great thing about them is that they are all available to watch for free on TED's website TED.com. You don't have to be a member; you don't have to pay a subscription. For me, this is what education is all about. If you'd like to try it out, then here are my Top 10 TED Talks for anyone wanting to become more passionate about perseverance.

1. *Grit: The Power of Passion and Perseverance* - Angela Lee Duckworth
2. *Never, Ever Give up* - Diana Nyad
3. *Programming Your Mind for Success* - Carrie Green
4. *The Skill of Self-confidence* – Dr. Ivan Joseph
5. *Forget Big Change, Start with a Tiny Habit* - BJ Fogg
6. *Tiny Surprises for Happiness and Health* - BJ Fogg
7. *The Psychology of Self-motivation* - Scott Geller
8. *The Power of Habit* - Charles Duhigg
9. *If You Want to Achieve Your Goals, Don't Focus on Them* - Reggie Rivers
10. *Inside the Mind of a Master Procrastinator* - Tim Urban

## Another Kind of Emotional Language

If you want a crash course on emotional language all you have to do is sit in front of the telly and watch as many adverts as you can stand. Many adverts work on the principle of creating a desire in the minds of the audience (such as a problem that needs to be solved, or an opportunity that can't be missed) and then presents you with the way to fulfil that desire (buying the product). That's the logical part of the ad, aimed at the rational part of your brain, yet very few advertisers, if any, try to logically reason you into buying their products. That is because decades ago advertising executives cottoned on to the idea that your behaviour is far more controlled by your Grog than by your rational thoughts. So what techniques do they use? One way to observe this is to watch the adverts without sound so you can pay close attention to how those advertising executives communicate with your emotions. They want your Grog to like the product, or if not the product itself, something that the product will give you such as fresh breath or an absence of haemorrhoids. It might be that the product in itself is aesthetically desirable (like a new car or a smartphone) but often it is the benefit that the product gives that is emphasised (and usually vastly exaggerated). If there's no particular benefit, then they try to attach an associated emotion to the product (consider perfume adverts with their often bizarre emotional imagery as a good example).

Some common themes that are used to achieve this are:

✦ The feeling of sexual attraction (a car with a semi-clad model is more attractive than a car without one)
✦ The feeling of joy and laughter (we like things that are funny)
✦ The feeling of being liked (we like being liked)
✦ The feeling of being more attractive (ditto)
✦ The feeling of being part of an elite group (we like to be special)
✦ The feeling of being approved by our peers (we like fitting in)
✦ The feeling of being superior
✦ The feelings of happiness, elation, or ecstasy
✦ The feeling of fear and avoiding it. Adverts play heavily on the fears of things like:
  ✺ Social ridicule
  ✺ Social exclusion
  ✺ Negative social judgements such as being a bad parent or a bad partner or just a bad human being in general

You might be starting to get the idea. But hang on a moment. Aren't many of these just different versions of the same thing?

Most people want to feel liked, loved, valued and even desired by others. At the same time, it is a universal trait in humans that we want to be part of a group, whether a family, a team, a social group, a political group or whatever. We seem to naturally form our own 'tribes' and view the world according to who is in our tribe (us) and who are not (them).

So as we have seen, we can influence Grog by the use of positive images, by reframing our point of view, by imagining or visualising images which reinforce our desired behaviour by watching, reading or listening to inspirational material, but there is one part of Grogarian that is just as strong if not stronger than all of these put together. It is the feeling of being included in our tribe, being approved by our colleagues and consciously or unconsciously succumbing to the mental and behavioural patterns of those that we love and respect. It's called peer pressure.

## Things to Think About

✽ In this book I call the emotional part of your brain 'Grog'.

✽ Grog (which is a combination of several important parts) deals with your emotions: fear, love, hate. It controls your passion.

✽ Grog is 'illogical'. Grog does not listen to reason - only to emotions and feelings.

✽ Grog is also very powerful. Grog has much more control over your behaviour than you might realise.

✽ Trying to consciously control Grog is like sitting on an elephant and trying to 'steer' it - if Grog doesn't want to go somewhere, Grog ain't gonna go - and vice versa.

✽ You can only communicate with Grog via emotion such as an inspiring film, a motivating story, a disgusting image or a shocking experience.

✽ Reframing techniques can also help you view your goals in a more emotionally motivating way.

✽ Finding the right way to 'persuade' your Grog to feel passionately about doing what you want it to do is a major factor for success with the Sorites Principle.

✽ Just having the right passion can move a small mountain.

## Top Tips

✤ Reframe the way you think about the action you want to carry out so that it is fuelled by a strong emotion.

✤ Attach a strong emotion to your actions.

✤ Use visioning techniques such as visualising yourself having succeeded. Imagine the positive elation, the celebration, all the great things you could do, be and have, once you've succeeded.

✤ Gain inspiration from films, biographies, TED Talks, poetry or inspirational quotes.

✤ Celebrate your progress.

## Questions to Ask Yourself (and Answer)

- Do a bit of soul-searching. How does your Grog feel about achieving your goal?
- Is Grog being a help or a hinder to achieving your goal?
- If Grog is a help, how could you make the most of Grog's enthusiasm to get more pieces put into place?
- If Grog is a hindrance, how could you change the situation? What can you do using reframing, inspiration or emotional experiences to change Grog's feelings about things?
- What is the single biggest emotional obstacle you have to overcome to achieving your goal?
- What do you need to do? Who do you need to talk to in order to overcome this obstacle?

# 10 Peer Pressure

Alcohol. Alcohol is great isn't it? It comes in a wide variety of easy-to-swallow flavours, is easily available at most of your friendly local pubs and is modestly priced. It also relaxes you, livens you up, reduces your inhibitions and makes you more sociable, flirty and fun.

One part of my history that I am proud of is that I was able to go for almost a whole year at university as a teetotaller. This was no easy achievement. While my fellow classmates we're discovering the joys of getting completely hammered, I sat among them drinking my Coke or lemonade and black trying to join in the frivolities and revelry the best I could. Not exactly the life and soul of the party, though. Looking back, I have to admit that I can't really remember why I didn't drink. I remember that it seemed like an expensive and unhealthy way to behave like a dickhead. But if I could go back and live my first year again I assure you that things would've been very different.

My friends weren't that bothered by my abstinence. They'd occasionally try to persuade me to 'Go on. Have a drink!' but by and large the peer pressure was low. One detail that softened my teetotalism in their eyes was that I was one of the few students to have a car: a Citroën Dyane (cream-coloured with a soft rollback roof). I loved that car. For me, it was the embodiment of freedom - not just for me but also my friends. Having 'wheels' allowed us to head out to the country pubs and get away from the crowd. Saint Andrew's is a small university town and you can't go anywhere without everyone else knowing about it. So because I was 'the designated driver' by default, being sober was a more socially acceptable state to be in. Nevertheless, the occasional 'Go on. Have a drink' was never-ending and the student culture made alcohol constantly enticing. I stuck it out all the way till the end of third term and to the end of my first-year exams when finally, I succumbed to peer pressure and got completely wasted at the first post-exam room-party I attended. So much for resistance.

It's amazing how strong peer pressure is. The current world population is approaching seven and a half billion and I estimate that of this enormous multitude there are about three people who genuinely don't give a toss about what anybody else thinks about them. They are all aged over a hundred and each live out hermitic existences in inhospitable separate corners of the planet each in the middle of nowhere. For the rest of us, peer pressure is up there with the other 'force majeures' such as earthquakes, tsunamis and planet-busting meteor impacts. There is no escape: Resistance is useless!

How we deal with peer pressure is not a rational process. It's Grogarian. Grog considers herself an expert on other people and is confident about what those other people think of you[43] and cares very much about it. Peer pressure is why Grog gets us to do the most irrational, self-harming and life-threatening actions. She can make us jump from hotel balconies into swimming pools, she can make us disfigure our bodies and consume the most unlikely of products. All because of peer pressure. Peer pressure is the number one reason why people start smoking, take drugs, become bulimic, anorexic and suicidal. Grog is hardwired to be highly attuned to what she thinks people think of us - far too highly tuned at times.

---

43- In spite of this confidence, Grog is frequently wrong.

On the subject of suicide, history shows that if someone commits suicide in your society, the likelihood that you or someone else there commits suicide increases, especially amongst those of a similar age. In his book The Power of Others, Michael Bond[44] points out that the main factor which influences whether someone volunteers to be a suicide bomber is not religious fanaticism, nor a burning hatred for the enemy. It is peer pressure - the following in the footsteps of peers; copying the behaviour of friends or esteemed colleagues who have already blown themselves to smithereens in the name of righteousness and justice. So never underestimate the power peer pressure has over our behaviour. After habit, I would say that peer pressure and social pressure[45] is the biggest factor that influences our daily behaviour and the choices we make - the ones we are aware of as well as all of those that we aren't. The things you do, say, eat, drink, wear, buy, value and believe are all heavily influenced by how you view others and how you think they view you. Peer pressure can be so strong, so overwhelming a force that it can cause us to carry out actions without requiring willpower and certainly in spite of prizes and punishments that are set up to deter such behaviour.

We are all different and yet we are all the same. We all have a natural preference to see ourselves as being part of a recognised group - our tribe, or to be more accurate 'our tribes' as we have several depending on where we are and whom we are with. We have our family tribe, our work tribe, our social tribe and even our extended political or religious tribes. Your tribe can be intimate - just you and one other person - or it can be massive - a group of thousands of people. Whether our tribe is real or simply perceived, it is a group of people with whom we identify. A group whose opinions, behaviours, circumstances, experiences, beliefs, physical appearance, values and/or lifestyles are similar to our own. A tribe can be a tight knit group of friends or a vast multitude who share a common interest (such as Justin Bieber, Greenpeace or bondage).

---

44- No, not the one who wrote all those Paddington Bear books but another one.

45- Social psychologists will point out here that Peer Pressure and Social Pressure are two separate things. I acknowledge this but for the sake of simplicity I'm putting the two together. Call it what you want, it still influences our thoughts and behaviours.

To be part of a group we need several factors in place. We need to be recognised, perceived or acknowledged. The opposite is to be ignored. We then have to be accepted into the group; that if we approach the group we are welcomed - the opposite would be that others withdraw or bar our entry. We need to be included in the group, to be treated as the others. The opposite is to be discriminated against, to be forgotten or overlooked. We need to be valued, which is to feel important, worthy or given some sort of status rather than being seen as useless or worthless. If we contribute in any way, it is important that our contribution is also acknowledged and praised and not ignored, ridiculed or condemned. We have a deep emotional need for these social factors - recognition, acceptance, inclusion, approval and value - and we can experience a strong emotional pressure to do whatever it takes to get them. This is what peer pressure is. The need to enter a group and remain there as a valued member. We are prepared to go to extraordinary lengths to achieve this even if it kills us.

### Figure 12: A summary of social bonding

| If you want to bond | If you want to alienate |
| --- | --- |
| Acknowledge | Ignore and overlook |
| Accept and approach | Reject and withdraw |
| Include | Exclude |
| Treat equally | Discriminate against |
| Give approval and praise | Criticise and condemn |
| Value and give status | Belittle and ridicule |

Groups who actively seek to acquire and influence new members use these factors to optimise the leverage peer pressure has over them. Put like this, it might sound rather ominous and sometimes it is. After all, just look at some of the stupid things people do in the name of peer pressure. But as we shall soon see, peer pressure can also be benevolent; providing us with the necessary motivation to do what is best for us.

Now, I don't want to turn this chapter into a class on social psychology. What I do want to consider is what can happen when the actions you have to do to get recognition, acceptance, inclusion, approval and value from your perceived tribe and the actions you have to do to achieve your goal are one and the same thing.

## Alcoholics Anonymous

Being an alcoholic is not nice. One of the worst problems alcoholics have to cope with is the disintegration and failing of their interpersonal relationships with everyone outside their drinking environment - their partner, their children or parents, with their non-drinking friends, colleagues and neighbours. Slowly but steadily their tribes are eroded. It's a common observation by alcoholics that they feel rejected, isolated, desperately lonely and that 'non-alcoholics just don't understand what they are going through'. This is why organisations such as Alcoholics Anonymous (AA) can be such a relief to alcoholism sufferers and such strong support - they use the power of peer pressure.

There is no direct pressure to be a member of AA or to attend the meetings. There is no register, no forms to fill in, no attendance sheets. Once there, people are treated with respect, they are treated equally. The attendees are free to choose to participate, to talk if they want or to just listen. But each person is given the recognition as someone who has made an important and gruelling first step: to recognise that they are an alcoholic (which some alcoholics resist vehemently). As they sit in a circle and are given the same opportunity to share their experiences, the members are given equal status and value. Nobody is judgemental. Nobody criticises. The senior members have all been there before. Each contribution is accepted. Each contribution is valued. Suggestions might be given, ideas shared. Everyone is listened to. News of success and progress is praised. News of regression, of turning back to the bottle and failure to stay sober is met with sadness but never ridicule or criticism. The overarching factor is that they are all in this together. They have common experiences, vulnerabilities and challenges. They understand each other better than anyone else - anyone from outside the group. But because of this benevolent peer pressure, millions of people have managed to strengthen their willpower to say no to alcohol, to remain sober and rebuild their lives. Consider the testimony of Kevin from Bournemouth as posted on AA's website. You can feel the peer pressure in his words:

"That's where being a member of AA comes in. People that are not 'alcoholic' just don't understand. In AA I don't feel like I'm different any more, I have something to belong to, I have found new meaningful friendships. I am also reminded if I ever start to think I can drink like "normal" people, I will end up right back where I came from. Best of all, I found that by following a few simple suggestions on a daily basis, the desire to drink alcohol has completely disappeared. I have discovered that I can solve, or at least cope with, any problem that comes along today by using the tools I found in the fellowship of Alcoholics Anonymous. The people in AA really care about what happens to me and I have a life way beyond my dreams. I have been able to get my life back on track and make up for a lot of things I felt guilty about in the past. My one small regret is that I enjoy my life so much today that I wish I had done something about my drinking problem a little bit earlier."

Kevin talks about how he is understood, how he is given recognition and accepted by the group, how he has made new friendships. He talks about being valued and supported. He clearly states that due to their help he has managed to stay sober and rebuild his life - something that just using willpower he would have been unable to achieve. So peer pressure can be a blessing or a curse depending where you get it from.

## How to Get Benevolent Peer Pressure

Now that we have established the power of peer pressure, the next step is to look at how you can get more of it in a form that would be beneficial for you. This is a bit more complicated than everything else we have done until now. So far everything we've done depends on you. You are the one on this journey. You are the one calling the shots. You are the one in control. But other people have their own ideas, agendas and ways of doing things that don't necessarily dovetail perfectly with your plan. In short, people are a problem. But, with a bit of effort, charisma, patience, back-scratching and bribery it can be done. And believe me - the effort is worth it. Here are seven different ways to get positive peer pressure.

1. Get a goal partner. Find someone who has a similar goal to you and team up. Whether it's jogging, dieting, going to the gym, learning the guitar or honing your presentation skills, doing it with someone else can be fun. Put the word out. Ask the people you know or put an ad up on notice boards to contact people you don't.

2. Join a group. Unless you have some perverse obsession, the probability is high that there already exists a group of people that are trying to do the same thing you want to do, right now. Weightwatchers, study groups, writing groups, build-your-own-house groups, they all exist and in greater numbers than you might think. Google them and check them out. There may just be a group near you.

3. Set up your own. If there isn't a group in your area, start one yourself. Just because there isn't one doesn't logically imply that nobody else shares your type of goal - it just means that no-one's taken the initiative to set one up. Brenda wanted to improve her Spanish but couldn't find any group in her area. So she decided to set up her own. She got half a dozen friends together and started informal practical Spanish classes learning the language needed for normal conversation. All of them are keen to improve as much as possible. They all exert peer pressure on each other to come up with useful phrases and to do their homework. Brenda did this through her network of friends living locally, but there is an abundance of suggestions about how to set up your own self-help/support group available on the internet. My recommendation is to find someone who has already set up a group in your area and ask them for help and advice. After all there's no point in reinventing the wheel, is there? And you might just get an extra bit of peer pressure straight away.

4. Follow people on internet. Social media such as Facebook and Twitter allow you to connect with your peers and develop a virtual tribe on-line. Reading other people's blogs or even starting your own can allow you to share hopes and fears, to celebrate wins and commiserate setbacks. You can give and receive praise and encouragement and develop social cohesion without ever having to leave the comfort of your own home.

5. Choose a role model. Peer pressure doesn't just come from our peers. It comes from people that we might know of - people that we might have

seen on the media but have never met in real life. In fact, they don't even have to be real-life people. I remember watching a talk given by what I can only assume was a German professor of psychology who explained that in order to be a good husband, one of the things you can do is to arrive home as James Bond would. 007 doesn't arrive home upset and stressed, complaining about what a gruelling day he has had being beaten up, chased, shot at, thrown off trains, pushed off buildings and falling through plate glass windows. He arrives home, immaculately dressed and perfectly groomed. He playfully throws his hat onto the hook, smiles, gives his wife a loving kiss and offers to mix her a dry martini while genuinely enquiring about her day.[46] So, as far as achieving your goal is concerned, who would your role-model be? What would they do in your circumstances? What should you be doing to be more like them?

6. Get a coach. A good coach understands the importance of peer pressure. Although a personal coach would not be someone in your circumstances sharing a common goal, coaches know about giving moral support, giving non-judgemental feedback, reframing techniques, assigning value to your efforts and dishing out lots of praise (not indiscriminate praise but recognising that even the most 'insignificant' of steps forward is an achievement worthy of recognition and approval). Your coach understands what it is that you need to strengthen your resolve and makes sure you get it.

7. Actively seek support from the people you care about. Finally, and possibly the simplest is to recruit support from your nearest and dearest. Now you have to accept that your closest friends and family are unlikely to want to achieve the goal you want. Just because you've decided that losing a few stone or giving up smoking is for you doesn't mean that they are going to enthusiastically fall in line. But they can give you moral support, especially if you share your sentiments with them. In chapter 7 we talked about getting a Praise Sponsor. You can ask them for moral support and encouragement, too. Or you could just put your reputation

---

46- I tried this with mixed results: firstly, I'm not of the hat-wearing persuasion and secondly, the wife usually implies that my alcohol intake has already reached its limit and that personally she'd just prefer a cup of coffee and did I remember to get some milk (which I inevitably haven't). Nevertheless, it's the thought that counts and the talk I saw did have a long-term positive effect on my behaviour when I arrive home from the office.

and pride on the line and solemnly promise them you will meet your next deadline, complete the next part of the puzzle by Tuesday or follow through with your next chosen challenge, just like Leo did.

## Leo

Leo was a short, skinny little fellow with a desk job. He was intense and the sort of person who blinked too many times for comfort when he got nervous. He suffered from asthma and in spite of his size, he still struggled with more than one flight of stairs, which would leave him gasping for breath. At only 57, this was not good. But what definitely didn't help was the smoking. He knew it was bad for him but he was sick and tired of trying to give it up. He'd been smoking for about thirty years and was all too well aware of the negative aspects to his "nasty, little habit." He'd tried will-power and concluded that he didn't have any. The shock tactics of looking at lung cancer photos had worn off as had the photoshopped image of his own gravestone - "Here lies Leo Bolton, who died of lung cancer aged 55", which he still carried around in his wallet but had seemed to become immune to. He'd tried going cold-turkey by refusing to buy cigarettes but the craving was more than he could stand. He'd tried nicotine patches, nicotine sweets and lollipops. He'd tried smoking with the opposite hand, at different times of day and avoiding situations that were conducive to smoking (like meeting with his smoking friends) but the peer pressure from his smoking buddies didn't help at all and in some perverse way he felt bad about letting them down. Then during one of those days when he was feeling frustrated about not being able to give up he realised that the peer pressure that was causing him to keep going might also be used to his advantage. He decided to draw up a contract which he then printed off about twenty times.

*"I, Leo Bolton, hereby promise to you, (insert name), that, upon my honour, henceforth I shall never smoke a single cigarette, pipe or other similar form of tobacco ever again"*

He then filled them in, one copy for each of the people most important to him: his wife, his two daughters, his parents, his brothers and sister, his closest friends and his boss.

"Just writing it down felt different. It was like something really deep and powerful had happened," he said. "But it was making this public promise to the most important people in my life that did it for me. I admit it. I went through hell and back several times, but the amazing thing was that each time I got to the point where I would have previously given in, I thought of all those faces, my friends and family who cared about me, and what it would be like having to look them in the eye and say 'I'm sorry. I've let you down.' Leo stopped smoking on the 3rd of March 2012 and as far as I know, hasn't smoked since.

## The Cop-out Clause

If you happen to be involved in the legal profession or have experience writing out contracts, you will have already noticed that in Leo's contract there was no reference to what would happen if Leo failed to meet his promise. You might think it would be better to have some sort of clause that specified what would happen if he failed. I would like to recommend against including any such clause in a document like this for two purely psychological reasons. The first one is that just by mentioning failure you are in some way endorsing it. You are recognising that the possibility of failure exists and in the same way that saying to someone 'Don't look down!' guarantees they will do just the opposite (usually when crossing a rickety old bridge), mentioning failure increases the chance that they will think about it. The second is that you are placing a value on it. If the penalty is, let's say, to give a hundred pounds to charity then that could be viewed as the price to pay for being allowed to break your promise (a price I'm sure Leo would be happy to have paid at some moment). The real penalty is in being viewed negatively by your peers. This is priceless and goes without saying. So if you think that following in Leo's footsteps might help you then go for it, but don't add any clauses about copping out.

Maintaining our honour in the eyes of people we care about is a strong form of peer pressure. In a similar way to the websites mentioned in the chapter on prizes and punishments for forfeiting money if you fail to follow through, there exist websites like Fatbet and DietBet which use peer pressure by helping you set up a weight-losing competition amongst friends and GymPact and HealthRally use similar ideas in order to get you going to the gym. Proving to your friends that you are keeping to your side of the bargain is a powerful technique that you might like to try.

## Positivity Spreads

One final note is that it's an interesting observation that emotions and feelings, just like chicken pox and syphilis, are highly contagious. If you have a person (or group of people) and put them with someone who is in a really good mood, then their mood will also improve. Similarly, if you put them with someone who is enthusiastic, their level of enthusiasm will increase. This also works for negative emotional states, too.[47] Without mentioning names, I know of someone who is so negative, so critical, pessimistic and demotivating, that they can suck all the joy and laughter out of a room just by walking into it.

It works for positivity, too. As we shall be covering later, when you are trying to apply the Sorites Principle every day, often with insignificant results, it is a natural tendency of ours to become despondent; the feeling of general futility will sneak in and we will start to wonder whether everything we're doing is a complete waste of time. To prevent this natural tendency from becoming a significant problem, it is highly recommended that we maintain a positive mental attitude and one of the easiest and most enjoyable ways to do this is to spend time in the company of people who already have a positive mental attitude. You know who these people are. Seek them out. Make an effort to spend time with them. Talk to them about your goal and all the things you're doing and bask in the glow of their positivity. Absorb as much of it as you can get and store it, because later you're going to need it.

---

47- It is important to point out that the people involved here have a neutral or mutual respect for each other. If there exists contempt between the parties, if they don't get on with each other, then the enthusiastic incomer is just perceived as an annoying twat and exacerbates the situation rather than helping.

So peer pressure can help us go even further than we can by using willpower, prizes, progress and passion. But people have their own agendas and at some point, for one reason or another, their positive peer pressure will end and you'll find yourself adrift, wandering about, looking for the right path and hoping that what appears to be the right path isn't the path of least resistance. Or at best hoping that the two lead you in the same direction. In such cases what you need are clear and carefully positioned signposts that tell you what you are supposed to be doing and how to do it when you are too lost or tired to know for yourself. I call these signposts 'Pointers' and they can be really, really useful.

## Things to Think About

✤ Peer pressure has a powerful influence both positively and negatively.

✤ Whether you like to admit it or not, your behaviour is very much determined by what 'other people' think of you.

✤ In terms of perseverance we can turn this peer pressure to our advantage.

✤ Making social connections with people who have shared objectives can give your motivation a real boost.

✤ By publicly promising to carry out a certain action or to refrain from doing it, our personal motivation can be greatly increased.

## Top Tips

✤ Do not underestimate the phenomenal power peer pressure has over us all.

✤ Find someone with whom you can share your feelings and your goal.

✤ Get a buddy, join a group, start a group, follow people on social media, get a role model, a coach or a peer pressure donor.

✤ Share your ideas of your goal with people you care about, making sure these are the right sort of people who will morally support you and your cause.

✤ Set it in writing. Write out a contract or some sort of personal pledge stating what you are going to do, how you are going to do this and when you are going to do it.

✤ Don't include a form of punishment or recompense. If you do you will see it as a 'get-out' clause which you might then use to justify letting yourself out of the promise.

## Questions to Ask Yourself (and Answer)

✹ How could you use peer pressure to your advantage?

✹ Are there any groups of like-minded people trying to achieve the same thing that could help you?

✹ Who can you follow on social media to increase your perseverance?

✹ Who would be your perseverance role model?

✹ What's stopping you from joining?

✹ If there is no such group available, what can you do to set one up?

✹ Would making a public promise help?

✹ What would the promise be, and who would you make it to?

✹ Who are the most positive people you know of, and how could you spend more time with them?

✹ What else could you do to get benevolent peer pressure?

# 11 Pointers

*"Sometimes when you're too tired to think, all you need is someone or something to point you in the right direction."*

In much of the western world, twice a year we play the game called 'Daylight Saving Time'. As you probably know 'Daylight Saving Time' (or DSL) is the practice of disrupting your sleep pattern, international travel, medical devices and record keeping all for the sake of saving a few bob on the electric bill. Now, leaving aside whether or not DSL is overall a good idea or not, I'd like to take DSL as a wonderful example of one important aspect of human nature.

Most of Europe and North America follow DSL and quite a few other places, too. As there are no major protests or civil unrest over the matter, it seems that by and large people accept the idea and are prepared to cooperate; we willingly get up earlier when there's lots of daylight (moving the clocks forward an hour in the spring) and have a nice cosy lie-in for an hour when the nights start to draw in (setting the clocks back an hour in autumn).

The acclaimed advantages of getting up earlier in the summer are that it saves energy and allows us to enjoy more of the daylight after work, thus allowing people to go out more. This is considered a good thing as it promotes outdoor activities such as sports, shopping and socialising. These, in turn, are good for your physical and mental health and good for local business too as you spend your hard-earned cash in pubs, shops, restaurants, cinemas etc.

But much of the criticism for DSL comes from the actual changing of the clocks so that an hour is skipped or that the same hour is repeated twice. This can cause international travel to become quite confusing. If your flight gets in at 2:10 in the morning when clocks go back, then is that the first or the second 2:10? And how can you tell the difference? The administering of precise medical treatment needs to be very carefully monitored to avoid disruption and of course detailed record keeping such as when a crime was committed and when was the suspect seen entering his home can become a bit of a minefield.

So if we generally agree that adapting our timetable to the seasons is a good idea but find that it's the actual changing of the clocks that causes all the confusion then why don't we just stop messing about with the clocks and simply all agree to get up one hour earlier regardless? For example, if you usually get up at 6:00, then setting the hour back means that in reality you're actually getting up at 5:00. So why not stop messing about with the clocks in spring and autumn and just decide as of today you're going to get up at 5:00 am for the next six months? TV stations just broadcast their programmes an hour earlier. Schools, businesses etcetera all start an hour earlier. In practice, it would all be exactly the same as in previous years but without the confusion and problems caused by shifting the hour forwards and backwards. Wouldn't it be all much simpler?

The answer is no and it's all Grog's fault.

As we have seen, Grog controls what you like and what you don't like. There's no logic involved with Grog. Regardless of how much reasoning or logic you apply trying to convince him that something is reasonable and harmless, Grog has other ideas.

And so it is for getting up in the morning. Most of us aren't capable of logical thought until after that first cup of coffee, but our Grog is on fine form from the very second we open our bleary eyes. If you're used to getting up at 6, then your Grog is satisfied with that. Have you ever missed your alarm on a work day and opened your eyes to see the clock saying it's 7:55? Remember that jolt of panic? That's Grog saying that something is not right and worth panicking about. Well, it's pretty much the same when you open your eyes and see the clock say 5:00. Getting up at 5:00 is not a good thing. Grog doesn't like it. Grog likes 'warm and cosy until 6:00'. So by setting your clock back an hour, you cunningly trick him into thinking it's just doing the same as before. As I said, there's no logic involved here; your PFC, the reasoning part of your brain, knows it's an hour earlier. But Grog doesn't and somehow it's all so much easier if you just play along with it.

What is there to learn from this?

Well, for one thing we are undoubtedly creatures of habit but in some ways pretty stupid creatures at that. Regardless of what the time actually is, regardless of how much sleep we've really had or how tired we are, we still get up by following what the clock says even if we know that it is wrong. In fact, after the first couple of days we don't even remember that it is 'wrong' anymore. We just get on with fixing breakfast in the dark and thinking about other things.

This is a rather interesting bit of our psychological programming. We human beings seem quite happy to go through our daily activities doing what we're 'guided' to do when we're not giving it much thought. Thus, applying the Sorites Principle of doing a little bit every day, then setting up Pointers to guide us through our day could be just what we need.

## My Morning Pointers

My morning routine at the moment includes the waking of two sleepy 5 year-olds, Alex and Sol, dressing them, fixing breakfast, preparing their lunch box, gathering bags, papers and other belongings, rushing out of the house and driving them to school. I go through this routine in some sort of daze - half thinking about what I'm doing and half thinking about the day I have ahead of me: the people I have to talk to, the errands I have to run and the objectives I would like to achieve. So maybe it's not surprising when Alex points out as he walks out the garden gate that he hasn't got his shoes on or that I have to unlock the door to go back and collect something I've forgotten[48] or double check that I locked the front gate. It's a one-hour operation and there isn't really much time for speculative contemplation. It's go, go, go.

What I learnt early on in this routine is that it's worth preparing things in advance. On a good day, if I had the energy the night before, I would have already prepared the area for the morning's assault. I would have set the table: bowls, spoons, cereal packet, etc. I would have set out the lunch boxes and checked that their little bags contain the standard requirements for nursery: smock, bib, change of clothes and a knuckleduster (just joking). Anything else such as important paperwork, letters to post, library books to return are placed next to the door. Less to remember.

All of these are 'pointers'. They are physical manifestations of 'signs' that say 'do this' at the moment when 'this' has to be done. They require no willpower, no prizes or punishments, no passion and no peer pressure. Another advantage about pointers is that once put in position, they don't even require any mental effort on your behalf. You don't need to make a decision. If the pointer says 'do this now', then you do it. If the light says 'stop' then you stop. No decision is made. It just magically happens. And this is good because sometimes making even a simple decision is just too much for us to bear.

## What Are You Going to Have?

Restaurants. Restaurants are great, aren't they? I love eating in restaurants - lots of mouth-watering food, cooked while you wait, brought to you at the table and with no washing up to do afterwards. Brilliant! And usually in pleasant company, too.

---

48- Usually my phone

It seems that we are naturally programmed to eat socially. It turns a meal into a special occasion, doesn't it? And eating out can also be highly entertaining. Apart from the food and the company you are with, there's the environment to observe, the ambience to absorb, the clientele to study and the menu to consider.

The next time you go to a restaurant, pay attention to how you and your fellow diners decide what you're going to order, because it's a great opportunity to see the decision-making process in action and once you are aware of it, it's hard to forget.

In order to select from a restaurant menu we are unfamiliar with, we have to look at each of the options in turn, read it, visualize it and rate how appealing it would be to our senses, store that information in our short-term memory and then pass on to the next. This is actually quite hard mentally speaking, because they are all tasks carried out by our PFC and our PFC doesn't work very well when tired and expecting to relax. It was looking forwards to chilling out with a few friends when suddenly it is being asked to do several tricky tasks all at once. Your PFC has to make a considerable mental effort if you want to end up with the dish that scores highest on your value rating.

As far as I have observed, choosing from a menu in a rational way rarely happens. People associate a mealtime with relaxation and don't want to have to tax themselves too much when they're trying to relax. So they become lazy. They don't make the best decision by selecting the highest rated option from all the options. They use another tactic that I'm sure you might have used yourself from time to time.

1. You pick something you are already familiar with.

2. You pick something your partner is having.

3. You pick something you've seen on one of the other tables that looks tempting.

4. Close your eyes, stab at the menu and take pot luck.

5. Ask your partner or the waiter for a recommendation.

I don't think that any of these are unusual. In fact, I think that this sort of behaviour is normal. Check it out the next time you're in a restaurant and see for yourself.

The reason I bring the issue up is it's a wonderful example of how reluctant we are at times to make decisions. Yes, we like to feel we have options. Yes, we like to feel we can choose and therefore, in some way, influence and control our destiny. But I can't help but feel that this is often just an illusion. Making a decision requires mental effort, just the thing we are low on after a hard day's slog and looking forward to some quality leisure time accompanied by a bottle of the house-red. And when it is difficult for us to make a decision, we find a way not to, by delegating the decision-making process to someone else, by postponing the decision if possible or by going for the default option which is the easiest, safest or simplest option available to us.

The behavioural economist Dan Ariely points this out by analysing the organ-donating statistics of European countries. He looked into why countries such as the United Kingdom, Germany, the Netherlands, Denmark have a low percentage of organ donors (about 20% or less) and yet neighbouring countries such as France, Austria, Belgium and Sweden have a relatively high percentage of organ donors (about 90% or more). After considering and discarding factors such as culture and religion he discovered that the main factor influencing people's decision whether or not to donate was how the form[49] they filled in was written. On the forms in the U.K., Germany, the Netherlands and Denmark, the form had a box that said "Tick the box below if you want to participate in the organ donor programme" while France, Austria, Belgium and Sweden had forms that said "Tick the box below if you don't want to participate in the organ donor programme." Ariely points out that the issue of donating organs and saving lives is a difficult and complex question which we find difficult to answer. The result is that we are mentally paralysed. We find it very hard to make a rational decision based on the reasons for being in favour or against. Instead we defer making a decision - we put off actively deciding (which means not ticking any box) and therefore maintaining the

---

49- It is common to have this question about being an organ donator on applications for driving licences, which was the source Dan Ariely was referring to.

status quo. When the decision is complex or difficult, or when we do not have the mental energy to decide on what to do, our natural tendency is to go with the flow. So in the U.K. for example, most people don't tick the box and as a result, opt out of the donor scheme while across the channel most people in France don't tick the box either and, as a result, opt in.

Can we take advantage of this reluctance to make decisions?

Happily, the succinct answer is 'yes'.

If you know that sometime later on you should do an activity you find challenging, such as eating a healthy lunch, jogging round the block or cold-calling potential clients, and that you know in advance you are going to be mentally tired or stressed, then you can increase your chances of carrying out that activity by making it the default option.

For example, let's say that you've decided that you're going to forgo the oven pizza and fix yourself a curried chicken salad with apples and raisins. That would be much healthier, wouldn't it? Yet you know full well that in spite of having the best intentions in the world, the last time you tried this, you ended up just popping that deep-pan pizza in the oven (enjoying a beer and a packet of cheese and onion crisps while you waited) which was so much easier. So this time you plan your strategy. You write out what you are going to do at lunchtime BEFORE you get there. "The menu for today's lunch is curried chicken salad with apples and raisins with fresh orange juice, a caramel yogurt for desert followed by a cup of Earl Grey (white, no sugar)." You then set out the ingredients (or even better, prepare it beforehand) and set out the plate, cup, cutlery and so on. Thus, when you get to lunchtime, you wander into the kitchen and there is your lunch already decided and laid out ready for you to get stuck into.

In this case, the written menu (or Post-it) along with the food already prepared and set out served as pointers. They guided your actions in such a way that you barely needed to make any decision. You just went with the flow.

So the observation here is whatever you can do to set up your daily routine beforehand, which will reduce the decision-making progress later on, will be of great help. In the next section, we are going to be considering the use of periodic actions and habits. A habit is something that we do when given a prompt (e.g. you get nervous so you bite your nails, or you come to a red traffic-light so you stop the car). If you like, pointers are the prompts for your desired behaviours and habits. You are intentionally organising your surroundings so that when the time comes you will have your prompts, your reminders and signposts all pointing you in the right direction making it effortless to decide what to do next. Here is a list of the resources you have at your disposal.

Smartphones

Apps

Post-it notes

Calendars

Laminated notes

Graphs

Magnetic whiteboard

Pre-positioned stuff

Internal pointers

## Smartphones

Let's assume you have one. If you don't, let's assume that if you want to conquer the world then you're going to get one. As far as modern day organizers go, they're about as good as you can get. I remember when I used to carry around a personal organizer - the sort that looked like a big thick ring-bound book. Not anymore. A good smartphone (or even a mediocre one) has a personal organiser beat hands down. As well as the apps, your smartphone will have the following features: multiple alarm facility, a smart-calendar and some means of recording your memos either by noting them down or recording them with audio or video. You can programme your phone to send you reminders at a set time, or when you arrive or leave a destination: from the mundane 'buy some milk' to 'now it's time to go to the gym!'

# Apps

The tech era moves pretty fast and so by the time you read this book, the apps available to you will have no doubt increased, but my firm favourites are Reminders, Notes and Things. Whatever your long-term goal it's more than likely someone has written an app to help you. There are health apps, language-learning apps, productivity apps. Take time to investigate what's currently on the market and take time to learn how best to use it. Just having it on your home screen can be a pointer to use the thing.

# Post-it Notes

I'm a big fan of Post-its. They're bright, colourful, cheap and easy. Use them to optimal effect by sticking them where you can see them in the right place at the right time: on your front door, on your briefcase handle, on the dashboard of your car, on your computer screen, bathroom mirror, bedside clock. Brenda, the lady whose goal was to learn Spanish the Soritean way, labelled everything in her home with Post-its and decorated her walls with useful vocabulary and phrases so she could see them every day. These brightly coloured bits of paper serve as excellent short-term reminders, not so good in the long-term as they lose their stickiness and fall off.

# Calendars

As well as the sort of calendar on your phone or computer, I'm referring to the wall calendars that you hang on the kitchen door. Whereas the virtual ones are only there when you have your device switched on, wall calendars are always visible. You can use it as your Progress Calendar if it serves your purpose. Keep a variety of coloured markers nearby so you can make notes and cross off the successful days. This is an excellent way to increase the sensation of progress and develop habits.

## Laminated Notes

Where Post-its fail, laminated paper takes over. By 'Laminated' I mean any piece of paper (and it doesn't have to be A4 sized) passed through one of those machines that melts plastic onto them and then cut to the desired size. Laminated notes are more durable and versatile: you can stick them to surfaces, carry them around in your pocket and they are resistant to dirt, water and grease. Pointers that are referred to frequently or handled frequently, such as checklists, benefit from being laminated. The only danger is that as you become familiar with it, you become desensitised and start to ignore it.

## Graphs

As we saw in chapter 8 on Progress, graphs are a great way to measure, plot and visualise our slow but steady success. But also having your graph in an easy-to-see place serves to remind you what you are up to. Once you see your results heading in the right direction - and they will head in the right direction - you will gain impetus to maintain the successful trend.

## Magnetic Whiteboard

I swear by these. We have a large one in the kitchen covered with an array of colourful little magnets I got from Amazon, and which the kid's try to pull off and play with when given half the chance. There's also a tray along the bottom where we keep a variety of coloured whiteboard markers and a rubber. The board gets filled with notes, things to add to the shopping list, receipts, reminders, dates, and all sorts. It's next to the door and is referred to as the family's sacred altar of planning.

## Prepositioned Stuff

Every night, before I go to bed, I set out my writing material. I set out my notes, chapter proofs (printed off with comments scribbled in pencil) and my laptop, which I plug in, leaving my Word document already opened and the screen on stand-by. This means that the following morning when I come downstairs, all I have to do is sit down, touch a key and 'hey presto' it's all there ready for me. I know of cases where people put their jogging clothes next to the bed so they are there the next morning - no thinking required, you just get up, get dressed and you're ready to run. Setting out your material, your work, your gym bag or whatever you need can help guide you towards that activity and also make starting it that little bit easier. If you're on a diet, then setting out your breakfast things the night before helps you keep to the Fruit 'n' Fibre and away from the biscuit tin.

## Internal Pointers

Up until now, this chapter has focussed on how you can organise and arrange your environment (your home, work etc.) to increase the likelihood of doing the right thing at the right moment. There does exist, however, another way of placing pointers that will help you do the right thing at the right moment. These are internal pointers.

Do you remember flow charts? A set of interrelated instructions designed to carry out some process. The 'If...then...' command says 'Here is a question. If the answer to this question is X then do this, if the answer is Y, then do that'. An example would be 'Are you thirsty? If yes, then have something to drink. If no, then don't bother'. If there is no option regarding a command, then it is not an 'If...then...' command.

**Figure 13: Example of a simple flow chart**

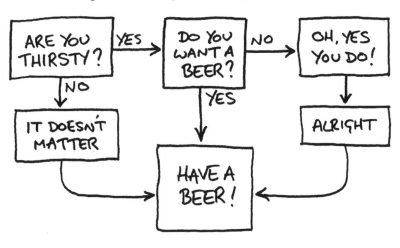

The 'If...then...' command is the most important ingredient of a flow diagram and one of the basic cornerstones of programming and, if you play your cards right, it can become a cornerstone of your mental programming, too. I refer to them as 'When/then' commands. To me, the word 'if' suggests there is a possibility of an event happening which implies there is a possibility that they might not, whereas 'When' is talking about a situation you know is going to happen at some point, which for our use of the When/then command is much more appropriate.

Your brain's Achilles heel is that it requires energy in order to think properly. By properly, I mean the sort of thinking that considers all of the relevant factors, takes each one into account, considers the options available and the merits of each option and then decides the optimal course of action - just like choosing from the menu mentioned earlier. All this is done by your PFC. However, it is important to remember that the activity of self-restraint through willpower also requires mental effort, sometimes a lot of effort in order to avoid succumbing to what is most likely to be one of the more basely pleasures (usually one of the seven deadly sins and if I had to put my money on it, I'd go for sloth and gluttony). What this means is that if you are in a position of deciding whether to continue trying to figure out how to continue with a task that you've been working on or just lie on the sofa and watch the telly for a little bit more than your PFC is having to fight on two fronts; on the one front, it is trying to consider what to do, what the next task should be, how to go about that next task, what would be the best way to start and what would be needed in order to do that. On the other front, it is resisting the urge to do a bit of channel surfing and maybe have a little snooze after all it has been a hard day and there'll be plenty of time later.

One way to solve this problem is to reduce the effort needed on the first front. This can be done by preparing yourself WHEN/THEN commands well before the time when temptation will be rearing its enticingly attractive head. An example of this is as follows: After I've taken the dog for a walk, then I will sit down at my computer, and the first thing I will do then is to connect to my internet banking service and note down my expenses for this month. What this means is that come six o'clock you won't have to think what you need to do. You have already decided. So you just need to deploy your mental energy reserves to overcoming the urge to catnap which is substantially easier. You can set up such WHEN/THEN commands for whatever you want and you can do it during a period of calm so you know when things get a bit strained you'll be doing the right thing. The beauty of this method is that the command doesn't have to be based on time or geography (as are most of the external pointers previously discussed). Internal pointers can be based on circumstances and are ideal for choosing the right course of action during times of duress such as 'When I feel a snack-attack coming on, then I will have a glass of water, do ten push ups and fuss the dog for five minutes to calm me down'.

## The 2-Minute Rule

Another great example of an Internal Pointer is given by David Allen, not the brilliant Irish comedian[50] but the American productivity guru and author of *Getting Things Done*. If you haven't already read, I highly recommend as it is another example of how applying the right simple ideas can lead to powerfully effective results. The Pointer that David Allen refers to is the '2-Minute Rule'. Namely that when the next action you have to take to advance in your project, the next piece of the puzzle you have to put in, only takes two minutes or less, then do it now; Deal with it immediately and get it over and done with. The simple beauty of this idea is that as well as taking yet another insignificant step towards your intended goal, you are also avoiding adding it to your list of things to remember and do. You get it done straight away and then get on with the rest of your day. Such examples would be cancelling a meeting, booking a table at your favourite restaurant or making an appointment with the dentist. However, there is a danger to the '2-Minute Rule'. There is a whole set of 'actions' that can be taken that are less than two minutes, actions such as checking your e-mail in-tray, texting, checking your Facebook account, looking up the latest football score, the weather or such like. Can you guess what the danger is with these things? The danger is what I call

---

50- If you haven't seen it, or even if you have, I strongly recommend looking up 'Dave Allen on teaching your kids the time' on YouTube. It is a comedy masterpiece and continues to make me laugh every time I see it.

the concept of 'Minimal Entry' which we will consider in more detail in the next chapter. But the general idea of Minimal Entry is that once you start an activity which you expect to be quick and easy, there is a natural tendency to continue doing that activity, which then expands much further than you had originally intended. What this means is that 30 seconds sending a simple text turns into 10 minutes of chatting, or just checking the weather forecast on the web turns into half an hour of internet surfing. Also, the frequency of these less-than-two minute activities is another factor. What David Allen is referring to are activities that once done are not going to creep up on you again in five minute's time, especially when dealing with new incoming stuff such as dealing with e-mails. So here the Internal Pointer is: 'When a situation occurs which I can deal with in less than two minutes, then I will do it immediately'.

Other examples of Internal Pointers could be...

✱ When it comes to desserts I will say 'no thank you' I'll just have a coffee.

✱ When I feel that I want a cigarette, I will remember what happened to Uncle Tom (an agonising death from lung cancer) and go for a walk around the block.

✱ When the kids start to make me angry, I will acknowledge that I'm angry and slowly count to ten before exploding.

✱ If I feel that I'm weakening in my resolution, I'll phone my mum/ friend/coach who's great at bucking me up.

✱ If I'm offered an alcoholic drink, I'll say 'thank you, but I'm on medication. But I'd really like a cup of tea (or whatever).

## What to Do with Your 'To Do' List

In our student days, my friend John loved to make lists. A list of what music he was going to put on his next compilation tape, a list of ideas for his next money-making venture as well as the inevitable 'to do' list. The zenith of his 'listorial' achievements was when he proudly showed me a list of all the lists that he was going to make when he had the time to do so. All this during our university day when we were supposed to be studying. As he frequently observed "Isn't it amazing what you can find to do when you don't want to do any work?"

Since then I have learnt the error of making 'to do' lists. A 'to do' list is just that: a static reminder that you have stuff to do that you're not doing. One way of leveraging the Pointer technique is to transfer your 'to do' list onto your agenda. Give each one a time and a date. If you put it into your smartphone's agenda, you'll even get a nice pop-up reminder telling you what you're going to do when you need to do it. And as we have seen, if you have a clock or an agenda telling you that it's time to do something then it's much more likely that you will automatically go and do it.

## Deadlines

From the very beginning, the word 'deadline' has an ominous sound - it's those first four letters, isn't it? I know we sometimes consider deadlines as something negative. But a deadline is just another form of pointer and I hope you are already starting to recognise the positive power of pointers. A deadline is simply a pointer that indicates a time on the calendar by when you have to have completed a certain task. The disadvantage of a deadline is that although it is clear about specifying by when a certain task has to be complete, it is notoriously vague on the subject of when the task is actually going to get done. What is missing here is a set of secondary pointers that guide us towards the timely realisation of the task. Without these additional pointers it is all too easy to let things slip, to forget one or two important pieces of the task along the way (or all of them) and to wake up one day to the too-often surprising realisation that you've left it too late and suddenly you have to rush.

This sort of thing can occasionally happen to you when you do the shopping at the local megamarket. Assuming that you have your list, you trundle your wobbly trolley up and down the aisles, slowly filling it to the brim. Your deadline here is more of a geographical one, represented by the checkout: you have to have completed the list by the time you get to the end. So you get to what you deem to be the end of your forage for

175

groceries, studiously analyse which queue of happy shoppers is going to warrant the least time waiting (paying careful attention to stay out of the 'ten-items-or-less' line (always embarrassing that one) and put yourself passively in the queue to pay. In order to pass those happy minutes, you idly contemplate the lifestyles of your fellow queue members by observing the contents of their shopping trolleys (cat litter, nappies and five bottles of vodka). You then calmly mull over your own shopping list just to double check that all is under control when suddenly you notice that you've forgotten the toilet paper. The toilet paper is on aisle 10 and you are in the queue opposite aisle 568 and there are now 5 shoppers behind you with overflowing trolleys. The adrenaline starts to flow. You are now faced with the dilemma of losing your place while doing the 400m dash or staying put and praying that there honestly was one roll left on the top shelf. You don't need this type of stress.

The solution to avoid this sort of experience is to put your list in 'geographical' order; the order in which you come across the different sections as you glide through the store. This way you can bung your booty into the trolley without having to backtrack to get the loo-roll. Your newly organised list avoids that last minute panic and I seriously recommend approaching your deadlines with the same ruthless efficiency. Whether it's your exam next term, your presentation next month or your house-guests that are arriving a week next Wednesday (tidy the house, prepare the guest bedroom and get in a bottle of Cointreau for Aunty Mabel, once you have your deadline stating by when things have to be done, if you don't then take the next logical step of deciding the programme for when the things are actually going to get done, then you're simply asking for trouble because your Grog is going to take one look at the deadline and feel "Oh, 'next term!'. That's an eon away. No worries there!" Those famous last words: 'Don't worry - there's plenty of time.'

While we're on the subject of deadlines, there are two other points I think are worth mentioning that have an influence on our perseverance.

The first of these is to consider how our deadlines are set. Some occur naturally, some we choose and some are thrust upon us. With the natural deadlines (like getting the harvest in or making it to the airport before your plane takes off) or those thrust upon us (finish this report by Monday or else!) there's not much flexibility involved; you just have to grin and bear it. But there is the other kind of deadline - the kind we set ourselves. And I'd like to question how we go about doing this. The reason I'd like to do this is because I think we could improve on how we set out deadlines.

In his book 'On Writing', the American novelist Stephen King wrote that he gives himself just three months to write the first draft of a novel. Three months!?!? I started writing this book giving myself a year! I chose this timeframe because it seemed like a large round comfortable figure. But when I signed my contract with my publisher, it was under the condition that the book would be finished within three months (cue small heart attack). At that point I was six months into writing and about half way through. Completing the manuscript in just three months was therefore doubling my productivity. What surprised me was that I seemed to gear up my productivity almost effortlessly and while writing these words I happily see from my progress plotter (see Progress chapter) that I'm actually ahead of schedule. So guess what? I did it. Most people like challenges, but just like Goldilocks, the challenge shouldn't be too hard, as this creates stress and it shouldn't be too easy, as this is not inspiring. The challenge has to be 'just right'. And if you can find that sweet spot, the point where the difficulty of the task is perfectly balanced with your capacity to do it, then your passion can be kindled to optimum effect. So the next time you set yourself a deadline, consider whether you're making it too easy for yourself. Could you do it in less time? Your knee-jerk reaction will most likely be 'No way, José!' but that is your Grog expressing himself. Give Grog a while to calm down and consider things with composure. If you brought your deadline forward, could you do it? You could, couldn't you?

The second point about deadlines is about not underestimating how motivating they can be. If we want to persevere we need all the motivation, we can get and therefore I think it is useful to embrace deadlines positively rather than fear them. Douglas Adams is quoted as saying "I love deadlines. I love the whooshing noise they make as they go by." But seriously, there are several reasons why we should love deadlines. Firstly, as a pointer they provide clarity and definition to a task. You know exactly when you have to have the job done. Secondly, as we've just established above, setting the right deadline can provide the optimum challenge which stirs up our passion which in turn provides motivation. Thirdly, achieving your deadline is intrinsically rewarding. It gives us that little shot of dopamine that makes us feel great. Fourthly, it is a clear sign that you are making progress. Without the sensation of progress, we become frustrated and disillusioned (see Progress chapter). A deadline, just like a finishing line or a benchmark demonstrates that in this world of insignificant change, definite progress has been achieved. Finally, it gives us the feeling of success. This is a positive experience and as we shall see in the corresponding chapter 'Positivity' is a key element regarding perseverance and fighting off those dark moments of gloom and futility.

In short, deadlines can provide you with a clearly defined challenge that can feed your motivation by providing reward, passion, the sense of progress and positivity. However, a good deadline must be carefully chosen and supported by a well thought-out programme. Otherwise the inevitable will happen: procrastination will take over and turn your dreams into nightmares.

So Pointers help set us going in the right direction without having to think about it too much. Pointers bypass the need for willpower, prizes, passion and peer pressure. They serve as a prompt to get us going and if we use them regularly they become part of our routines and habits, and once our Soritean actions become part of our daily routine, then we really do have the Sorites Principle licked.

## Things to Think About

- Our brains are lazy and prefer to run on automatic if given the opportunity.
- Our natural response is to do something without question if there is a pointer telling us.
- We can use pointers to help us carry out small actions instead of relying on willpower or motivation.
- Pointers can take many forms such as clocks, signs or Post-its.
- Pointers can also be internal, self-programmed When/Then commands.

## Top Tips

- Program activities into your agenda, Google Calendar or similar.
- Set alarms as reminders.
- Leave yourself signs, notes, Post-its or messages of encouragement.
- Program your computer to boot up opening a certain document you need to work on.
- Objects can also be pointers. Leave your running shoes by the bed.
- Set up 'Internal Pointers' in your mind 'When X happens, then I'll do Y.' Such as, 'If an action takes less than 2 minutes, I'll do it immediately.'
- Program what and when you are going to eat, drink, smoke or whatever to alleviate the decision-making process when your willpower is low.
- Don't keep a 'to do' list. Programme your things to do in your agenda - preferably with a reminder to let you know it's time to do them.
- Use deadlines intelligently to not only serve as a pointer but to give you the optimum challenge, and a sense of progress and positive success.

## Questions to Ask Yourself (and Answer)

- What Pointers do you already use?
- What Pointers could you start using?
- Where could setting external Pointers help ease your decision-making process?
- What objects could you pre-position to encourage your desired behaviour?
- What When/Then commands could you set for yourself?
- What deadlines are you facing? How could you make the most of them?

# 12 ● Periodic Actions, Habits & Routines

## The 21-year diary

When I was ten years old, my big sister gave me for Christmas a Five-year Diary. Dark turquoise leather bound with its own little lock (the key lost long ago) it had at the beginning a brief foreword which read as follows:

*"Perhaps none but the most determined will achieve an entry for every day in the Five Year Diary, but even if only the special days and the important events are entered its pages will grow more interesting with the passing of each year."*

I distinctly remember reading this when I was ten. The word 'determined' bothered me, partly because I didn't know how to pronounce it (I deduced that it was pronounced 'detter-mind') and partly because I don't think that I knew what it meant.

Nevertheless, despite of my lack of vocabulary, not only did I manage to write an entry for every day of those following five years but also went on to fill another 3 diaries writing an entry every day for another sixteen years until I was thirty-two.

For most of those years I kept writing not because of willpower nor because I had some sort of biochemical reward after completing each entry (the novelty of that had worn off years earlier). The thing that kept me going was that writing my diary had become a deeply ingrained part of my bedtime routine, like cleaning my teeth or going to the loo. It was part of the night-time ritual that I did, almost without thinking about it, like getting up and ready in the morning or commuting to work. It all happened in a sort of automatic way, without any sense of mental effort. An action that I had repeated so many times that it had become habit, a basic routine that required no 'detter-mindedness' at all.

In fact, it wasn't that easy to stop. It felt strange not writing it, as if there was something missing - something not quite right. But keeping a personal diary of your most intimate thoughts and having a suspicious and nosey girlfriend don't combine well together.

Here is another answer to the question 'What is there left when willpower, rewards and emotions have faded?'[51]

The answer is in the actions that we have learned to do that require no mental exertion whatsoever. Activities we carry out without giving them a second thought: our periodic actions, habits and routines.

Periodic actions are things you do that are repeated regularly after a certain period of time has passed. Celebrating your birthday is an example. Getting up on a Friday looking forward to the weekend is another, it happens every seven days. Taking your antibiotics every six hours is another.

Habits are things that we usually do when we are provided with the right stimulus. The way you answer the phone, the way you blow your nose, the way you bite your nails when you're nervous or the way you snack on comfort food when you're stressed.

---

51- The first one was 'Pointers' covered by the previous chapter.

Routines are groups of actions that usually go together. Getting up in the morning is an example. The way you shower, prepare a sandwich, drive to work or sit down to watch the telly are all probably examples of a set of actions that you do the same way each time.

These three concepts are not mutually exclusive. Routines can often be periodic, such as getting up in the morning. And when one action is the prompt for another which then becomes the prompt for yet another then a routine could also be regarded as a series of habits.

However, the overlap is not always there. Sniffing or coughing when you are nervous is a habit but not a routine.

## Nervous Cough

One of the lecturers during my university days was a wonderfully sweet man who was an expert in his field and from whom one could learn a great deal, but when put in front of a group of students he turned into a quivering wreck. His hands would tremble slightly, he would perspire more than appropriate, and unfortunately he had the habit of a nervous little cough. Half cough, half clearing the throat; it was a quiet little action that if done occasionally would not have drawn attention. However, as he did it at least once a minute, it started to become an annoying distraction. It got to the stage, where I started to make a mark in my notes every time he coughed, and sometimes it got to over eighty times in an hour's lecture. Not being one to miss an opportunity it occurred to me that instead of regarding this as an annoyance I could to turn it into an entertainment and started to run a competition every week with my peers guessing how many coughs he would produce. Of course once the stakes were down everyone started to count each cough to make sure all was fair and correct. The sudden interest in his little habit however must have been felt by the professor because as he could sense there was something afoot he became even more nervous. I still have my notes and the record stood at 216 coughs in one hour. At that point I think I was berated by one of my female colleagues for being a prat and so I decided that getting a degree was probably, in the long term at least, more important than having a bit of fun.

Although habits, routines and periodic actions are not necessarily the same thing, they do have at least one thing in common: They are all carried out with minimum mental effort. They come easily to us. We don't have to think about them too much. "It's six o'clock. Time to pop a pill." You just do it. It doesn't require a mountain of willpower, mental effort or passion. In fact, they can be actions that are carried out so often that you find yourself doing them without any thought at all.

Carrying out actions without any thought at all has its advantages and disadvantages. How often have you had to go back to see if you locked the door or turned off the oven? When you do something very familiar which doesn't require concentration we often take the opportunity to think about other things. Sometime after you have carried out the action, you might not be sure that you did it or not. Can you remember? Did you really do it or are you confusing it with the memory of a previous time? At times, we catch ourselves in a daze or wandering around like a zombie. How often have you found yourself driving to work instead of driving to where you should be going? It might sound funny, but sometimes it can happen with heart-breaking results.

## Samantha

In August of 2014, Samantha, a senior accounts manager of a plastic manufacturing company and mother of Alan, a 15 month-old toddler, was distraught when she returned to her car after work to find her little boy still fastened in on the back seat. She had forgotten to take him to nursery in the morning. As the car had been parked in direct sunlight for almost seven hours, the little boy had experienced excessive temperatures and had passed out. In spite of attempts to resuscitate him, the little Adam never regained consciousness.

Some would find it easy to criticise Samantha for being irresponsible. But you don't need many scientific tests to prove that we are all guilty in some way of the same thing. It's the way our brains are. Over forty percent of our behaviour is automatic; one action automatically leads to the next action which are all carried out without much mental effort at all. And if we are particularly preoccupied with something out of the ordinary, if our attention is fully taken by some major worry or important distraction, then we are especially vulnerable to the rest of our brain running on automatic taking over our regular actions and carrying them out without consulting the conscious 'thinking' part of our brain.

In spite of the dangers of acting 'unthinkingly' the fact that we can (and regularly do) carry out so much without conscious thought is great news for you if you want to apply the Sorites Principle to its full potential. As we have seen, the third part of applying the Sorites Principle involves carrying out small actions all the time. Periodic actions, routines and habits are just that; things that we carry out almost every day. No need for willpower, prizes or a sense of progress. These actions are carried out with minimal conscious thought and therefore require no motivation, no emotions and no peer pressure. If we can incorporate these small actions into our regular activities, then we can be sure of a constant trickle of 'insignificant' progress that will gradually build up to get us to where we want to be.

## How Do We Put This into Action?

There is no mystical magic formula here. The answers are mundane and 'obvious'. In spite of this, I would suggest you consider your track record at this point and ask yourself how often you have actually put these 'obvious' answers into practice. Be honest.

## A Periodic Action

Programme it. Write it down. If you have a part of the puzzle you want to carry out at a particular time on a particular day, then put it in your agenda. Programme it into your smartphone so you get a reminder. Put it on the calendar, set an alarm, get your secretary to discretely point out "in five minutes it'll be time for you to do your special thing."[52] You might be sceptical of this - all that bother over something so straightforward. You'll think, 'I don't need to do this! It's too simple, too obvious!" This is you talking while you are calm, rested and focussed on your goal, but once

---

52- While trying not to smirk

you put this book down you re-enter the real world of stress, distractions and temptation. Your attention is in constant demand. Making the mental effort to carry out your new regular action requires willpower and concentration - precisely those things you know you are not always going to have. So take the effort out of having to remember and decide; programme your periodic actions in whatever way works for you and stick to it.

## The Key to Habit-forming

As the habit-experts point out, a habit is an action that is automatically carried out when the right prompt (or trigger) occurs. A popular myth is that it takes twenty-one days to develop a habit. This is not true; a habit very much depends on how frequently the 'prompt' and the corresponding 'habit' occurs. Take my writing as an example.

A few months ago, the comma key on my computer at home finally realised it had had enough of this mortal world and decided to give up the ghost. It would no longer cooperate despite all my creative efforts to press it in all the ways that occurred to me. The comma key became a mere decorative feature that simply gives balance and harmony to the keypad layout. This was a problem. But as I am nothing if not resourceful,[53] I programmed the Autocorrect facility to put in a comma every time I typed a double full stop '..'[54] This was a most satisfactory solution - quick, easy and didn't cost a penny! That first day I merrily tap-tapped away adding double full stops that magically turned into commas where ever I fancied. Lovely!

The next day I found myself working from my office which has a nice all-singing, all-dancing computer connected to the 'server' along with everyone else's computers in the company. As I set myself to the grindstone and started typing, I found myself automatically typing double full stops every time I needed a comma in spite of the fact that the comma key at

---

53- ...and too tight to buy a new laptop.

54- And before it might occur to you to ask, I got it to put in a semicolon (;) every time I typed a double colon (::). Sometimes I have to sit back and marvel at my own ingeniosity.

work functioned perfectly well. It actually took a concerted effort to stop doing it. This was after just one day of typing. This proves that habits don't need twenty-one days to form. They just need to be repeated enough times to sink in. In the case of my 'comma' habit, it took just a few hours.

So the 'key' to developing a habit is to do it so often you start to do it automatically - something you do without thinking like biting your nails or lighting up a cigarette. In order to achieve this, to carry out an action so many times that it becomes a habit, you have to overcome your two biggest obstacles: your unreliable willpower and your Grogarian resistance.

For example, if you want to develop the habit of practicing the Ukulele for three hours every time you get home from work, these two obstacles provide you with two challenges. The first is that dedicating three hours to studying is tough. It requires mental effort and, as I've pointed out and shall continue to point out, willpower will not power you towards your goal. When you get home, absolutely shattered after a gruelling day, the last thing you need is to try to 'willpower' yourself into action. It simply is not going to happen. The other is Grog, constantly eyeing the environment and... "Oh, look! That sofa looks soooo enticing and comfy. Three hours of study? Sod that for a game of soldiers! A little well-earned relaxing break feels much more like it. And if we just adorn it with a nice beer out of the fridge, like this, and a tube of Pringles, like that, and just put the telly on for just five minutes, voila! That's us sorted out until it's teatime!" Difficult to resist? You know the answer, don't you?

So what's the solution?

The Sorites Principle is all about insignificant change and here, 'insignificant' is the operative word. In his book *Mini Habits*, Stephen Guise emphasises the practical advantages of establishing new habits that are embarrassingly small. After all, doing even a little is much better than doing nothing. Examples of the kind of mini-habits he refers to are doing just one press-up or typing just fifty words or practicing the Ukulele for just one minute. The main advantage that this has is that these activities are so pathetically small that they require hardly any willpower and generate almost no Grogarian resistance. Doing them, or to be more specific, 'starting' to do them is easy, and once we are down there doing our push-ups, or writing at the computer or sat with our instrument in our hands, then doing a bit more is even easier. So start small and work your way up.

The use of Soritean tools such as Star Charts, Progress Calendars and Progress Plotters are great for this as they serve as permanent pointers to carrying out your desired new habit. In fact, any of the pointers we mentioned in the last chapter can be used to point you in the right direction until your habit sets in.

Just putting these theories into practice could be seen as a habit in itself. There are a couple of ways that you can do this and trust me, they work wonders!

## Minimal Entry

Here's an interesting little habit I would recommend to anyone. I call it the habit of 'Minimal Entry'. This is a technique that is as simple as it is effective: a powerful little productivity tool that you can apply to any goal (or chore) that can be done piece by piece. I use the habit of Minimal Entry as much on a domestic level, if not more, as I do when I'm dealing with my larger projects and goals.

On many occasions, we put off doing some activity because we see it as a 'large chore'. Here I'm specifically referring to such chores as loading or unloading the dishwasher, tidying the living-room after my twins have run riot through it, cleaning the kitchen work surfaces, emptying my in-tray, hoovering the house etc. (you get the idea, don't you?).

So the prompt for this habit is when you realise that a chore has to be done, but you don't feel like doing it because there's too much to do.

The action is to focus on carrying out the smallest action you can do to start dealing with the 'chore' - one that your Grog finds acceptable. It is important that you have no intention of doing anything more than this single action because Grog doesn't like doing chores. If she did, then it wouldn't be a chore, would it? So an example of this would be to unload

ONE glass out of the dishwasher and put it away or to pick up ONE cushion off the floor and put it back on the sofa or look at ONE e-mail and deal with it.

The curious thing about the technique of Minimal Entry is that 9 times out of 10, once you've done your minimal entry task your Grog will feel 'Oh, that wasn't so bad. Actually, that was much easier than I was expecting. In fact, now that we're standing here with the dishwasher and cupboard open we might as well do a few more glasses (or cushions or e-mails). And before you know it - hey presto! - you've done the whole task, little by little without realising it.

I frequently use this trick for washing the dishes. I say, well, I'll just do those cups and maybe a small plate or two and then I might move on to the big plates and so on and before you know it 80% of the washing up is done.[55]

I also use it for writing. When I've got a spare half hour I'll sit down with my notebook. Grog will feel 'No, no! Not that bloody writing lark again! We want to relax! We want to have a rest!' But I calmly reply that that's fine and I point out that all we're going to do is "open that little notebook and jot down just a couple of tiny ideas and then we can rest, okay?" And Grog feels "Okay. If that's all it is, then let's do it." And so we get out our little notebook and jot down a few ideas that have occurred to us and Grog feels "Oh, that was easy" and I say, "Well, as we're here with the notebook open and pencil in hand, how about writing just a little more?" But actually I haven't got to the end of the sentence because we are already scribbling down the next idea and so one thing flows into the next.

## The One-minute Blitz

Another version of Minimal Entry is the One-minute Blitz Habit. Here again you're faced with a chore that you can do little by little. The difference is instead of focussing on the minimal amount of work to be done, you focus on a minimal period of time in which you have to do it.

---

55- I usually leave the cheese grater, the fondue and the greasy oven tray for the wife.

You say to Grog "Look, we have this chore to do but we really don't want to spend a lot of time doing it, do we?" "Too bloody right!" feels Grog. "So how about we see how much of it we can get done in just one minute (or however many minutes you think you can get away with). After that we'll do something you like such as relaxing on the sofa or eating chocolate." "Done", feels Grog, "Let's do it!" Once again, just like Minimal Entry, one minute turns into two, which turn into five and so on until you suddenly realise you've completed the entire task.

I use this method while I'm waiting for my twins to put their shoes on in the morning before I take them to school (which usually takes 10 minutes and most of my patience) during which time I've loaded the washing machine, watered the plants and defrosted the fridge.[56] Nevertheless, if you do actually just spend one minute doing your chore it's still one insignificant step in the right direction.

The curious thing I find with the One-minute Blitz Habit, as with that of Minimal Entry, is that it's like shooting fish in a barrel. It's so easy to fool Grog into believing you. She has the memory of a sieve. She never once feels she's been used. She never feels that she's been tricked, conned or diddled. She just happily continues on the lookout for something to eat, fight or fornicate with.

## Seize the Opportunity

While we are on the subject of Soritarian habits, I'd like to add one that I rediscovered for myself when I was halfway through writing this book. To an extent it goes against everything that has been said about the importance of doing regular periodic actions, of setting routines that are conducive towards your intended objective.

It is the habit of seizing the opportunity. It is the habit of arranging your surroundings to allow you (dare I say 'encourage you') to achieve a little bit of your objective, to get a little bit closer to your goal, to put in another tiny piece of the puzzle whenever the opportunity arises. Here, the prompt is when you have a free moment while you're having to wait

---

56- Just joking! It defrosts itself.

somewhere or find yourself in the right place with a few minutes to spare and now even easier in this day and age of smartphones and broadband. It was only several months after I started writing, that I began carrying around a notebook and pencil with me at all times (except in the shower) this includes by the side of the bed, in the car, while out and about in town, at the dentist's, doctor's or waiting for the kids to hurl themselves out of school gates and come joyfully (joyfully for them, that is to say) barrelling into me at breakneck speed. When I first started writing I followed the advice of other writers who recommended sitting down at one's computer in uninterrupted silence for several hours until 'the pixie of inspiration' comes to visit. For me, this technique seemed logical, but in practice, finding several hours of uninterrupted silence proved far more challenging than I had imagined. Furthermore, the pixie of Inspiration often seemed to have her own ideas about when and where she was expected to appear. The whole process was, at least for me, somewhat less than satisfactory. What I then discovered is that I can usually double my productivity if I'm simply prepared whenever the pixie of inspiration comes to visit, whether it's when I'm sat at my computer, in my car or on the loo. If I get an idea I can jot it down and as we saw before, once you start writing then sometimes the ideas just keep coming. I've written on trains, in bars and cafés, while delayed at the airport and even while queuing up at the post office. My note book and pencil allow me to put little pieces of my puzzle in whenever I feel the urge. Of course, this habit is not ideal for all tasks. If you're building an extension, you can't carry around a few bricks and half a bag of cement just on the off-chance you get inspired. But you can carry revision cards around with you. You can take the opportunity to walk up the stairs instead of taking the lift. You can look at your app for learning your theory test for driving. You can choose to get off the metro and walk that extra stop. You can take that extra minute to go out of your way to compliment someone on a job well done.

## My Favourite Habit

To conclude this section, I'd like to share a little habit that I have passed on, and will continue to pass on, to all my friends, family and clients. It's simple, easy and - believe it or not - works better than you might think. It's a little trick I got from behavioural psychologist Dr. BJ Fogg who refers to it as the Maui Habit in his TED talk on 'Tiny surprises for happiness and health' and goes like this:

When you wake up each morning, sit up and just before you stand up, say to yourself (out loud or just think it inwardly) "Today is going to be a great day." It might sound like one of those hackneyed Americanisms like "Have a nice day!" but if you say it quietly to yourself with sincerity, the effect can be palpable. I say it to myself on most days - except for the ones I know are going to be bloody awful, and it sets me in the right frame of mind for the whole day. Just this one little habit can help put you in a better mood, be more positive and optimistic, and open to more opportunities.

## Habits Are Like Lego

I love Lego. The stuff I had as a kid (kept in one of those big square metal biscuit tins) were essentially a collection of four-by-twos, two-by-twos, one-by-twos and those little individual one-by-ones that got found under the sofa three months later. They mostly came in red and white with a meagre scattering of blues, blacks and yellows. It wasn't much, but I was happy with them. Today it's completely different. The Lego my kids have is absolutely wonderful with so many different shapes and colours I could sit down and build stuff with (or without) my kids for ages. I live in wonder of what it must be like to work in Lego HQ and spend all day coming up with imaginative new ideas to get parents to fork out small fortunes for a few coloured bits of plastic.

The reason why I bring the subject up is that habits, just like Lego, are something that you can put together and build on. I earlier mentioned that we can look at routines as a series of interconnected habits - each one the prompt for the next. My diary writing is an example of an activity that became a habit incorporated into my bedtime routine. So if there is one simple action that you would like to start doing regularly, one trick is to stick it onto one of your existing routines, as if it were another piece of Lego being added onto something you've already made.

Most of us have at least four rock-solid routines: getting up, commuting to our place of work or study, returning home and preparing ourselves for bed. If there are any 'insignificant' habits you can do to nudge you a tiny bit closer to your goal, then you might like to consider adding them to one of these.

To be blatantly specific such examples could be to increase your positivity to do the 'Maui Habit', saying that today is going to be a great day when you get out of bed. You could listen to a relevant podcast or audio-book on your commute to work. You could remind yourself of your internal pointers (your When/then commands) or go over your newly learnt Italian vocabulary as you return home. Or you could write out tomorrow's programme of all the little pieces you are going to put in tomorrow before you turn out the bedside light. BJ Fogg explains how he manages to keep fit by incorporating his physical exercising to his going-to-the-loo routine. Every time he went he'd do five press-ups which meant him doing over 30 press-ups a day.[57] Not at all bad, if you ask me.

Periodic actions, habits and routines are another key part in our armoury in our battle for perseverance and a way to keep on moving forward. Along with prizes, progress, passion, peer pressure, and pointers, they can form a formidable combination to slowly but surely take you relentlessly towards your goal.

There is, however, one factor that can jeopardise all this important work. One factor that can bring everything you have accomplished so far tumbling down. It's called 'lack of patience' - the feeling of suddenly wanting too much, too soon. You might not have a lot of patience, but it is worth cultivating the little that you do, because without it, your Soritean journey is doomed.

---

57- Not all habits work for everyone. I tried this one for myself, but without much success. Our bathroom is quite small and I kept banging my head against the towel rail.

## Things to Think About

✱ Periodic actions and habits don't need willpower or passion.

✱ They are activities we do almost without thinking.

✱ We are most likely to carry out periodic activities if we programme them and set reminders.

✱ If we do something enough times it becomes a routine - something we do without thinking.

✱ Habits have a prompt, a trigger.

✱ It's easier to establish a habit by starting embarrassingly small. This requires minimum willpower and generates minimum resistance from Grog.

✱ You can increase the likelihood of turning an action into a habit by incorporating it into an existing routine.

## Top Tips

✦ Use current routines to help develop new ones.

✦ Cultivate habits by modifying your environment.

✦ Write out your routines. Have them clear in your mind.

✦ Learn to incorporate routines into your current one by having an open mind.

✦ Cultivate routines by ensuring you have the necessary resources to hand as often as possible.

✦ Use the habit of Minimal Entry to facilitate starting a task by doing the minimum action required.

✦ Use the Blitz Technique by doing as much of a task as you can in just one minute.

✦ Use the Seize the Opportunity habit to do a little bit whenever the moment arises.

✦ Strengthen your positivity by starting each day by saying "Today is going to be a great day."

## Questions to Ask Yourself (and Answer)

🧩 When are you going to start programming your important periodic actions?

🧩 Where would you write them down and what reminders would you set?

🧩 What embarrassingly small habits could you start doing that would benefit you?

🧩 What activities could you do more often by applying the Habit of Minimal Entry?

🧩 When could you use the Blitz Habit to put in another piece of your puzzle?

🧩 What could you add to your morning routine to help you apply the Sorites Principle?

 **13 ▸ Patience**

*"By the time it came to the edge of the Forest the stream had grown up, so that it was almost a river, and, being grown-up, it did not run and jump and sparkle along as it used to when it was younger, but moved more slowly. For it knew now where it was going, and it said to itself, "There is no hurry. We shall get there some day."* — A. A. Milne, *The House at Pooh Corner*

Kids. Kids are great, aren't they?

They're young and full of a sort of naïve positive energy. They're often cute and prone to activities such as play, laughter and exploring the world in general. Annoying but relatively harmless, it might come as a bit of a surprise to those of you who haven't heard about it yet to learn that in the late 1960's, a group of researchers at Stanford University in California thought that in the name of science it would be a good idea to psychologically torture a group of kids at the local nursery school to see their reactions.

# Marshmallows

Lead by psychologist Walter Mischel, the idea was beautifully simple and indeed lead to some very interesting results. The basic idea was to take some poor unsuspecting child, between 4 to 6 years of age, to an almost empty room, free from distractions furnished with nothing more than a table and chair. Upon the table was a small tray and on the tray was a single marshmallow. Presumably there was some sort of secret observation facility such as a two-way mirror (like you get in all the good cop interrogation scenes). The child would then be offered the solitary marshmallow for doing nothing but being there OR double the reward (e.g. the aforesaid marshmallow plus another one) if the child would be prepared to wait for fifteen minutes. Sometimes the prize was changed to a chocolate biscuit or similar but the principle was always the same: the child wanted it and wanted it badly. The psychological torture bit came from what happened next: After explaining the 'deal', the experimenter would then leave the room so that the child was alone with the succulently tempting marshmallow for the fifteen minutes while the rest of the team presumably hid behind the two-way mirror and had a good laugh.

For some of the poor little souls, the temptation of the undefended marshmallow was too much to bear; their resolution crumbled and they scoffed it before the time was up. No extra prize there, then. But others had different ideas. Some covered their eyes or turned their backs to avoid seeing the prize. Others distracted themselves by doing some sort of physical activity.

Out of the 600 children who underwent this test, only about a third were able to resist temptation and wait for the bigger prize.

The really interesting part of the test was that the development of these 600 children was then surveyed over the following years, and what the researchers found was that the children who were able to patiently wait tended to be better students, got better exam results and were more successful in other life measures.

In other words, being patient is not only a virtue, it is a desirable trait that is worth cultivating for your own benefit.

Without a doubt, it is lack of patience that is one of the main reasons why we don't apply the Sorites Principle more often than we do. When we want something we want it now. Occasionally, I give my children a version of the Marshmallow Test: "You can have one sweetie now or you can have two sweeties when we get home in ten minutes." This almost inevitably ends with my kids choosing to have the one sweetie now AND the two sweeties when we get home: another victory for the psychological attrition from two five-year-olds.

As with the children who succeeded in getting their two marshmallows, the key to success is to avoid thinking about what you're patiently waiting for. It seems ironic that I'm proposing one puts so much effort into pondering and deliberating over one's long-term goal only then to try to put it out of one's mind. But, yes, that's exactly right. Your goal, and hopefully it will be a large one, will seem quite formidable and, in comparison to where you're currently standing, will also seem such a long way away. This observation can create the sensation of General Futility even though success is a mathematical certainty. And General Futility has Despondency as one of his main allies. Despondency, the lack of hope, will make you feel that all this is a waste of time, that all those little pieces of the puzzle are so insignificantly insignificant that they can't amount to anything. "What's the point?" you'll find yourself saying.

The point is that regardless of how insignificant your actions might seem at the moment compared to their final objective, they WILL get you there. If you're still struggling with this concept, re-read the first part of this book again. Sir Edmund Hillary (along with his trusty Sherpa Tenzing Norgay) didn't pop up to the top of Everest by magic. They struggled step by step. But every step was a step closer to where they were going. Garry Kasparov is one of the best, if not THE best chess player in the world. From 1986 until he retired in 2005, he was ranked the world's number 1 for 225 out of 228 months. An incredible achievement. However, there was a time when he had no idea how to play chess (admittedly when he was in kindergarten). His journey to ultimate chess supremacy was taken game by game, move by move.

These sensations of General Futility and Despondency are natural. We all suffer from them, time to time. Hell, I know for myself, even when writing this book, even after writing half of it, even when writing these words here, the final goal seems so far away. My patience is stressed. I want it done; I want a hardback copy sitting proudly on my bookshelf now!

## Second Breakfast

The other day I went to my local bar. It's a quiet, intimate place where everyone is on first name terms and with just one or two 'permanent residents' slumped at their usual tables midmorning before the lunchtime crowd arrive. I usually wander in about eleven o'clock to get my second breakfast (a *café con leche* and freshly baked croissant - lovely!) and idly mull over the morning's proceedings. But yesterday was different. Just before I got to the bar, a group of half a dozen 'youths'[58] who had been wandering along the pavement, instead of taking the expected route of continuing up the road, had the audacity to decide that they would enter the bar (my bar) to presumably partake of some refreshment. By the time I realised their intentions, it was too late to make a dash for it. They were already at the door and I had no option but to smile through gritted teeth and let them all pile through ahead of me. I was livid. There I was, looking forward to calmly and quietly ordering my fresh coffee and pastry - individually served and quietly enjoyed, when suddenly I find that I am going to have to 'queue up and wait!': Queue up and wait for a bunch of idle layabouts - who clearly had no intention of being in a hurry - to slowly discuss what they might feel like having, what each other might feel like having and how the latter might influence the former. All multiplied by six. I was dismayed. For a brief moment I thought they might say "Oh, we don't know what we want so why don't we let this nice gentleman who is waiting behind us order because he looks like the sort of person who knows exactly what he wants and doesn't need to wait for a bunch of indecisive fuckwits like us in order to enjoy his second breakfast." But no. No such luck. I then thought of jumping the queue (not that the troop of six had formed anything even remotely resembling a queue) politely pointing out that 'Actually, I do know what I want, so would you mind if I

---

58- Yet another example of the Sorites Principle is how the defining age of a 'youth' slowly creeps up over the years. The 'youths' in question were probably in their late twenties and wearing suits. As far as my mother-in-law is concerned, I am still a 'youth'.

ordered now while you continue to struggle with your mental-processing skills?' But my English blood and upbringing forbids me to queue-jump. For me, queue-jumping is one of those things that one simply doesn't do along with aggravated murder and high treason. It's one of those values that makes me a better person (or so I keep trying to tell myself). My third thought was to go to another bar. But there are only two and the other one is crap - the croissants are made out of cardboard and the coffee has a distinctly unpleasant aftertaste. My final thought, however, was "Hang on! I'm writing a book with a section on patience. How could I apply what I know to cope better in this situation and could I use it as an example?

The answer was clear and immediate. Yes, and yes. The art of patience is distraction. Instead of focussing on the thing one wants now (second breakfast, getting to your destination ASAP or becoming rich and famous) simply focus on something else, something that you can do right now that you don't have to wait for. The watched pot never boils[59] - the more you intensely focus on something that takes time, willing it to take less, then the agonisingly longer the time is going to feel. So back in the bar, I started to think of how I could incorporate the experience into this chapter. I got out my Goal Diary which also serves for jotting down ideas and started the 'seize-the-opportunity' habit mentioned in chapter 12. I started scribbling down a few notes when… hey presto! as if by magic, the troop of six had been served and migrated to the rear of the bar out of harm's way allowing me to sit at the bar and enjoy my second breakfast in peace.

## The Art of Intentional Distraction

The art of intentional distraction can be extremely useful in a variety of circumstances ranging from dieting to road-rage. My father suffered from road-rage. He spent most of his autumnal days as a serene and thoughtful human being. But put him behind the wheel of a car and he turned into a rabid tyrant with the patience of a starving whippet. Everyone who drove faster than him (and there were a few) was an irresponsible idiot, and everyone who drove slower than him (and there were a lot more)

---

59- This is patently untrue. It takes my kettle two minutes and forty seconds to boil two mugs-worth of water even when you stare at it constantly. I know this because I've tried it.

were 'wiff-waffs' who shouldn't be allowed on the road if they don't know what the pedal on the right is for. His road-rage became so great that even he realised he needed help - and so he sought the services of a hypnotherapist who claimed he could help with that sort of thing. True to his word, that is exactly what he did and he achieved it by using the art of intentional distraction. In my father's case, the hypnotherapist got him to redirect his attention. Instead of focussing on getting to his destination as fast as possible with the minimum of hindrance, my father was to focus on another subject close to his heart: saving money. Instead of trying to plough up the motorway at 70 mph (or faster if he thought he could get away with it), my father was to focus on trying to save money by driving at the optimum speed for maximum fuel efficiency. This, according to the car's handbook, was 62 mph. Unfortunately, he embraced this new attitude to driving with the same zealousness he previously had for terrorising fellow road-users. This resulted in him driving at 62 mph even on motorways. He would even take the car out of gear and freewheel on the motorway when going downhill and with the wind in the right direction.[60] As I hadn't done hypnotherapy, being in the car with him went from one extreme to the other. Instead of being one of the fastest vehicles on the road (which I have to admit I rather liked) we became one of the slowest, being constantly overtaken by lorries, Citroen 2CVs and donkeys pulling carts. I confess that it was extremely frustrating for me to be my father's passenger, especially when it was to be driven to the airport to get my flight back to Barcelona and we were running a bit late. Nevertheless, it is a clear demonstration of how the art of intentional distraction - redirecting the focus of our thoughts from something that we can't control to something that we can - is able to increase our patience, improve our behaviour and save us a few pennies to boot.

## You Will Get There in the End

In the northern part of Spain, the council have had the wisdom to install pedestrian crossing lights with a countdown facility: a visual indicator that tells you how many seconds you'll have to wait until you can cross

---

60- Yes, honestly. Freewheel along motorways. I promise you. I'm not making this stuff up!

and thus reduces the urge to risk life and limb crossing before the little green man lights up. This is a brilliant idea. I understand that they are thinking of introducing the same thing for the drivers. I think that would be a brilliant idea, too. It would allow drivers to turn off their engines as they would be able to see how long they had to wait. It would also reduce road-rage because you know what is happening. With a visible countdown system, you know how long you have to wait and you can see the numbers getting closer to zero. I think they are a great idea and should be installed everywhere - for pedestrians, cars and husbands waiting for their wives to get ready to go out.

This system combats our lack of patience by giving us information. Whether you know how long it's going to be or not, the waiting time is exactly the same. But how much we know about that time makes a big difference. It's not the same waiting for an indefinite period (which can seem eternal) as it is to waiting for a known length of time - as anyone who has flown low-cost can verify: Is my departure gate going to announced imminently or have I got time to have a couple of beers and then do my daily hour of meditation? The expression 'I don't mind, so long as I know' springs to mind. Having a definite timeframe helps us to calm down and deal with it.

This is another tool we can use to our advantage. If you use the progress plotter in a responsible and realistic way, you can see that so long as you keep moving forward, step by step, progressing little by little, you will achieve your goal at the designated time. You know how long the process will take and therefore when it will become a reality. With this knowledge, the part of your brain responsible for impatience can sit back and enjoy the ride. Having this information from the very start makes the task much easier. If we had no idea how long a journey was going to take, it would cause uncertainty and doubt which in turn would produces stress, worry and frustration.

So remember, as we said in chapter 4 on goal planning, giving yourself a clear time-frame is important as it also helps strengthen our patience and to stay in a positive frame of mind.

Controlling your patience while keeping frustration and general futility away from your door works like this: Set yourself a concrete and realistic date for your goal (maybe by using your Progress Plotter) and then just focus on the task at hand, and, if possible, only on the task at hand. Live each moment in the present. Focus on what you can do today to put a few tiny insignificant pieces in place. Think about doing it, do it, acknowledge that you've done it, tick it off and move on. That is all you can realistically hope for. The future is another time, another place. You have no control over it. In fact, you have no idea what the world is going to be like in just a few years' time. In those immortal words of Tolkien - "All you can do is to decide what to do with the time that is given to you." And by the 'time that is given to you' I take to mean the present moment. After all it is the only moment you can control, the only moment you can be sure of.

If you do this, if you focus your attention upon what you can achieve today and carry it out, then you can go to bed with the sensation of accomplishment, the satisfaction of a day well spent, of having made progress and that is a very good thing.

It is important that you get your reward, your dose of dopamine from today's activities, from today's successes and the small but important progress that you have made.

So don't obsess about your goal. Try to keep it in your sights while at the same time being indifferent about it and just like A. A. Milne's river at the start of this chapter, you will get there in the end.

## Things to Think About

✚ Patience, the ability to postpone gratification, is one of the key characteristics not just for the Sorites Principle but for success in general.

✚ If you become impatient you will become negative about your goal, your capability and your chances of success. You will become frustrated, disillusioned and get the feeling that the whole thing is futile.

✚ The key to strengthening your patience is in two steps...

❧ Give yourself a clear time-frame: Set a realistic date when you will achieve your main objective.

❧ Use Intentional Distraction: Stop thinking about your large goal and just focus on the little objectives that you can carry out today.

## Top Tips

✚ Don't expect miracles: Expecting too much, too soon only leads to problems. Be realistic... and patient!

✚ Use the Progress Plotter to clearly see how long your goal is likely to take.

✚ When you are feeling impatient, try using the art of Internal Distraction to focus your attention on something else that you can control now.

✚ You will have moments when you want things to happen more quickly. Hold in there, it will happen. Re-read this book if necessary.

✚ Look at the progress that you have made and will continue to make.

✚ Slow and steady wins the race.[61]

---

61- I'm sure the likes of Lewis Hamilton, Florence Griffith-Joyner, Lance Armstrong, Jessica Ennis-Hill, Seb Coe and Mark Spitz would debate this point. But even if slow-and-steady doesn't win you the race, it will definitely get you over the finishing line - even if it's when everyone else has packed up and gone home.

## Questions to Ask Yourself (and Answer)

✿ In what situations does impatience cause you problems such as unwanted stress, frustration or negative thoughts?

✿ Could you use Intentional Distraction to focus your attention on something else that you have immediate control over?

✿ Could setting yourself a specific waiting time help?

✿ How could you apply it to make yourself feel better and become more positive?

✿ What do you need to put into place to help you get into the habit of using these methods?

 # Positivity

*"When you walk through a storm*
*Hold your head up high*
*And don't be afraid of the dark*
*At the end of a storm is a golden sky*
*And the sweet silver song of a lark*

*Walk on through the wind*
*Walk on through the rain*
*Though your dreams be tossed and blown*
*Walk on, walk on*
*With hope in your heart*
*And you'll never walk alone*
*You'll never walk alone!"*

- Rodgers and Hammerstein
"You'll Never Walk Alone" from the musical Carousel.

When you start out on a new journey towards a new goal things are fresh and exciting. You acquire tools for the job. Maybe new equipment, new clothing, a new set of routines, a new way of looking at the world and the vision of a new destiny. You are motivated. This can continue for quite a while but at some point you are going to come across a barrier. Something will happen to dampen your enthusiasm, to rain on your party, to piss on your bonfire.

These psychological barriers can be external or internal. They can come from outside such as criticism, derision, rejection or plain abuse. They can also come from inside such as the sensation of failure, the fear of making a fool of yourself or a sense of futility.

There will be times when you feel like chucking in the towel and giving the whole thing up as a waste of time.

Don't.

The Sorites Principle is not only based on experience and the fact that millions of incredible feats have been achieved through steady and unrelenting accumulation of small gains but also on logic.

It works because of the simple laws of mathematics. If you constantly move forwards towards your destination you will inevitably get there. It won't be tomorrow. But just like the removal of a million grains of sand, with patience and dedication you will get there. Through perseverance and the application of the right prizes, maintaining a sense of progress, harnessing passion and peer pressure, setting up pointers and periodic actions and cultivating patience you can achieve your goal, you can reach your final destination. However, nobody is going to promise you that it's going to be an easy ride. You are going to meet a variety of hazards and obstacles along the way. There will be stumbling blocks, potholes and hurdles. There'll probably also be dead ends, false turns and even restless natives. You have to be prepared for them. You have to acknowledge that there will be 'dark' moments when you will feel like chucking it all in and giving up. "What's the point?" you'll cry out, "It's never going to happen!" and proceed to wallow around in your own despondency for a while.

In order to overcome each negative psychological barrier, it is important to maintain a positive mental attitude. Positivity is like the fuel used to transport all the different weapons you will use to fight negativity during those dark moments.

This is easier said than done.

Have you ever been depressed? I have. Being told to smile and be happy when you're depressed is completely counterproductive. When you are feeling depressed, happiness is an inconceivable concept. You might as well be told to learn to levitate. It's not going to happen. But, unless you are suffering from clinical depression it is worth remembering that feeling down is a temporary state. You haven't always felt like this in the past and you're not always going to feel like this in the future. Accept feeling down for what it is: a temporary drop in morale, a momentary lack of motivation, but nothing more. Certainly don't make any decisions about packing it all in. During these dark moments, it is your Grog that is talking to you. Grog is complaining about how she misses her comfort zone, how frightened she is of social rejection and how nice and easy it would be to go back to all that familiar stuff you left behind a while ago (remember it is exactly all that familiar stuff that got you here in the first place). Bear in mind this is the same Grog that would tell you to bash your boss over the head with a chair and staple his genitals to his desk or that would tell you to run off to the Caribbean with your personal assistant, leaving your poor family to fend for themselves or that would tell you to lounge around all day stuffing yourself with Martini's and Ferrero Rochers and tell the bailiffs to go and fuck themselves. Grog is full of some wonderfully colourful suggestions but her advice is rarely based on a rational universe and usually lacks a certain logical foundation. Grog's ideas need to be taken with a very big bucket of salt before giving them serious consideration and those feelings of despondency are no exception.

## Carly and Her Mum

How's your memory? Good? Bad? Most people say that it's okay but admit they have occasional lapses. But how do you know if your memory is okay? After all, a memory is just a configuration of neurons in our brains.

These configurations are here and now. They are merely representations of our past and not very good representations at that.

The mother of a friend of mine, Carly, often got depressed and frequently lamented her husband's death, about how wonderful he had been and how much he had loved her. This perplexed Carly because she only remembered the arguments and the fighting and how often her mother would threaten to take the kids and leave 'the bastard'. Although their memories of the same person are apparently contradictory, they are both probably remembering with a certain degree of accuracy events that really happened. There is no paradox here, no contradiction. The mother and the daughter selectively choose to focus on different moments, different experiences that produce differing emotions. It's like the example of the glass of water - is it half-empty or is it half-full? Our experiences and, consequentially, our memories of those experiences are greatly affected by our emotions and we are naturally skilled in selecting just the 'right' memories to self-justify the feelings and emotions we are experiencing at the moment.

In moments of despondency, your brain will dig out its memories and paint them all with all the gloom and despair it can muster. It will shrink or simply ignore all the positive and motivating things you have achieved so far and enlarge and focus in on the bad ones, thus magnifying the negativity of the whole situation.

This will happen and will happen regularly, so be prepared for it!


## Look How Far I've come!

The surest way to stop your positive memories from being manipulated by negative emotions is to set them down in stone. Or, if not stone, to set them down in writing. This is one of the main reasons for keeping a goal diary. Maintaining a record of all the things you've done, all the things you've achieved, what your life was like just a few months ago and all the excitement, joy and other positive emotions you've had, then it is much more difficult for a despondent attitude to distort those facts.

Have you ever been on a hike up the side of a large hill, step by step, up you go chatting to your friends, trampling the bracken with the wind in your face and the pale sun on your back? And at some moment you stop, turn round and see the amazing distance you have come. There in the distance you can just spot the little grey rectangle of the pub where you set off from and presumably those tiny coloured spots next to it is the car park where hopefully your car is still parked.[62] You've not got to the top yet, but nevertheless the feeling of seeing how far you've come so far is usually one of awe and amazement. To suddenly see the immense distance, you have come is inspiring and euphoric. As you had been concentrating on watching your step over the rocks, ruts and rickety fences of your hike, you had not been thinking about the full distance you had to travel but just on the step-by-step progress that you had straight in front of you.

So, one way to improve your positivity is to review the progress that you have made so far. If you can, get into the habit of making a note of the little victories you have, the successes, the little steps forward you take, then over time these notes will build up into a formidable source of inspiration for those moments when a bit of inspiration is just what you need.

# Margo

Do you like smoked ham? Or what about smoked trout? Or maybe a bit of smoked goat's cheese? Smoking adds a subtle touch of finesse, turning good food into something exquisitely delicious.

A few days ago I went out to celebrate with a very good friend of mine called Margo. We were celebrating because she's just made her dream come true. For the last ten years, her driving ambition has been to set up and run her own successful gourmet smoked foods business. The name of her company is Fumont Gourmet and what it does is to take high quality raw ingredients (fish, meats, cheeses), smoke it, put it into beautiful packaging and then supply it to Michelin star restaurants and private customers.

---

62- I say this because one of my wife's workmates did something very similar in the Pyrenees only to witness from about a mile away, some git driving his car off into the hazy distance. It spoilt his entire day's walk.

Finally, after constantly slogging at it for all these years, struggling to put piece after tiny piece of her dream into place, she has done it. She put in the last piece of her jigsaw when she got the last piece of bureaucratic paperwork giving her a licence to officially operate as a vender of smoked products (if any of you have any experience of slowly wading through the quagmire of health and safety requirements, sanitary inspections, packaging licence, fiscal red tape, data protection acts and local as well as national licensing procedures then your admiration for what Margo has achieved might just have quintupled).

Starting from absolutely nothing, she now has her own premises - which started out as a derelict barn - which she has completely renovated. These premises include an impressive industry-standard kitchen area, a small smoker, an office with reception area and a tasting salon where her Michelin star chefs as well as other highly valued prospective customers come to sample the goodies on offer and quaff the locally produced house wine selection. She has her own webpage (www.fumontgourmet.com) her own line of packaging, including tiny hand crafted wooden boxes for her smoked salt and cute glass vials for her smoked olive oil. She has her own stationery, business cards and even a branding iron for marking the crates of smoked comestibles she ships out. She has investors and funding. She has developed and perfected her own way of hand-smoking foods (including olive oil, trout caviar, cured ham and quail eggs) using old vine-wood: last year's dead wood from the local vineyards. She now has the experience to smoke almost anything (as she says, "you bring it in and I'll smoke it for you, my darling!"). Before she got her premises running, her home was completely taken over with the business. She has suffered crippling arthritis due to repetitive work syndrome and the relationship with her partner has been put under years of constant strain. She has sacrificed not only her blood, sweat and tears, but also her time, her health, her finances and her relationships to turn her dream into a reality.

As we were getting to the bottom of our second bottle of house white (accompanied by a few 'tapas' of locally produced smoked mozzarella), the conversation turned to my book and I asked Margo about her perseverance and what had motivated her to keep going through all these years of hardship and mayhem. She immediately replied, "It was because I knew I could do it. I had a deep steadfast belief that it would work. All I had to do was to keep at it and see it through."

She used this positive belief to defend and motivate herself during those dark moments of tiredness and despair to keep herself going. The positive belief that it will work.

In her own way, Margo has followed her own Sorites Principle.

1. She identified a clear goal and decided what path to follow and what actions would be necessary in order to get there.

2. She broke each of those actions down into many thousands of tiny pieces.

3. She then spent ten years putting in one or two pieces every day until she had made it.

In truth, Margo has not just used positivity to keep herself going. She has used many of the techniques that we have already looked at. She has used a variety of prizes and punishments to coax and cajole herself out of bed and onto the workface. She has used passion: her pride, her insatiable curiosity and often her love/hate relationship with her smoker. She has a fantastic moral support from her friends, family and partner (who all get to be taste-testers of her latest gourmet experiments). She had her agenda chock-a-block with an intense work schedule. Her raw products served as their own pointers: 2 pounds of fresh fish waiting to be smoked is a clear indication as to what you have to do today. The very nature of her project was full of progress markers: her first successful batch of smoked produce, her first paying customer, her first order from a Michelin star chef, the signing of the lease of her premises, etc. But more than any of these, the thing that kept her going was her positivity. Well done Margo, you're a Sorites Star!

Positivity is part of a virtuous circle. Prizes, progress, passion, positive peer pressure and well-tempered patience all increase your positive attitude which in turn feeds our motivation and drives us towards more prizes, progress, passion and so on.

But what about when you're not feeling particularly positive? What if you're not the sort of person that regularly overflows with optimism? Is there anything you can do to cultivate your own positivity supply? Happily, the answer is yes. Maybe not the sort of euphoric positivity that gets you dancing on the table with your knickers on your head, but certainly a quiet kind of positivity that can simmer away feeding your motivation when required.

## Three Simple Questions

Scott Geller, the American psychologist who specialises in human behaviour, safety and motivation, points out three key questions that can greatly help with positive motivation. They are:

1. Can I do it?

2. Will it work?

3. Is it worth it?

If you ruminate on these three questions, deeply considering their answers in all their possible manifestations and still come up with a 'yes' to each of them - then you should already start feeling the embers of positivity beginning to be kindled into flame.

'Can I do it?' deals with your capability as a human being. Do you have, or are you able to acquire, all the resources, knowledge, skills necessary to get the task done? Can you put in all the tiny pieces?

'Will it work?' addresses the practical outcome. If you put all the tiny pieces together, a few each day over the period of time you have, will it get you to where you want to be? You can consider this as a question of simple mathematics: if you add all the pieces together, will it make the whole?

'Is it worth it?' This, of course, can only be answered by you. Nevertheless, it's a powerful question. Do you remember your Goal Diary? Hopefully you will have written down all the reasons why you wanted to go through all of this in the first place. You've decided what you want. You've identified what it's likely to take. If you see you've chosen your goal wisely, if your reasons are good enough, strong enough, then the answer should be obvious. Imagine what it will be like having your goal become a reality. Visualise yourself, your success and all it would beget. It should give you the positive kick up the arse to get you going. Try it for yourself.

## Affirmations

"Every day, in every way I get thinner and thinner and thinner."

When I talk to people about having a positive mental attitude, they occasionally come up with the subject of positive affirmations. As a coach I have been dealing with affirmations and witnessing the results, or the lack thereof, for years. I can't help but feel that affirmations are a concept that is misunderstood and much maligned.

According to the experts, affirmations work on the observation that our brains often struggle to distinguish what is reality from what is imaginary. Just this subject is complicated enough to warrant a whole book just by itself. In fact, one of the roots to many of our psychological problems, such as lack of confidence, insecurity and paranoia is our inability to distinguish between our imagined world (created by irrational suppositions, guesses and unfounded beliefs) and the real world. Our body is genetically wired up to respond in a certain way to certain situations (like running away from a snake or the desire to have an intimate physical relationship with your attractive tax adviser). These responses are physically manifested by biochemical reactions which cause the increase in your heartbeat rate or the dilation of your pupils. The conscious, thinking part of your brain has no control over these things, yet they happen. Curiously, they happen whether the stimulus (the snake or adviser) is real or just imagined.

## Lemons

There is a simple test you can do to show this. It's called the Lemon Test and if you've not come across it before, I have included it in full at the end of this book in the appendix. It's a nice little mental exercise you can do where you mentally 'experience' a lemon: you imagine seeing it, feeling it, smelling it and tasting it. If you do it right, you notice that your mouth starts to water. The glands in your mouth increase their saliva production. This physical reaction is not a conscious one - you cannot consciously decide to make you mouth water. It's not like scratching your ear or sticking your tongue out. Such actions are acts of direct will. But saliva production is an involuntary act; your body does it automatically when it deems necessary which means when it thinks it's getting the appropriate stimulus and this it does whether you want it to or not. You have no say in the matter. It's completely involuntary. There are quite a lot of involuntary acts your body does which can be quite inconvenient and/or frankly embarrassing at times (as I'm sure you're already aware of). The Lemon Test is an example of how the subconscious part of our brain can react when we consciously think of certain things. So, going back to the idea of affirmations, the argument tends to be that 'Just by saying an affirmation (i.e. something positive about ourselves) increases the likelihood that it will happen'.

## Bullshit

But it's not quite that simple. If you say to yourself that you're feeling a little sleepy, then the rest of your brain will probably go along with that without any problem (maybe you feel a yawn coming on), as with the suggestion that you're feeling a little peckish (in fact I might go and grab a small smackerel of something right now). But although your subconscious can be easily tricked, it's not entirely gullible. Your mouth might water but nevertheless there is still a part of you that knows that the imagined lemon doesn't really exist.[63] For most of us, we are only too well aware of our limitations. If you're the sort of person who finds it difficult to squeeze into an aeroplane seat or who can't read the bathroom scales without the use of a well-placed mirror, then saying to yourself 'I am thin, slender and light as a feather' is clearly a question of 'who are you trying

---

63- If you are the sort of person that finds it difficult to differentiate between reality and imaginations, you might like to consider professional help. If you're not sure, look up 'Father Ted Spider-baby' on YouTube to see how Father Ted Crilly explains it to Father Dougal McGuire. But it's just a suggestion.

to fool?'. This is not an affirmation. It is bullshit, you know it and so does your subconscious which will reject and rebel causing more harm than good. However, something along the lines of 'I am in control of my actions and every day I can choose to reduce my weight, little by little, to become a better, healthier human being' is something much easier to stomach - if you pardon the expression.

There are thousands of affirmations that you can repeat to yourself regularly each day to buck you up and spur you onwards and upwards. From quotes from the wise such as…

*"The man who moves a mountain begins by carrying away small stones"*

…to something more tailor-made such as…

*"The road is long, but so long as I move forward, step by step, day by day, my success is a mathematical certainty."*

Or you may make up your own. But whatever you do, don't try to fool yourself. Affirmations that work best need to be positive, realistic and, of course, frequently repeated. Stick copies of it about the house, on the bathroom mirror or your computer screen. Repeat it as often as needed to remind yourself that you can do this, it will work and it is worth the effort.

## Seven Positive Practices

Although being positive and persevering are not the same thing, the former is essential for the latter. Everyone has their opinion on being positive, the internet proves it. Just do a search on 'How to be positive'. I just did and got 1,290 million results (in just 0.62 of a second - isn't Google amazing?!). Compare that to 'How to lose weight' (just 83.3 million in 0.66 of a second, 'How to stuff an elephant' (24.2 million in 0.70 of a second) or 'How to cure hay fever' (a paltry 467 thousand in 0.71 seconds).[64]

Nevertheless, not to be perturbed by a vast quantity of opinions on the subject, here are my own top personal recommendations for keeping away from the dark side of gloom and despair.

---

64- Incidentally, I also Googled 'how to tell if your mother-in-law is an alien' which came up with an unexpectedly impressive 34 million results. Is there something somebody should be telling me about this?

1. Review your progress
2. Practise gratitude
3. Relaxation and mindfulness
4. Fresh air and sunlight
5. Spend time with positive people
6. Practise altruism
7. Physical exercise

## 1. Review Your Progress

On the days when I'm feeling a little low, I review my progress to see how far I've come. I do this in a couple of ways. Firstly, I use my Progress Plotter as described in the chapter on Progress. Now approaching the two-thirds mark of my writing journey I find myself buoyed up by how much I have achieved so far. Inevitably, this motivates me to push on and set fingers to keyboard. However, I also have kept a progress record in my Goal Diary. Here I have kept a sometimes brief, sometimes not-so-brief account of my thoughts, ideas and feelings about my writing as well as other topics both work- and personal-related. It can be fascinating to keep reviewing these pages as they reinforce the sensation of progress, not just in a numerical way (as does the Progress Plotter) but also in terms of how my thoughts, ideas and feelings have grown and developed (or, in some cases, withered and disappeared). As I pointed out in chapter 8, progress, just like justice, not only must happen, it must also be seen to happen. This, in itself, is a very positive experience.

## 2. Practise Gratitude

In his book *Authentic Happiness*, Martin Seligman demonstrates that one of the key techniques for maintaining a positive frame of mind is practicing gratitude: consciously expressing appreciation for the good things we have. I'm sure you are well aware of the unfortunate habit we seem to have to take things for granted, especially if you are on the receiving end and you are the one being taken for granted. Unfortunately, it's a natural tendency for all of us. Our attention is very limited; when you are paying attention to one thing then you are not paying attention to anything else - a fact that is exploited by pick pockets. In a world where our attention is constantly being bombarded from all sides, by people, media and our phones, it is no surprise we can go for weeks, months or even years without thinking about the good things we have going for us in our busy lives.

It's like the question 'How happy does your car make you?' (if you don't have a nice car then you can substitute 'car' with any other possession you have that makes your life easier such as the pair of glasses you are wearing or the legs you have that allow you to walk about). Even if your car is so marvellous that it makes your heart burst with joy, it only does so WHEN you think about it. The reality is that you don't actually spend that much time thinking about your car. Even when you are driving it, you are most likely thinking about some problem you have to face, some worry that is dogging you, or some mundane errand - basically anything but the car itself. We don't think about the good things in our lives because they don't demand our attention. Your wonderful car (or glasses or legs, etc.) only demand your attention when it stops being wonderful and starts becoming a problem by breaking down, getting stolen or unexpectedly bursting into flames. We have so many good things going for us yet we fail to be aware of them until it's too late.

The way to rectify this is to practise gratitude, to 'count your blessings' so to speak. Take a few minutes in your busy schedule to recognise all those positive things you have going for you that you take for granted: your family, friends, home, freedom, body, Pink Floyd albums. Don't approach the subject trivially. Give each one the attention it deserves. Think of what life would be like for you if you lost them. To truly appreciate the good things in your life can be a very positive experience, and if that good thing happens to be a person, then sharing that appreciation with them can be a powerful moment. Seligman explains how in his Positive Psychology class his students would take it in turns to bring along a guest one evening. There in front of the class, the student would explain to all the gratitude they had for this person, why they were special to them, how much they were valued. The positive energy of love and gratitude were amazing. The positive karma lasted for weeks.

So why not try it for yourself? Think of someone who has had a positive influence on your life but who you have never really thanked properly. Write a text of about 300-500 words explaining why you are grateful to them. Then get in touch, arrange a visit or coffee. Then read them the text. Seligman guarantees you will feel lastingly better.

## 3. Relaxation and Mindfulness

Many times in this book I've drawn attention to the idea that our prefrontal cortex (PFC), the thinking, rational part of our brain, is much more limited than we believe. Our conscious mental processing capacity is much less than we give ourselves credit. Prolonged, intense periods of thought: planning, decision-making, holding concepts in short-term memory, imagining, decision-making, willpower and creativity, can leave us suffering from brain ache from too many demands. Our thinking becomes fuzzy and fallible from the stress and strain of too much mental exertion. Constant stress is toxic to our mental wellbeing. We suffer burnout, breakdown and depression.

This is not a good thing.

One way to fight brain fatigue is to learn to relax our PFC. And it's not as easy as it sounds. For many people 'relaxing' is synonymous with sitting in front of the telly, or meeting up with friends or just having a quiet drink down the pub. Yet in such circumstances, we are just substituting one kind of thinking for another. It is said that a change is as good as a rest but regarding your PFC I beg to differ. Resting your PFC requires you to stop thinking (yes, I'm sure you've come across a few people who seem to have mastered this state permanently) but when you consider the list of tasks done by your PFC includes self-talk, day dreaming, judging, worrying, imagining and mental rumination you begin to see how occupied it can be - even when we think we are relaxing. So the way to give the poor little thing a rest is to turn it off, or at least reduce the number of tasks it has to do. This is what mental relaxation techniques such as mindfulness and meditation are all about. In its simplest form, mindfulness is learning to experience our surroundings via the sensory part of our brain without having our PFC intervene. This means being aware of your 'here and now' but without judgment, without worry, without generating ideas. Perceiving your environment but without any internal dialogue. This is very hard to do if you've never tried. But the effort is worth it. Everyone I know who has mastered mindfulness or meditation emphasises the fact that not only is relaxing the mind good for you, it also feels marvellous. You come out of your relaxed state feeling exactly that. Relaxed, refreshed and ready for anything. It is a great help to strengthen your morale, your willpower and your positivity. If I have managed to even slightly interest you in developing your ability to relax your brain in order to get more out of it, I recommend reading 'Your Brain At Work' by David Rock.

## 4. Fresh Air and Sunlight

Take a bunch of people and split them into two groups. Send the first group off to take a 'relaxing break' in the city and the other group to take a 'relaxing break' in a place surrounded by mother nature. It's probably no surprise to learn that when they return the second group is better off for their break.

What might be unexpected is just how much better off they really are. Getting quality time with lots of fresh air and sunlight has some profound effects on us and increasing our positivity is just one of them.

If you spend time in the countryside, on some quiet beach or some secluded forest, your brain starts to behave differently. Some scientists think that this is to do with a type of chemical emitted by plants called phytoncides, others say it's to do with increased oxygen levels while others point out that there are far fewer distractions in the middle of the woods than there are in Piccadilly Circus. Maybe it's a combination of all three. But whatever it is, it works.

Getting back to nature calms us down and cheers us up. It decreases our blood pressure and for some reason reduces the production of the stress hormone cortisol. It reduces anxiety, the risk of depression and even helps fight obesity.[65] When we get direct sunlight, our vitamin D levels go up

---

65- As a sceptical friend pointed out - maybe that's because you don't find many 'Big Macs' lying around in the middle of a forest and you can't put on much weight eating nuts, berries and squirrel shit.

which is a good thing (but don't overdo it - 30 minutes is good enough). Sunlight also lifts our mood in the same way that lack of sunlight causes winter depression (and I used to put it down to all that Christmas shopping). Outdoor activities tend to be synonymous with physical activity which helps produce serotonin which, in turn, also makes us feel good. So whether it's hiking, hill-walking, camping, birdwatching, fishing or just wandering about, whistling loudly and asking passing ramblers if they've seen your dog anywhere, they are all recommended ways to increase your positivity.

## 5. Spend Time with Positive People

When I first moved to Barcelona as an English teacher in 1990, one of the first people I befriended was Mark. Mark was a fellow English teacher. We both started working for the same school at the same time. He was intelligent, hard-working and very witty. But he had one major fault. He was exceptionally negative. For Mark, the world was a shit-hole: unfair and full of stupid, ignorant and selfish arseholes. His loathing of 'them' ('them' being everyone else in the universe apart from you and me) was only matched in his inventiveness in ridiculing them. At first it was funny and guaranteed an entertaining evening after work over a few beers. But after a while, I realised his negativity was starting to rub off onto me and I found myself being sucked into the dark abyss of his way of thinking: everyone is out to exploit you, you can't succeed without having rich parents, nobody gives a shit about you so why should you give one for them.

As Lillian Glass points out in her book *Toxic People*, there are those who seem to have been put on this planet with the sole objective of making your life more difficult, more disagreeable and more arduous; individuals whose default setting is to complain and criticise. Intentionally or not, they bring you down, they dampen your enthusiasm and drain you of your positivity like a vampire sucking blood. My advice here is to be aware of who these people are and to try if possible to stay away from them because conversely, there also exist people who are exactly the opposite. People who seem to radiate positivity out of every pore of their skin. After you spend time with these people you feel great. They are positive, optimistic and supportive. They lift you up. My advice is to notice these people, value them and spend time absorbing their positivity because, as we saw in the chapter on peer pressure, positivity is contagious, too. With the right energy you can get the right attitude you need to persevere and succeed. Having a positive attitude to your capabilities is important because just as Henry Ford said "Whether you think you can, or you think you can't — you're right."

## 6. Practise Altruism

One of the routes I take to circumnavigate the rush-hour traffic in the city is to take a road called 'Foix Avenue' (pronounced Fosh) which is a long winding road that leads down the hill into the city. Towards the top end, just where it crosses 'Monestir Street' is a set of traffic lights and on the opposite corner is the secondary school 'Frederic Mistral - Técnic Eulalia'. It was at these traffic lights that I once found myself in my car waiting, when all of a sudden a football landed in the middle of the road, in front of me but on the other side of the traffic lights. Now the junction of Foix and Monestir is not particularly busy at the best of times but it does have a steep slope. As soon as the ball landed on the tarmac, it began what according to the Newtonian laws of motion was to be a long trajectory down a long and steep hill. I must have been in one of my more charitable and adventurous frames of mind because in an instant I decided to do my good deed for the day: Carefully checking there was no oncoming traffic, I ran the red light, drove across the junction, overtaking the ball and continuing down Foix until I deemed it far enough to stop the car, get out and head off the ball in its bid for freedom. I stopped the car in the middle of the road and got out just in time to see that my calculation had been about half a second out and the ball merrily rolled past me just before I could get to it. I then proceeded to make a quick sprint for the ball - demonstrating to all the drivers waiting at the lights on the uphill side of Foix how crap I am at running and how badly out of shape I am. In spite of my physical prowess, or lack thereof, I managed to catch up with the ball, stop it, pick it up and took it back up the hill to the school fence. What I had failed to notice was that I had by now achieved the full attention of about two hundred school children, who from the playground, as well as the classroom windows were all watching the latest entertainment of some foreign bloke rescue a football. When they saw me approaching the fence, the apparent group to whom the ball belonged gestured to me and so I deftly threw the ball over the fence and to my pleasant surprise got a round of applause and cheers from most of the school. I took the opportunity to give them a modest bow, a cheery wave and then made it back to my car just in time as the lights changed.

The reason I mention this here is because after this event, I found myself in a surprisingly good mood for the rest of the day. In fact, just recounting this anecdote of simple altruism puts me in a more positive frame of mind.

This shouldn't come as a surprise. It is now well-established that carrying out acts of altruism - helping people without expectation of anything in return - makes us feel better. Just like Amélie Poulain, in the beautiful film Amélie, we can all discover that the very act of helping others can be highly rewarding in itself. If done in the 'right' way, it can give your life meaning, increase your feeling of self-worth, and increase your positivity and while you're asking, the 'right' way means that:

a)  You don't expect anything else in return

b)  Your reason for doing it is simply to help

c)  You have no underlying motives

d)  You genuinely want to

This implies the wrong reasons are:

w)  You do expect something in return

x)  You keep score

y)  You use it to show that you are better than others

z)  You do it because you feel obliged

So the next time the opportunity arises, do a good deed for the day and start feeling even more positive about yourself.

# 7. Physical Exercise

Another way to increase your positivity is to get some physical exercise. Let's face it - exercising is good for you in so many ways. Your body was designed for moving about, not for sitting down all day at your computer.[66] Moving about a lot helps us burn off those unused and unwanted calories. It develops our muscles. It gets our heart pumping, our blood flowing and uses up any excess adrenalin, which helps us to relax. But as far as feeling more positive goes, the most useful thing that physical exercise does is to produce endorphins. Endorphins are a type of neurotransmitter that help us cope with pain and also make us feel great. They are produced by the brain during strenuous exercise - the sort of exercise that leaves you with sweat pouring down your face as you gasp for breath. Having said that, gasping and sweaty is what I experience if I have to go up and down the stairs more than three times in close succession and I don't feel that euphoric about it. But the experts say this is the case. In fact, some would go even further and say that the benefits of regular strenuous exercise are even greater pointing to numerous studies that suggest that exercise can make us think better, improving our learning capacity, decision-making, concentration and our ability to relax.[67] But one thing is clear: If you exert yourself physically once in a while, then you'll feel all the better for it.

---

66- At least this is what my chiropractor tells me each time I go to see her with my dodgy back.

67- If you are interested in learning more on this subject, I recommend 'Spark!: The revolutionary new science of exercise and the brain' by Dr. John J. Ratey.

## Things to Think About

✦ The main obstacle to succeeding with the Sorites Principle is mental rather than physical.

✦ The mental obstacles are of the negative emotional kind such as apathy, self-doubt and futility. A negative emotional state naturally stirs up our negative memories and fuels our negative feelings.

✦ By keeping a positive approach to the Sorites Principle we can keep on track, stay focussed and motivated every day.

✦ We can strengthen our positivity by reviewing our progress, practicing gratitude, learning relaxation techniques, going out into the countryside to get fresh air and sunlight, by spending time with positive people, helping others and getting exercise.[68]

---

68- A friend of mine who reviewed one of the earlier drafts of this book asked if this meant that if you "raised a million pounds for a deserving charity by going on a sponsored cross-country run with a positive friend and halfway along stopping to do 30 minutes of meditation, 30 minutes of gratefulness and then had a shag behind a bush," would this make you one of the most positive people in the world? To be honest, I don't know. Why not try it and write in with your experiences?

## Top Tips

- Be aware of your positivity level and recharge it when necessary.
- Remind yourself of how far you've come by reviewing your Goal Diary.
- When you're feeling down, ask yourself the 3 questions about your goal: Can you do it? Will it work? Is it worth it?
- Choose yourself an affirmation. Something to repeat to yourself 50 times a day to drum into your head the effectiveness of the Sorites Principle.
- Set time aside to reflect on all the things you have going for you.
- Learn to meditate or to be mindful.
- Make an effort to go for a long walk in the countryside when the weather is nice.
- Identify at least one person who positively inspires you. Arrange a time to enjoy their company, talk to them about your goal and absorb some of those all-important positive vibes.
- Make a habit of doing at least one good deed a day - just like boy scouts.
- Do regular strenuous physical activity. How you do it is up to you, but get that heart accustomed to pumping hard.

## Questions to Ask Yourself (and Answer)

- How is your positivity level right now? Why?
- When do you feel your most positive? Why?
- What brings you up?
- What brings you down?
- How many of the 9 positivity boosters[69] can you implement?
- What else works for you that hasn't been covered here? How could you make the most of that more often?

69- The 3 Simple Questions, Affirmations and the Seven Positivity Practices.

# 15 Problems

"Isn't it amazing what you can find to do when you don't want to do any work?" - John E. Firth

Consider the following. Imagine that you have arranged to visit a friend who lives 100 miles away in a village you've never visited. You get in your car and start driving along the familiar roads of your neighbourhood, but after just a few miles you find yourself on an unfamiliar road. You look at the clock which says you've done 17 miles; you've still 83 miles to go. "83 miles is a long way" you say to yourself, "a long, long way." You keep your foot down but when you get to 20 miles, the thought comes back. "I've been driving for about 20 minutes and yet I've still got so far to go." You start to get very anxious about the whole journey. Your start to think things like "What if I get lost? What if I break down? What if I run out of petrol? What if my friend isn't there when I arrive? What if my friend doesn't want to see me?" You are overcome with doubt and uncertainty.

You give up. As soon as you can you swing the car around and head back to your comfy home mopping the sweat from your brow and feeling much relieved. It was all too much… It wouldn't have worked anyway.

It sounds a bit silly doesn't it? But this is actually how many of us think when we set out on some new venture by ourselves. We start off with all the right ideas and good intentions but slowly the negative emotions start to seep in under the door and fill up our head with invented reasons (conscious and unconscious) as to why our new goal is a really bad idea and why it's not going to work.

These come in several predictable forms, as follows:

## Futility

In chapter 4 on Planning Your Goal we looked at the importance of having a goal which has the right level of challenge - not too difficult but not too easy either. But the level of difficulty of your goal and your ability to rise to meet it are not static. They fluctuate - they go up and down and unfortunately not necessarily in the same direction, at the same time. There will be days when the level of difficulty of your objective will go up and your perceived ability to cope with it will go down. On such days you might feel that all your efforts are a complete and utter waste of time.

This is normal and nothing to be ashamed of. Try not to worry about it too much.

Several times it happened to me while writing this book. "Nobody is going to be interested in this. Nobody will be interested in publishing it. It's never going to work." Nevertheless, here it is.

These feelings of futility were created by Grog as a way of protesting the fact that you are out of your comfort zone. These feelings are irrational and they are wrong. Yes - you are out of your comfort zone but so what? You aren't going to achieve anything new and worthwhile if you don't start doing things differently.

Don't let Grog control your destiny. Don't let Grog make you confuse slow progress with no progress. In the chapter on patience, I underlined the importance of not focussing on your end goal too much. The Sorites Principle works because of the steady process of insignificant change. You might not be aware of it at times. You can't see anything happening. But if you stick to your logical and well-founded plan, it will happen. Remember your Goal Diary? Use it. Look back through the pages to remind yourself of everything you've succeeded in achieving so far - all those tiny steps forward that you have taken. So long as you keep taking them - getting those small wins every day - you are going to get there. Look at your Progress Plotter. Remember it's just a question of mathematics - it takes time but you only have to achieve a tiny little bit every day to inevitably succeed.

When things are looking too big and you're feeling too small it just might be time for a dose of positivity. Remember the tips from last chapter? Get out and away from it all for a while. Go for a walk. Get some fresh air in your lungs, some sun on your face and some blood pumping through your body. Count your blessings. Reflect on all the things you have going for you. Don't dwell on your goal. Remember how capable you are to have achieved everything that you have so far. Reignite your passion. Dig up all those examples of stuff that emotionally moves you from chapter 9 on Passion such as the people who have gone through what you're going through and have come out the other side. Find all those motivating stories, films, songs and TED Talks. Remember the importance of peer pressure. Use it in times of need. Spend some time with the right people and get things off your chest and allow yourself to be bucked up.

The sense of general futility is normal. But it is also irrational, mistaken and temporary. With a bit of conscious effort, you can endure it, overcome it and send it back where the ugly little bugger came from.


## Self-doubt

Whereas futility is the feeling that your goal is too big, self-doubt is the feeling that you are too small. That you are not capable, not worthy, you don't have what it takes. Where is this feeling coming from? Is it coming from inside of you - from Grog? Or is it coming from outside - from those around you? Your friends and family might seem nice enough, but if any of them are the sort who have given up on their dreams, given up on striving for anything other than what is dished up on their plate every day then they just might be exerting negative peer pressure on you, subtly or not so subtly. If any of them come out with stuff like "Are you still wasting your time with that silly goal of yours", then maybe it's time to find some different friends or relatives - these ones are no good for you. You either have to win them over to your way of thinking (difficult) or distance yourself from them and spend more time with those who do understand and admire the valuable work you are doing.

If the feeling of not being good enough is coming from within, you probably feel that you don't have the necessary knowledge, skill, experience or talent to get to your goal. Let's get this clear right now. Nobody who set out on a new and challenging goal had these things. If they did, it wouldn't have been truly challenging, would it? You only need the knowledge, skill, experience and talent to get yourself up that next tiny step. As you continue to put in place all those tiny pieces of your goal, you will grow, you will learn, you will practise your skills and you will rise to meet the occasion, to meet the challenge that you have facing you today. Forget about the future. You can't suddenly spring up to the top of the Empire State Building. You'd probably struggle with just half of the 1576 steps that would take you up the 56 flights of stairs to the very top. You wouldn't be able to do it. Not all at once, no. But you could do one flight of stairs, couldn't you? And then another? You might not get yourself up there in one go, but little by little, it would be no more difficult that going up and down the stairs at home 56 times. So focus on the challenge you have to face today - you will rise to your future challenges when the time comes.

Be patient, realistic and positive. Focus on how far you've come rather than how far you have to go. One way to do this is to find someone who is trying to do what you are doing, but is a few steps further behind you. If you know someone like this, you can help them with your knowledge, experience and encouragement. This, in turn, will boost your own morale and strengthen your self-confidence. It will help you remember what you used to be like and how far you've come.

You can't go far without making the odd mistake here and there. Making mistakes is inevitable. I have deleted thousands of words from this book, whole chapters on neuroscience and psychology that I felt with hindsight were too complicated and unnecessary. I spend ages writing it and ended up binning the lot. It was background information that served no practical purpose. Whether it was right or wrong to do that is irrelevant. I spent time and effort doing something that I later saw as a mistake and I saw my measurable word count backslide as a result.[70] But just because one thing I did was a mistake doesn't mean my entire goal was a mistake, too. Unless you're perfect (which you aren't) you're going to make a pig's ear of something sooner or later. That's absolutely fine and nothing to be ashamed of whatsoever. Accept it, learn from it. Take it as a useful experience and move on. Some call it 'failing forwards': failing is not a setback - it is a necessary part of the journey to get to your goal. It doesn't mean you're not capable. You are just as capable as everyone else - more capable actually, as you have had the guts to set yourself a goal and go for it. Just that one simple but profound detail already marks you as being more capable than many others. Well done! Keep going and show all those doubting Herberts just what exactly you are capable of.

## The Fear of Failure

Down by the Barcelona sea front there is the Mar Bella Skate Park. An open public area it was built as part of the redevelopment of the coastal area when the city hosted the summer Olympics back in 1992. Especially designed for skateboarders it is full of ramps, slopes and large rounded hollows all lovingly crafted out of something similar to polished Portland - a satisfyingly smooth cement surface upon which the youth of today can perform their death-defying exploits without worrying too much about how much skin they are going to lose when things don't go as planned.

On most days the Skate Park is populated with an assortment of 'youth culture' on an assortment of 'gear' ranging from the traditional skateboard

---

70- Even this can be seen as a step forward. Although it was a severe blow to my measurable progress, it strengthened the structure of the book and was, in a way, a step forward. I once gave a speech in public where I blanked: I completely forgot the text that I thought I had memorised for the event. It was an awful experience and an excruciatingly embarrassing mistake. But whereas someone in that situation could have said "That's it. I'm never going to talk in public again." I took it as an important learning experience. I now no longer try to memorise my public presentations. I prepare and structure the content, but I let whatever words that occur to me at that moment come forth. I've never had to experience going blank since.

to stunt-bikes, blade-skates and scooters or whatever the latest trendsetters deem as being cool. All enjoying the Barcelona sun, while practising their manoeuvres and showing off their skills.

So it was just the other day I found myself down there with my little cherubs. We'd taken the morning as an opportunity to get some bicycle practice (which only recently have had the stabilisers taken off). We had driven down to the beach with the bicycles in the boot, parked and then, with the twins precariously mounted and myself following behind on foot, we wended and wobbled our way along the flat, wide promenade that accompanies the beach for about a mile and a half from the Old Port all the way up to the Forum at the edge of the city limits. Tired of terrorizing our fellow pedestrians with our somewhat erratic cycling techniques we decided to sit and rest for a while by the open-plan Skate Park and marvel at the exploits of the bigger kids while slurping juice and scoffing bananas.

One of the things that struck me was how often these kids fell over. This was definitely practice time as opposed to showing off time where the focus of the participants was to stretch and improve their skills. All the kids were pushing themselves to learn things they hadn't yet mastered. They were frequently falling over, some far more spectacularly than others, but without exception, each time they fell they picked themselves up and got on with it.

For skaters, falling down is part and parcel of the day's business. As with all other sports, falling down, falling off, stumbling, tripping, slipping, sliding, skidding, crashing is all part of the learning process. Taking the wrong turn, making the wrong move or even making the right move at the wrong moment are all small steps up the learning curve. As they say, "Those who never made a mistake never made anything."

Yet in my experience, too often I come across examples of people who perceive a mistake as a sign that things are not meant to be. Their lemma is "If at first you don't succeed, give up and don't make a fool of yourself." Rather than embracing the idea that overcoming difficulties is part of the development process, they see difficulty as a reason to quit.

This is not a good thing.

The Sorites Principle is about achieving big important things by frequently carrying out lots of easy insignificant things which requires the application of focussed perseverance. Sometimes we try to do this and it all goes well for a while. But then at some point, inevitably, we'll slip up. We find that something doesn't go according to plan. Something doesn't work and we just give up. "I tried to give up smoking but I can't." "I tried learning to ski but I can't", or "I've tried to lose weight but I can't." Bollocks! Just because you don't succeed the first, fourth or tenth time doesn't mean you can't. It just means that you haven't found the way that works for you. J.K. Rowling was rejected by twelve publishing houses before her first novel was accepted.

Can you imagine one of those skaters down by the Barcelona beach falling over and saying to himself as he got up "Oh, that didn't go as expected. I tried to skateboard but I can't. I'm giving up and going home." No, of course not. That's not how it works. These kids fall down dozens of times a day and each time they get up and get on with it, each time having learnt an insignificant bit more about skateboarding which, little by little builds up and makes them into skateboard champions. Life works that way, too.

If you're trying the Sorites Principle and it's not working for you, don't give up and consider yourself a failure. Like those skateboarders and all sportspeople of today - consider WHY it's not working for you and what you need to do in order to make it work. What went wrong? What can you do differently to make it go better? What can you learn from your experience? Is it really not working or are you confusing slow progress with no progress?

If you find yourself saying 'What's the point?', if you are feeling like giving up, please, please, bear in mind that you are probably feeling down. You are feeling demotivated, defeated and demoralised. At such times when you are overcome by a wave of negativity your thoughts will be along the lines of "I can't do this. It's too difficult. I'm not capable. I'm too weak. I'm not good enough." This is natural. It happens to everyone at some point. But it is just a feeling - not a reality. Just because you are feeling frightened of something doesn't make it life-threateningly dangerous. So temporarily feeling incapable doesn't make it so either. If it did, there would be no

Olympic Champions. There would be no Beatles, no four-minute mile, no Virgin Galactic, no conquering of Everest and no discovering of the North Pole. There would be no cures for diseases, no computers, no World Wide Web, no Rolls-Royce, no Concorde or Flying Scotsman, no smartphones, no Lord of the Rings, no James Bond, no Hamlet, no Mozart, no World Cup, no Wimbledon and no Wombles. None of these happened easily. If you are having a low point, recognise it and let it pass by. Then, when the negativity has subsided look around for a source of positive inspiration (see chapter 9 on Passion), get yourself up and get yourself going again.

Although we are all generally motivated by similar things, in practice, the detail can vary considerably from one person to another. One person is inspired by a group of friends, the next by their own personal vision of success. One is inspired by a yearning need to feel comfortable in their own body and the next by the fear of not having enough money to feed their own family.

Accept that finding the right way to persevere is neither easy nor obvious. Try one way and if it doesn't work, learn from your experience. Observe, change, tweak, modify, adapt. Try another way, another route, another variation until one day 'click!' it all comes together, it all falls into place and you find yourself slapping down piece after piece of your puzzle into place, day after day, month after month until the whole picture begins to take a definite form. The light at the end of the tunnel starts to become clearer and clearer until finally you find yourself out of the tunnel, standing on the summit of your conquest, euphorically celebrating your final and inevitable success.

Failure is not 'not succeeding'.

Failure is giving up before the right way to succeed has been found.

## Lethargy

One of the advantages to writing non-fiction is that you don't have to work 'linearly'. By this, I mean you don't have to write by starting at the beginning, continuing in a straight line and finishing when you come to the end. The chapters in this book are mostly mutually independent, so each day I have the luxury of being able to choose which chapter tickles my fancy and I work on that.

Although yesterday was a comfortably productive day (1,792 words), this morning I feel uninspired. I did well yesterday, didn't I? So I deserve a rest. A break. I have earned a day of relaxation, of loafing on the sofa and scratching my arse all day, don't I? As you can gather, today is turning out to be one of those 'tough' days, motivationally speaking. So, sifting through my chapters I see that this section on Lethargy seems to be rather appropriate for today's theme. I was finding it hard to get myself going. It's a problem and quite a common one from what I see.

## Martin

Martin was having a similar problem of getting his new money-making idea off the ground. He wanted to break into the field of 'voice work' (recording voice-overs and narration work for television and advertising). He'd had a few lucky breaks and wanted to build on them. The idea was viable and realistic. He had a luxurious velvety voice. He could be charming and ooze charisma. All he had to do was to make a 'demo' recording (a recording which showed the range and styles of the voice work he was capable of) but he was finding it surprisingly hard to get round to doing it. He was suffering from lethargy, a lack of motivation. He felt it was all a bit too hard, a bit too far out of his comfort zone. He was continuously procrastinating, finding (inventing) new reasons (excuses) to not do what he had promised himself he would do. What was worse, he realised what was happening but felt powerless to do anything about it.

So what is the solution? How can we deal with a bout of lethargy or procrastination?

Happily, I have an answer. The first thing to do is recognise that the feeling of lethargy is not a 'rational' thought process. It's a feeling and therefore it comes from Grog. Grog is lounging around his comfort zone feeling very happy, cosy and snug. The proposal of doing whatever it is you want to do is threatening to take him out of his comfort zone and Grog finds this idea very scary. Naturally, he puts up resistance in the form of a myriad of well-rehearsed excuses that have all been tried and tested in the past. "We deserve a rest", "Having just one day off won't hurt", "I'll start tomorrow, maybe, if the circumstances are favourable, when I've got the required time, energy, confidence, when the right stars are aligned." Putting it off until tomorrow is not an option. Doing it little by little leads to success. Not doing it, little by little, leads to nowhere. The problem with accepting one little excuse for postponing your action is it's never just one. Excuses are like vermin - they both breed like rabbits. When you are at odds with Grog you only have 3 options:

1. Coercion: Take him on directly. Rely on your willpower to overcome resistance and force him to do as you command.

2. Persuasion: Find a way to convince Grog that to do what you want is actually something he will find interesting - something that he will enjoy.

3. Indifference: Find a way to do what you want but in such a way that Grog doesn't resist.

Let's get things clear - option 1 is a bad idea. Trying to force Grog to do what you want is highly counterproductive. He's bigger, stronger and more stubborn than you will ever be. The more you try to fight Grog, the more Grog will fight back by cranking up the levels of doubt, lack of self-confidence and anxiety. It just results in more frustration, resentment, self-sabotage and the feeling of failure. Admit it. We've all been there before.

Option 2 can work very well but it requires a high degree of creativity. There is the possibility of using prizes and punishments as a motivator, but these work best when Grog has a comparatively neutral opinion on the matter. Besides, coming up with a suitable prize or punishment requires a certain degree of thought, so there is the danger Grog will resist by feeling that prizes are stupid ideas which aren't going to succeed this time. Punishments for resistance is just another form of coercion (see option 1 above). A tactic more likely to work is that of finding some way to tickle Grog's fancy. Reframing the situation - finding some way of looking at the actions which you need to carry out and finding a new viewpoint that is more attractive to Grog. Is there some inspirational image, vision or concept that can motivate Grog to action? (see chapter 9 on Passion). Go back to your Goal Diary. Look at your Goal and reread all the reasons why achieving your goal is important. Are those reasons still valid?

The third option is a bit sneakier. Here you find a way to do what you want WITHOUT Grog resisting. The Sorites Principle is very appropriate for this way of working. Here you make the action you want to do seem so small and trivial, so insignificant, it is hardly worth resisting. This can be done by the second step of applying the Sorites Principle: breaking it down into the tiniest steps possible so that as far as Grog is concerned they are easy, painless and entirely insignificant. So, going back to Martin, instead of him thinking, 'I've got to make a demo recording and take it round all the recording studios', he could make a list of much smaller steps such as...

🐾 Scripting just one track of the demo recording

🐾 Identifying just one person who could give good advice on making a demo

🐾 Finding just one person who could record and edit a voice demo

🐾 Recording just one track for the demo

🐾 Contacting just one person who might have some useful contacts in the business

🐾 Doing just one search for 'recording studios in my area'

🐾 Writing down the contact details of just one recording studio

🐾 Making just one call to ask how to present a demo

🐾 Visiting just once to present yourself face to face

I'm sure there are other similar steps Martin could add here, too.

We become lethargic because we see the next step as being too challenging. Grog feels it is too big and so it's no surprise that we find ourselves resisting. However, when broken down to smaller pieces, it's not the same.

Other methods to get you underneath the lethargy barrier are the methods of 'Minimal Entry' and 'Blitz' explained in chapter 12 on Periodic Actions, Habits and Routines.

# Apathy

Yesterday was another great day.

It was warm and sunny. I had a productive writing day. I also gave one of my first productivity workshops for this book which I'd spent a few days preparing. It went very well indeed. To tell the truth, I'd gotten myself quite anxious about it, it's quite a big step to find yourself for the first time talking to a large group of people about something that up until only recently had just been in your head. But my presentation went very well and so I had good reason to celebrate with a few friends and a few beers in the evening. Yesterday ended on a high.

But today is different.

It's a Friday morning and it's been a long slog of a week. It's not warm and sunny, either. It's a grim, rainy day. It's that sort of persistent rain that requires an umbrella but is not sufficiently heavy to make it dramatically exciting. It just persistently falls out of heavy, ironclad clouds that blot out the daylight requiring the use of artificial light even at midday. The euphoria of yesterday's success has been washed away down the drain. To summarise: I'm feeling down. And because I'm feeling down, my attitude to everything else is down, too. I'm experiencing another unwanted visitor: Apathy.

Do you remember that apathetic experience? You can't get yourself motivated. You can't be bothered. 'What's the point?' you say to yourself. It happens, admit it. Here it's useful to bear in mind that, once again, the part of our brain that is responsible for this feeling is Grog, and Grog is highly fickle. Things like rain, cold, the absence of sunshine or even just natural light can, and often does, affect his mood. There's also what I call the 'Euphoria Hangover'. Let's say you've been working towards some important stage of your goal such as a presentation, an exam or some sort of important event like a marathon or competition. If on the day of the event, you do well, if you pass or win or get a standing ovation, then you feel absolutely fantastic. You get a burst of euphoria which makes you feel marvellous. But, the next day is different. Paradoxically, the day afterwards you feel surprisingly down.[71] Your task is done and finished.

---

71- This happens even without the after-effects of alcohol.

Up until the day before you had a driving mission; you had a concrete goal that demanded your full attention. It motivated you. It inspired you. It got you bouncing out of bed in the mornings. But now it's gone, finished, dead. It leaves you with an emptiness that your friends and family simply don't understand. If you're not expecting it, then it can catch you completely off-guard.

It was for this precise reason that my graduation was such a bittersweet experience. I worked bloody hard to get my degree (in spite of what anyone else has to say on the subject). I thrived at university. My days were packed and eventful. We worked hard and played hard. Yet when it ended with my final exam (which went very well, thank you), I initially celebrated my success but soon found myself lamenting the very thing I'd spent four years striving to achieve. There was suddenly a vast hole in my life that I hadn't had the time or forethought to prepare myself for. It wasn't until a few weeks later, when the full reality of the need to find a job hit me, that I finally pulled myself together and started out on my next challenge.

I now know that this 'euphoria hangover' is perfectly normal. Especially for people like mountain climbers, Olympic gold-medallists and even newly-weds. You spend so long looking forwards to that 'big day' that when it's over you feel an unusual numbness that leaves you feeling apathetic and down.

We all experience low points in our motivation, both for external reasons (e.g. bad weather) as well as internal reasons (e.g. disappointment). It happens and is nothing to be overly concerned about - we all feel it from time to time. But it's also important to be aware of why we are feeling a bit 'off' and not to get it confused with other factors. As I explained in the previous chapter, it is easy to use a negative mood as a filter through which everything else we consider seems equally negative, futile or pointless.

In such cases I suggest revisiting your list of things that will increase your positivity. Be kind to yourself. Have a cup of tea, put on some great music and start to think about more positive things. Get out your Goal Diary and browse through it, looking at all the stuff you've succeeded in doing and all the progress you have undeniably made, which will help those clouds of apathy pass by and to allow you to start enjoying warming rays of positivity[72] which, as I look out of the window, I'm pleased to see has already started to happen.

## Distraction

*"I have two kinds of problems: the urgent and the important. The urgent are not important, and the important are never urgent."*

- Dwight Eisenhower, Former President of the United States

One of the worst enemies of the Sorites Principle is distraction. That is to say, consciously or unconsciously directing our attention to something other than that which contributes to putting in the pieces of our puzzle.

In his book *First Things First*, Stephen Covey uses what is referred to as the Eisenhower Matrix to address this problem of distractions. The matrix divides our activities into four types as illustrated below. Things that are 'important' or not and things that are 'urgent' or not.

### Figure 14: The Eisenhower Matrix

---

72- A word of warning. If your 'temporary' apathy has lasted for a few months then maybe, just maybe, you should seek medical advice.

By important, we are referring to any activity that is beneficial to us in the long term. Things that are good for our health and things that take us further towards achieving our long-term goals. Any action that helps put one of your pieces into place.

By urgent, we refer to things that demand our attention now regardless of whether we want them to or not, such as the doorbell ringing or someone in the street asking for directions.

When Dwight Eisenhower said that he had two kinds of problems: the urgent which were not important and the important which were never urgent. What he was failing to point out is that he also had a third kind of problem: The ones that were neither urgent, nor important.[73]

The important but not urgent problems are the ones that we should all be focussed on. By spending time on the truly important stuff we can avoid a lot of the other sorts of problems. They are the sort of problems that require calm and careful planning, steady work done without duress. Working towards your long-term goals using the Sorites Principle is an example of this kind of problem. As it produces insignificant change, the work cannot be considered urgent as it apparently has no effect on the present. But it is important - very important.

The urgent but not important activities are mostly due to external demands, which usually means helping others achieve their objectives by putting yours aside for a while. Such activities are writing a report for your superior, replying to texts from a friend, going to the shops for your partner or lying on the floor and pretending to be a monster for your kids. These can be classified as interruptions and how you deal with them is up to you. If you feel the person interrupting you is as important or more so than your current task, then by all means give them your attention. However, if you have truly worthwhile work to do, then close your door, turn off your phone, pretend you're not there and allow yourself the time needed to do your thing.

---

73- There is of course the fourth kind - the problems that are both important and urgent. But these are self-regulating in that they scream for your attention because if you don't give into them then things could turn out really nasty. It is worth pointing out that while important and urgent problems are perfectly valid, many of them could be avoided by careful preparation. Potential crises can be foreseen and steps taken to prevent them from happening. House fires can be avoided by installing safety measures. The same applies to many others. Prevention is better than cure. Lurching from one crisis to the next might feel that you're doing worthwhile work saving the world from disaster, but the real disaster is finding yourself in that situation in the first place. The really important problem is how to prevent the world from having to be saved at all - which brings you back to quadrant 2.

The worst problems, however (and it's the one that Dwight forgot to mention in his classic quote) are the ones in quadrant four: the ones that are neither urgent nor important. These are what we call 'pastimes' and others call 'time-wasters'. They are a problem because as they are not urgent they don't shout for our attention and you don't notice them. They are subtle, sly and get your attention not by calling to you directly. Instead, they have a hotline directly to Grog.

Such problems are the response to the question 'What shall I do now?' when you are feeling a bit lazy/tired/stressed. The answer is often to do something like watch the telly, surf the internet, use social media, reorganise your music library or play a video game. While these activities are not particularly bad in their own right, the danger they pose is the disproportional amount of time they take up of your life. They are activities that once started, suck up hours of your time while giving you precious little in return. This is why we innocently call them pastimes. The other danger with these pastimes is that Grog loves them. They are at the epicentre of Grog's comfort zone. Grog's desire for pastimes is so strong that they can become addictions. Refraining from wasting your valuable time on pastimes is not easy - in fact it can be downright painful.

I hereby solemnly confess that for almost a year, I was a Candy Crush addict. For those of you who have managed to avoid it, Candy Crush is a get-three-in-a-line video game. It's simple, attractive and highly addictive. I got up to about level 800, which, I'm sad to say, must have taken up more than a thousand hours of my life. I was even playing the damn thing on Christmas Day 2014 when I could have been spending quality time with my family. I finally realised what was happening and in a moment of fortitude and resilience, I deleted the game from my phone without backing the level up.

Time-wasters are therefore activities that serve no constructive purpose other than to satiate Grog's need to be comfy. Tell Grog to fuck off! If it's rest you need (as is perfectly normal when you are tired or stressed) then rest. However, rest properly. Real rest. The sort that leaves you feeling refreshed and replenished. The sort that involves sitting or lying down and not having your brain do anything. Having a quiet power nap is fine, half-an-hour's meditation or mindfully sitting in the park can work wonders. They are not the sort of activity that is going to suck hundreds of hours from you every month while leaving your brain with that fuzzy feeling after staring at a screen for so long.

There are perfectly good reasons for using social media or watching T.V. but please, do yourself a favour and control the amount of time you dedicate to such pastimes. Watching your favourite series, documentary or a good film for a couple of hours once in a while is fine but if its four hours every evening then that's 28 hours a week - the equivalent of over a whole day you've spent while getting nothing tangible in return. I find it so unbelievably ironic that many of us struggle to find 30 minutes a week to do real strenuous exercise, yet can effortlessly dedicate dozens of hours to unproductive time-wasters.

So what are we to do?

There's no point denying it: trying to suppress Grog is a herculean task. Grog is going to have his way eventually. So the most practical and effective way of limiting your distractions and making sure that your important, but not urgent, tasks (i.e. the activities that get you closer to your goal) are going to get done is to use the Pointers mentioned in chapter 11. As pointers work without the need for willpower or passion, they work automatically and can be immune from distractions.

The best way to do this is by using a little tool I recommend called the Weekly Piece Planner.

This is a document you prepare each weekend. Here you identify what important-but-not-urgent actions you are going to carry out this coming week, which pieces of your puzzle you are going to put into place. These pieces you list along the top of the planner. You do this because identifying these as your priorities stops them from getting lost, postponed or simply forgotten on a normal calendar. You then assign each one a place in your weekly schedule. These planned activities are then sacred and should not be replaced by interruptions (quadrant 3 activities) or time-wasters (quadrant 4 activities) - see figure 14.

## Figure 15: A Weekly Piece Planner

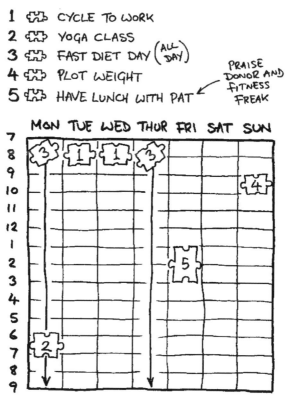

Once you have programmed in your important Soritean activities, then you can fill the rest of your time to your Grog's content, happy in the knowledge that you are not letting the unimportant get in the way of the important.

This is only part of the solution. For when the day arrives and it's time for you to do your thing, Grog will be there feeling a bit miffed and having quite forgotten the deal about letting him have his own way apart from these sacred moments of Soritean progress. Grog feels the whole thing is a pointless waste of time and will never, ever come to terms with the little by little principle. He therefore will resort to one of his predictable and well-rehearsed excuses for wriggling out of the deal.

1. I can't do it because I'm too busy.

Too busy? Too busy doing what exactly? Whatever it is, it's not as important as achieving your one chosen life-changing goal. Remember that the important should never be at the mercy of the unimportant. Use visualising to remind Grog how wonderful reaching your goal will be. Whatever you're doing at the moment is unlikely to be as important as your programmed task (though it might seem to be more urgent). Use the 10-10-10 decision-making tool described in chapter 4 on Planning Your Goal to help.

2. I won't do it today; I'll just leave it till tomorrow.

No. Tomorrow never comes. Tomorrow Grog will say the exactly the same thing. If there's room for it on the calendar tomorrow, great! You can do it now, where it was scheduled AND tomorrow! It was planned for now and it will be done now. Get used to it!

3. I won't do it today because I have a good excuse.

Any reason for Grog is a good excuse. Recognise it as an excuse and treat it as such. Which takes priority, your long-term goal or a pathetically improvised excuse? If it wasn't improvised, then why did it only just pop up now just when you are about to do your programmed activity?

4. I can't do this now because it will upset someone.

What? Someone will get upset because you are trying to achieve your life's ambition? You're the one who should be getting upset. Your activity was programmed. Who is going to get upset by that? If you couldn't devote your time to them because of a hospital appointment or a job interview, would they still be upset? If it means arriving late for an impromptu meeting, party or get-together then they should have given you more advance notice. Let them know that you're not available, you have a prior commitment. If they ask, tell them it's personal, important, serious and none of their bloody business. If it's peer pressure trying to stop you doing your important-but-not-urgent thing, then use peer pressure to support you. What would your Praise Sponsor, Support Group, Coach or Supportive Mother say if they could hear you?

5. It won't hurt if I don't do it just this once.

Oh, yes it will. In precisely the same way that the Sorites Principle works, so does back-sliding. One little slip won't hurt if it is just ONE little slip, but if it is one little slip every other time, then these build up until 'just this once' becomes such an effortless excuse that it becomes the default reaction to your call to task. Better to follow the rule of no exceptions, no excuses, no backing out. Use the Progress Calendar to increase the pressure never to break the chain.

The problems Grog sets before us are so unimaginative and easy to anticipate they would be considered a joke if it weren't for the fact they can have such a negative and harmful effect on our lives. Without exception, they are all pathetically predictable excuses that can be overcome by determination, creativity and stealth.

Suffice it to say, you are your own biggest obstacle you have to overcome and you are perfectly capable of doing it. Millions of people have discovered this for themselves and millions more will do it in the future. You can be one of them if you choose.

## Things to Think About

- There are a set of obstacles that you are going to encounter along the way to achieving your goal.
- These obstacles are no secret. In fact, they are well known and highly predictable. They are:
  - Futility
  - Self-doubt
  - The sense of failure
  - Lethargy
  - Apathy
  - Distraction
- These feelings are perfectly normal to experience from time to time.
- Our morale can be brought down by external factors like bad weather or an unpleasant argument.
- Be prepared for them. In this case, forewarned is forearmed.
- It is vital to distinguish between Urgent and Important activities.
- You can fight against distraction by recognizing urgent but non-important activities for what they are.

## Top Tips

- If you're struggling to persevere, try to observe your feelings and identify which of the six obstacles is blocking you. It's easier to find the solution if you know what the problem is.
- Address futility by remembering success is simple maths: a little every day adds up to a lot. You'll benefit from boosting your positivity, too.
- Self-doubt is faced by remembering your capabilities gradually grow along with your challenges. Right now, you only need to be able to get up that next step. Mix with the right people to get a better mind-set.

- Fear of failure: Recognise that failure is not the same as not succeeding. Failure is giving up before you have found the way to succeed. Brush up on inspiring stories or find a role model.

- Lethargy affects you if you see the task you face as too much effort. Break it down into easier parts.

- Apathy is a temporary low. Be patient and kind to yourself. It's Grog resisting. Try to entice Grog by remembering why your goal is worth the effort.

- Distraction. Isn't it amazing what you can find to do when you don't want to do any work? Don't let urgent things get in the way of your important actions. Use the Piece Planner.

- When you are thinking of giving up, recognise that you are feeling temporarily down. Wait until you're feeling more positive (see chapter on Positivity), learn from your mistakes and press on!

- Keep a progress diary. Referring to it occasionally can be very motivating to see how far you've come.

- Identify the important actions you are going to do in the forthcoming week and programme them into your agenda.

- Print off a copy of 'My Weekly Piece Planner' and use it.

- Avoid being interrupted or distracted by turning off your phone and consciously refraining to check social media, e-mails, etc.

- Learn to recognise Grog's excuses and be prepared to stand up for yourself.

- If you find the Eisenhower Matrix useful for prioritising your time, there are several apps now on the market. Search 'Eisenhower' or 'Priority' to find your preferred choice for keeping your important tasks above the urgent ones.

## Questions to Ask Yourself (and Answer)

✻ What causes you to feel that your potential goal is futile? How could you reframe the situation to reduce the feeling of futility?

✻ What obstacles have you encountered previously that have stopped you from persevering with a project?

✻ What obstacle is stopping you from progressing?

✻ What do you need to do, what problem do you need to solve in order to overcome this obstacle?

✻ How are you going to do that? If you're not sure, what would somebody else do to solve your problem?

✻ The most common obstacles to the Sorites Principle are futility, self-doubt, the fear of failure, lethargy, apathy and distraction. Which ones are you most troubled with? What are you going to do about it? When are you going to start?

# 16 Case Studies

The previous chapters have been scattered with examples of how the parts of the Sorites Principle have been put into effect. While facts and explanations engage the thinking part of our brain (our PFC), examples of real living people are useful because they connect with us on a more emotional level and when we are talking about emotions, we are talking about Grog. Grog loves stories, anecdotes and case studies. If you're listening to somebody give a boring talk and they start to tell a story, you can feel how Grog suddenly sits up and starts paying an interest. Stories in such cases are simply the ideas that the speaker wants to convey put into some social context. The way we 'feel' about them is different, we can relate to them more naturally and so they are easier to absorb and remember. As I pointed out before, getting Grog on your side is a really good idea. So to reinforce the practical application of the Sorites Principle, here are three examples set out in a little more detail for you and your Grog to absorb.

# Brenda

I first met Brenda while I was giving a presentation in Marbella. She has an unstoppable sense of humour and more than her fair share of 'laughter-lines'. She is what you might consider a modern day 'Shirley Valentine'. She took early retirement, told her husband to go stuff himself, sold up and moved to the Costa del Sol where she joined a group of friends living the Life of Riley on the Mediterranean Coast. That was five years ago. For the first few years she tried to learn Spanish with little success. One of her problems was that she was living in a cocoon of Englishness. All her friends were English speakers, she watched the English TV channels, got English newspapers and even the local restaurant was owned and run by English speakers. Another of her problems was that she was regularly visited by General Futility. In spite of annually enrolling in Spanish classes at the local Civic Centre, her teacher 'tried hard but was dull and boring'. Uninspired she didn't feel that she was making any real progress. She got frustrated by 'constantly' having to go over the same things in class (I'm sure her teacher felt the same). She had come to believe she was incapable of learning another language and that it was all a complete waste of time. Of course, one of her main handicaps was that she spent most of her time speaking, hearing, reading and writing in English. Her Spanish studies were sporadic and half-hearted and, predictably, her perseverance was less than satisfactory. One of Brenda's mistakes was that she was relying on her own opinion to gauge whether she was making any progress or not. Nevertheless, Brenda felt very bad about not speaking the language of her new place of residence and she was determined to set things right.

Following the Sorites Principle Brenda embarked upon a coherent plan of action which included the following:

✱ She needed to engage her Grog. She needed to make improving her Spanish interesting and fun. She also needed peer pressure. So she started her own group of three friends, which soon became seven. The magnificent seven they called themselves, quite appropriate for a bunch of retired women. From the very start, they were all similarly frustrated by their lack of Spanish and were keen to make some 'real' progress. They would meet twice a week: once in a 'Not English' restaurant (which was a different venue each time) for a study-lunch and once in the home of one of the members where they would watch a Spanish film on DVD with Spanish subtitles.

🌸 When they met in the restaurant, they would insist that the menu would be in Spanish and that the waiter would talk to them in Spanish. They took it in turns to translate the menu. Anything on the menu that they didn't understand would be noted and learnt for the following week.

🌸 They made an effort to get to know the local Spanish population by having a guest speaker come to their meeting who would talk about their interests. It turned out that the mother of the girl from the Post Office was the winner of the prestigious local Spanish Omelette competition and they got her to come round and give them a cookery class one day.

🌸 Once word got around about the Magnificent Seven, they started to get invited to various places. They got taken round a local vineyard and were shown how wine was made. They got shown round a local paper manufacture and learned how paper was made. One old neighbour came round and tried to teach them how to play the guitar. They even got this woman to come round to give them a presentation about sex-toys which she said was absolutely hysterical. Even though they didn't buy anything they did learn a lot of new vocabulary!

🌸 Instead of a study-book each of the group would carry a little notebook - their version of a Goal Diary - where new vocabulary and useful expressions were noted down and shared at the meetings.

🌸 Brenda bought a set of multi-coloured Post-its which she used to label things around the house and for useful phrases of the week.

🌸 They also started to discover Spanish music. They would listen to songs and try to understand the lyrics. Sometimes, one of them photocopied the lyrics and then tippexed out some of the words as a sort of gap-fill exercise. As they started to discover Spanish music Brenda would listen to it for pleasure instead of her usual listening selection from the 60's and 70's.

✤ There was real peer pressure to improve. Everyone made an effort to come up with ideas, activities or games. One of them brought in Trivial Pursuits in Spanish, and as Brenda admitted, "We were all rubbish at it, but it was a laugh anyhow." Anything that was new and seemed useful was presented and noted down. Anyone who didn't contribute at the 'useful words I've learnt this week' part of the meeting was 'severely chastised'.

✤ They actively helped each other. If someone knew something that the others didn't, then they would teach it to them. It made everyone feel useful. There was real learning and progress taking place.

✤ Rather than estimating her own progress, she started to count how many hours 'studying' she had completed each day on the understanding that any mental application to speaking Spanish was positive.

✤ They got hold of past exam papers for the Spanish as a Foreign Language Diploma or DELE (*Diploma de Español como Lengua Extranjera*), the A1 level and practised the parts they didn't know.

✤ All six of them sat their first official Spanish language exam and all six of them passed with flying colours. As Brenda said "It was like being a kid again. It was so exciting. When I saw my result it was like YES! I've done it. I've done it! We were all just a bunch of giggly girls."

## Ivan

When I spoke to the director of my local gym about the research I was doing for this book, he immediately suggested I talk to Ivan, a fitness coach who works there. I described Ivan in chapter 5 on Prizes and Punishments when I explained how he uses judicial praise to motivate his clients. But his work and coaching techniques involve much more than just giving out praise. Over several coffees in the neighbouring bar, Ivan was keen to earnestly underline the importance of everything he does as a sports and fitness coach. He lives for what he does and approaches his subject with a natural passion and positive enthusiasm that are so contagious they almost make me want to leap into some Lycra and start pumping away.

✹ The first thing Ivan does with a new coachee is to establish rapport. Peer pressure between coach and coachee only works if the two connect and get on with each other. He tries to find out as much about the person as possible, partly because he is genuinely interested but also because it allows him to identify what the two of them have in common, such as hobbies, music or football teams. He knows that some people like to work out to music while others don't, some like being talked to while working out, others find it distracting. He knows that some people respond well to being touched (e.g. on the shoulder or upper arm or a motivational pat on the back), while others shy away from physical contact. He tries to understand what makes each person tick. He uses that to increase the rapport he has with each and thus, to increase the perceived peer pressure. He then leverages that pressure further by establishing that from here on, it is the two of them working together. If the coachee doesn't follow through with the exercises or diet, then the coachee is letting both of them down.

✹ He also tries to find out WHY that person has come to him for help. What is it they want? What are their dreams and fears? What worries them or gets them out of bed in the morning? He's looking for what they are passionate about - what emotions are driving them.

✹ During those moments when they are struggling to complete their exercise programme he gets them to visualise what they will be able to do when fit, how they will feel to show off their bodies on the beach or fit into the clothes that they have always wanted.

✹ He works with the coachee to design a mutually agreed weekly routine. This is then printed out for the client to have as a pointer - a clear guide to what he or she shall be doing at what time and on what day.

✹ On the other hand, Ivan has learned not to be too demanding on his coachees. He's learned how far he can push them before their Grogs start to resist. In his early days as a coach he organised a Saturday morning cross-country running group, but he struggled to make it a success. He admits that at the beginning, he was far too demanding with punctuality, attendance and the effort his runners put in. People started dropping out as the whole thing became too serious. Ivan stopped being demanding and concentrated on what each of the runners wanted to get out of the group. The group became a success.

➕ He puts great importance on empathising the following with each coachee when they start each session: how are they feeling today, are they on a high or a low. He uses a colour-coding system where 'red' is highly motivated and positive and purple is the other extreme - feeling crap about everything. He monitors each person's colour (by asking, not by sight - I just wanted that to be perfectly clear), to make sure people's morale is heading in the right direction.

➕ He makes sure his fitness sessions are fun, that his coachees smile, laugh and enjoy themselves.

➕ As well as what his coachees do in the gym, he also works with them to consider what they do outside the gym, what good and bad habits they have, whether or not they use the stairs instead of the lift, or if they walk/cycle to work.

➕ Ivan also gets the coachees to observe and regulate their diet. He encourages them to set up a whole series of pointers and positive habits that are all pieces of the goal. He works with them to prepare a weekly menu. They work on not only what should be eaten but also when and how. For example, by eating their food more slowly and trying to savour it. He suggests that they should not only eat healthier foods but that they slightly reduce the size of the portions of food they have.

➕ He gives them lots of praise for keeping to their diet.

➕ He forbids them certain types of non-healthy foods. Sweets, chocolates and popcorn with the threat of a gruelling punishment if he finds out they have had any during their get-fit programme.

➕ He encourages his coachees to get into the habit of drinking water regularly - as soon as they wake up, before every meal and before going to bed.

✤ He gets them to stop buying sugary drinks and get the 'diet' version of their favourite soft drinks instead.

✤ If they insist on drinking alcohol, then he gets them to use smaller glasses.

✤ He helps them tackle snacking by getting the coachee to learn to postpone snacking for even just a few seconds to start with. Fighting the urge to eat between meals by just a few minutes at first. He also gets them to visualise the snack going directly on their waistline.

✤ If possible, the coachee substitutes snacking for some other activity. Instead of going to the bar or wherever those extra calories are a temptation, they should find a quiet space to meditate or to go and do twenty push-ups or sit-ups.

✤ He gets his coachees to text him when they have been 'virtuous', explaining what they have managed to do and he always replies with plenty of praise.

✤ If necessary, he suggests they join another group that will increase peer pressure and increase their desire to 'keep to the path', such as a weekend runners' group or cycling club. The gym has its own version of weightwatchers, which is also well attended.

✤ If he has two or more coachees that he thinks might get along together he encourages them to become get-fit buddies.

✤ He sets clear objectives. He uses several measurables. Apart from just the coachee's weight, he uses body fat (by 'pinching' the skin at the waist. I tried it, though my 'pinch' is more like a 'grope'), waist measurement, heart-rate recovery, blood pressure and running times for the coachees who go cross-country with him.

✤ These measurements are all charted to give a clear visual feedback about how they are progressing, each one with a clearly defined objective so they can see how near they are to completion.

✤ He always makes sure that his coachees have a clear idea of what they want to achieve, why they want to achieve it and how they are going to achieve it. He makes sure that they realise the journey to their destination is going to be a long and arduous one at times, but that it is well within their capabilities and ultimately worth it.

❖ And after all that, he gives them even more praise.

## Ian

As I pointed out in the introduction, this book is a testament unto itself. If it weren't for the material that I've covered (and to be honest there's more here than I originally expected), I would never have made it to the end. It's taken me the best part of a year of solid perseverance which has been very trying at times. To use a bizarre Back-to-the-Future type of logic - If it weren't for this book, this book wouldn't exist. Just to prove I walk my talk as far as the Sorites Principle is concerned, here are all the techniques I used to keep myself going.

❖ I started out with a clear objective: to write this book and get it published.

❖ I set myself a deadline of one year and an easily measurable target: a word count of 75,000. (6,250 words per month or about 1,500 words per week).

❖ I drew up a list of all the little pieces of the puzzle I needed to do, including researching how to write a book, how to get published, researching writing courses, putting the word out about my project, networking, improving my presentation skills, adjusting my timetable, making more time by reducing the number of coaching clients, improving my website and incorporating my book onto it, learning how to talk about my subject without coming across as a moron (I'm still working on that bit), setting times to read, write and research, learning new habits and unlearning old ones.

❖ I started new routines: getting up two hours earlier and writing while the family was asleep, carrying around my notebook and writing whenever the pixie of inspiration came to visit.

* On days when I wasn't so inspired, it helped to just type up my handwritten notes onto the computer - this usually led to more ideas.

* I drew myself up a progress plotter with the line of intended progress clearly marked, I kept regular track of my word count and I'm pleased to say I was almost always ahead of schedule, which my Grog really liked.

* In the first few months, I started by programming on my Google-calendar when I was going to write. Though again, after a while, I had got into the habit and no longer needed this pointer. In fact, towards the end, I found that on the days I didn't do any writing I started to get withdrawal symptoms - feeling nervous or as if I had an 'itch' that needed to be scratched.

* I did, however, keep up with the pointer/habit of setting up my laptop and setting out my notes the night before so when I came downstairs in the morning it would be all set out before me.

* At the end of each writing session I calculated what percentage of the book I had completed (based on a target of 75,000 words). Grog liked being able to see that I'd written (for example) 3.7% of my book.

* I made an effort to talk to people about my project which helped my morale as their reaction was almost always positive and supportive and often produced new examples.

* I got myself a Goal Diary, which I also used to jot down ideas.

* I gave out chapters to friends and family to review and to help with peer pressure.

* I made notes on my iPhone whenever I got an idea I wanted to include in my book.

* I reviewed old notes from my coaching clients about what had been stopping them from achieving their goals and how they had overcome those obstacles.

✦ I leveraged my passion by often thinking of what words of encouragement my father would have given me and how proud he would have been to have a book written by his son.

✦ I increased peer pressure by setting up a bet with a friend, who is also writing a book, on who could get published first.

✦ I did research. Lots of research. When I was too tired to write, I read or watched TED Talks.

✦ I interviewed people who were involved in Sorites Principle type activities.

✦ I read lots of books (see recommended reads).

✦ At the beginning, I kept a star chart of the days that I wrote with a prize for hitting my monthly quota. My first prize was getting my car professionally cleaned on the inside which it needed badly after years of ferrying the twins to school and back every day. The star chart proved useful to start with but I stopped after two months as I found the Progress Plotter to be enough.

✦ I made a conscious effort to sit down and write even when I wasn't inspired. This is one of the main takeaways from Steven Pressfield's *The War of Art*: a must read for any would-be author.

✦ I contacted other people who wrote and talked to them about their experiences.

✦ On the dark days, general futility came and whispered in my ear with a giant megaphone that nobody is going to be interested in this rubbish and that I was wasting my time. Fortunately, I had written down comments from friends who thought differently. I referred to my goal diary cum notebook often, as well as my progress plotter to keep general futility away from the door.

✦ I envisioned how it would feel publishing my book in the future - what it would be like to go around giving presentations, interviews and book signings. I imagined holding a freshly printed copy in my hands.

✤ I read up on how to get published and realised that I would need to sharpen up my public speaking, so I joined the local Toastmasters Club and rapidly learned how much I needed to improve.

✤ I started to research publishing companies in the area and started to build bridges, brush up my C.V., improve my website and network in the publishing sector.

✤ I'm pleased to say that the publisher I chose - or would it be fairer to say that she chose me, is marvellous. Gillian Pollock from Guid Publishing has been as great a source of peer-pressure and positivity as I could ever have asked from anyone.

✤ I actively sought to give productivity workshops about my subject before this book was published to get to grips with talking coherently about it in front of a public.

✤ As the days got closer to my deadline and it all started coming together, the emotional motivation of being within sniffing distance of the finishing line turned into a dominating factor. There were even days when I was so enthusiastic that I forgot to add my progress on the plotter. Just being able to tell those who enquired that I was 'almost finished' and see their impressed reaction was a real thrill.

# Questions

❉ Which parts of these case studies resonate with you the most?

❉ Which parts of these case studies could you adapt and include to help you persevere?

❉ How would you do it?

❉ Can you think of anyone you know who is persevering towards their goal? How many of the techniques mentioned in these pages are they using? If you don't know, why not buy them a drink and ask them?

 # 17 Conclusion

We have been on a journey. We have seen that apparently insignificant change when carried out regularly and in a constant direction will inevitably lead to impressive results. We have seen that this process can be divided into three basic steps: Planning, the Pieces of the Puzzle and Perseverance. We have identified eight techniques to increase our power of perseverance: Prizes, Progress, Passion, Peer Pressure, Pointers, Periodic Actions, Patience and Positivity.

I said at the beginning of this book I would like to propose that the journey of a thousand miles does not begin with a single step, but with a lot of planning and preparation. Applying what we have covered to this hiking metaphor, we can now be more specific by saying the journey of a thousand miles begins with clearly identifying your destination, by writing down its address so it will be obvious when you get there. You need to identify why you are doing this, why it is worth the effort and what the benefits are of reaching your goal. You need to consider each possible route and choose the best one. It should be clearly marked on the map - a good map showing all the necessary details. This route should then be broken up into simple daily stages with all the possible resting places marked.

You need to make sure you have all the necessary equipment (including cash, corn plasters and extra power for your phone) or check that at least you'll be able to acquire material along the way. You can give yourself little rewards for completing each stage if the satisfaction of completion is not sufficient. Praise yourself for every stage finished. Put a little gold star on your map or get praise from your Praise Sponsor. As you walk, you need to fix your sights on the next rock just ahead, or the next tree and put out of your mind that your intended resting place for tonight is still twenty miles away, and certainly try to forget that the number of miles to your final destination is still in three figure numbers.

Cross off each stage of the journey you have done to keep clear that satisfactory progress is being made and all is going according to plan. Find something that you enjoy about your journey, something to get passionate about. You could read the history of the places you'll be passing through or the stories of travellers who have been this way before you. Walk along in the company of others, talk to fellow travellers coming the other way who can inform you of the difficulties ahead, have people at the side lines who can cheer you on. Recruit the help of a hiking coach, someone who understands what you're going through and can help motivate you during those dark moments when general futility comes to visit.

Keep to a routine. Prepare your things the night before so that in the morning getting up, ready and off is easy and effortless. Cultivate good habits: look after your boots to keep them in good condition both outside and inside. Keep a Goal Diary, noting down your daily progress and the useful nuggets of wisdom you discover along the way. Get into the habit of smiling and saying hello to fellow travellers to keep yourself positive and sociable. Eat and drink responsibly.

Don't focus on the difficult part of walking: distract yourself by focussing on the local flora and fauna, chatting with your hiking friends or thinking about all the reasons why you are on this trip. Stay positive, don't complain about your aching legs and feet. Keep away from people who will demotivate you, bring you down or tempt you into bad habits. Keep getting up each morning, put your boots on and making sure that you keep taking one small step after another in the right direction.

If you can do all of these, you will enjoy your journey, which cannot fail to be rewarding, worthwhile and inevitably successful because, as we have seen, the constant application of insignificant actions when coherently focussed will inevitably lead to dramatically significant results.

This is the Sorites Principle.

 Appendices

# The Sorites Principle Summary

The constant application of insignificant actions when coherently focussed will inevitably lead to dramatically significant results

---

Many big important changes we want to make happen gradually, little by little over time

Paradoxically, these changes go unnoticed precisely because they happen gradually

This apparent lack of change leads to frustration, a sense of futility and low morale

We can improve our ability to achieve big things via little actions by following 3 steps

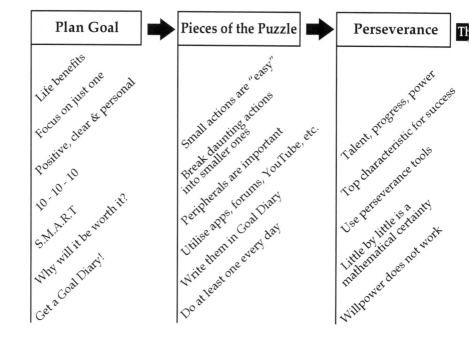

| Plan Goal | Pieces of the Puzzle | Perseverance |
|---|---|---|
| Life benefits | Small actions are "easy" | Talent, progress, power |
| Focus on just one | Break daunting actions into smaller ones | Top characteristic for success |
| Positive, clear & personal | Peripherals are important | Use perseverance tools |
| 10 - 10 - 10 | Utilise apps, forums, YouTube, etc. | Little by little is a mathematical certainty |
| S.M.A.R.T | Write them in Goal Diary | Willpower does not work |
| Why will it be worth it? | Do at least one every day | |
| Get a Goal Diary! | | |

## Prizes

Praise sponsors · Points system · Reward actions not goals · Certificates · Good for short term · Star Chart · ... and Punishments · Do it or burn it · Shame yourself into it

## Progress

Vitally important · Powerful motivator · Track measurables · Progress Calendar · Prepare progress · Deadlines · Set milestones · Use against futility · Log progress in diary

## Passion

Grog · Passion is a powerful motivator · Get to know your Grog · What inspires you? · Images: real & mental · Stories · Films, books, etc. · Heroes & role models · Quotes

## Peer Pressure

Powerful & underestimated · Promises/contracts · Toxic peer pressure · Goal buddies · Get a coach · Use forums · Join useful peer group · Set up your own group · Local or virtual

## Pointers

When too tired to think · Pointers prompt actions · Program into agenda · When/Then · Prepare in advance · Smartphone · Post-its · Objects · Clothes

## Periodic Action

We are creatures of habit · Periodic actions occur without having to think · Cultivate good habits · Replace bad with good · Routines are like Lego · Minimal entry · One-minute blitz

## Patience

Lack of patience is serious problem · Mathematical certainty · Avoid too much, too soon · Focus on next step · Review Progress Plotter · Internal distraction · Ignore long-term goal

## Positivity

Be aware of morale · Is it worth it? · Affirmations · Gratitude · Fresh air & sunlight · Exercise · Back to nature · Learn to relax · Altruism

 # Paradoxes

If you're still a bit unsure about it, a paradox is a statement that contradicts itself. It appears to be true and wrong at the same time. For example: consider these two sentences together:

*"The following sentence is true."*
*"The previous sentence is false."*

Some paradoxes are based on logic, such as Russell's paradox, which is to do with making lists of things. He asks the question "Would a list of all the lists in the world that do not include themselves, include itself?" which can give you a headache just trying to think about it. If Russell's paradox is too taxing, consider the more conceptually digestible paradox that says 'nobody shops at Sainsbury's because the queues are too long'. Does this tell us that people shop there or not? But not all paradoxes are based on logic.

Take the example of the *Ship of Theseus* from philosophy which considered the issue of whether a ship repaired over time by replacing each of its wooden parts would remain the same ship. A modern day equivalent is Trigger's broom. Trigger is a character out of the British sitcom *Only Fools and Horses* who claims to have owned the same broom for 20 years. He admits the handle has been replaced 14 times and the head 17 times but for Trigger it's still (paradoxically) the same broom (which he proves by showing a photo of when he bought it).[74]

Paradoxes can also take the form of images which appear to contradict themselves. The works of Maurits Cornelis Escher are great examples of this using perspective-based paradoxes where things apparently in the distance are based in the foreground or flights of stairs which ascend only to finally arrive at the point where they started, such as his 1960 work *Scaffold Ascending and Descending.*

---

74- For any Terry Pratchett fans there is also the dwarfish axe mentioned in The Fifth Elephant. The axe has been passed down through the family for generations: sometimes the head needed replacing, other times the shaft, still more times the eye or the bit, but it's still paradoxically considered to be the original ancestral axe.

My mother-in-law is another example. The temperature in our house is 20°C. On some days, she will proclaim that it's far too hot in the house and that we're wasting money on heating. On others, 20°C is far too cold and we don't know how to heat our home properly. Is 20°C too hot or too cold? Or can it be both at the same time? It's a paradox!

To get to the point, the Sorites Paradox (also known as the Paradox of the Heap) is a logic-based paradox derived from considering what happens when you start with a heap of sand and then one by one remove each grain of sand from that heap. The paradox arises from the combination of the two key ideas (or predicates). The first one is that a large pile of sand can indeed be considered a heap. The second one is that the removal of just one grain of sand is so insignificant that it does not stop the heap from still being considered a heap. Or to put it another way, if you were standing there looking at a large heap of sand, taking one grain away would not stop you from perceiving it to be a heap of sand.

To be more specific, if the heap were a modest one of say one million grains (which would merely be about a bucket's worth) then we could represent this process mathematically as follows:

1,000,000 grains is a heap.
Taking 1 grain from a heap makes no difference to it being a heap.
So if 1,000,000 grains is a heap, then 999,999 grains is also a heap.
Taking 1 grain from a heap makes no difference to it being a heap.
So if 999,999 grains is a heap, then 999,998 grains is also a heap.
Taking 1 grain from a heap makes no difference to it being a heap.
So if 999,998 grains is a heap, then 999,997 grains is…
…and so on until…
…So if 4 grains is a heap, then 3 grains is also a heap.
Taking 1 grain from a heap makes no difference to it being a heap.
So if 3 grains is a heap, then 2 grains is also a heap.
Taking 1 grain from a heap makes no difference to it being a heap.
So if 2 grains is a heap, then 1 grain is also a heap.

But obviously just one grain isn't a heap. So the question begged is 'What is the minimum number of grains of sand needed to constitute a heap? But, whatever number you come up with, it will be unsatisfactory because a) it would be an arbitrary number which other people might not agree with, and b) whatever number you came up with, it would not prevent the observation that one grain less is such an insignificant difference that the heap minus one grain would still be perceived as a heap, too.

You can even start the opposite way round. You begin with one grain (not a heap) then add one more grain (not a heap, either) and keep adding grains. However, as the addition of just one grain doesn't convert something that wasn't a heap into a heap, then you're really no better off.

I think the best solution to the Sorites Paradox is my own: the 'Gibbs Solution', which is also based on two predicates: 1) There are things in life which are important that deserve your attention, 2) The solution to the Sorites Paradox is not one of them. This is an elegant solution because it means that you can leave it and go and have a nice cup of tea, spend time with your loved ones or get back to work with peace of mind and concentrate on living the fulfilling and prosperous life of your choosing by putting in the pieces of your own puzzle one by one.

 # Free Resources

Free stuff. Free stuff is great, isn't it? Especially if it's something you actually want, rather than something that somebody else is trying to get rid of, or one of those 'freebies' that morally obliges you to buy something else. I'm happy to point out that neither is the case here, as a) I'm not getting rid of anything, and b) as you've bought this book already. It's more of a 'thank you' freebie than anything else.

So what's up for grabs?

Throughout this book I refer to certain perseverance tools such as the:

* Star Chart

* Progress Calendar

* Progress Plotter

* Weekly Planner

Each of these is relatively easy to produce by hand if you're the creative sort who likes making your own stuff. If, however, you're like me and prefer not to spend your valuable time reinventing the wheel, especially when someone has been kind enough to let you print it off free of charge (for personal use), then go to www.guid-publications.com/soritesworksheets/ and help yourself.

I hope you find that your new and improved powers of perseverance enable you to achieve some of those big, important things that until now, you might have thought beyond you.

All the very best,

Ian

# ⬛ The Lemon Test

The Lemon test is a simple demonstration of how your body can be 'tricked'.

Close your eyes... actually, it might be a better idea to read the whole of this first. Try to remember the general idea and only then have a go at doing it with your eyes closed. Anyway, as I was saying... close your eyes and imagine that you are holding a lemon. Visualise its shape, its colour. Notice the texture of its peel, how the light shines off it. Notice the little details of where the lemon was connected to the tree and any little blemishes on the body of the lemon. Feel the weight of the lemon in your hand. Feel its firmness. Squeeze it gently and feel its resistance to the pressure of your fingers. Notice its slight lemony smell. Now imagine that you have a small sharp knife in your other hand (swap hands if you prefer). Imagine that you slowly and carefully, without any risk of hurting yourself, start to cut the lemon in half. You feel the pressure of the knife on the lemon and you notice the slight muffled sound as you begin cutting through the body of the lemon. You notice how the blade of the knife is wetted by the juice of the lemon as it emerges from the lemon's centre. You might notice an increased resistance of the knife as it encounters a lemon pip or two, as it cuts through the soft, moist interior of the fruit. As you continue to slowly cut, the two halves begin to open and separate, revealing the flower-shaped interior of the lemon until the cutting is complete and you have two halves.

Put down the knife and one half of the lemon, keeping the other half in your hand. Again, change hands if you prefer. Bring the half lemon closer to your face so you can see it better. Notice the glistening detail of the exposed cut. Observe the thickness of the peel, yellow on the outside, whiter on the inside. Notice how the smell of the lemon has now strongly increased as the lemony fragrance pleasantly fills your nostrils. Observe how the juice of the lemon has started to trickle downward forming a drip along the bottom cut and watch, as you gently, but firmly start to squeeze, how this droplet increases until it inevitable grows so big that it naturally falls to the floor. Now bring the fruit up close to your mouth. Breathe in the lemon-soaked air. Feel the texture of the lemon on your lips and notice how the acidity of the juice can already be felt penetrating the tiny cracks in the skin of your lips. Now prepare to put the lemon fully to your mouth and to suck some of the juice...

Now you can open your eyes and stop imagining. By now, you should have noticed that your body, mental and physical reactions, your saliva production and the nerves of your lips, tongue and mouth have all reacted. Maybe you noticed an increase in stress as the juice dripped on the floor. Even though it was all imagined, your body reacted as though it were real.

#  Perseverance Quotes

(in alphabetical order)

"All good work is done the way ants do things: little by little." - Lafcadio Hearn

"A river cuts through rock not because of its strength but because of its persistence" - Jim Watkins

"Dreams are just ideas until you take the first step to make them real" - Ramona Foster"

"Every step towards your dream today is a step away from your regret tomorrow" - Dr. Steve Maraboli

"Failure will never overtake me if my determination to succeed is strong enough" - Og Mandino

"Go as long as you can and then take another step" - Anonymous

"Good, better, best. Never let it rest. 'Til your good is better and your better is best" - St. Jerome

"Grant me the serenity to accept the things I cannot change, the courage to change the things I can, and the wisdom to know the difference" - Reinhold Niebuhr

"Great works are performed not by strength but by perseverance" - Samuel Peterson

"I may not be there yet, but I'm closer than I was yesterday" - José N. Harris

"If you chase two rabbits, you will not catch either one" - A Russian Proverb

"If you don't know where you're going, you are never going to get there" - The Sorites Principle

"If you're going through hell, keep going" - Winston Churchill

"It does not matter how slowly you go as long as you do not stop." - Confucius

"Isn't it amazing what you can find to do when you don't want to do any work?" - John E. Firth

"Just like a jigsaw, if you put in a piece of your project every day you will inevitably achieve your dream" - The Sorites Principle

"Little by little, a little becomes a lot" - Tanzanian Proverb

"Little by little, one walks far" - Peruvian Proverb

"Little by little you fill the sink and drop by drop you fill the barrel" - A Catalan Proverb

"Nothing is particularly hard if you divide it into small jobs" - Henry Ford

"Permanence, perseverance and persistence in spite of all obstacles, discouragements, and impossibilities: It is this, that in all things distinguishes the strong soul from the weak." - Thomas Carlyle

"Put your heart, mind, and soul into even your smallest acts. This is the secret of success." - Swami Sivananda

"Setting goals is the first step in turning the invisible into the visible." - Tony Robbins

"Sometimes the smallest step in the right direction ends up being the biggest step of your life." - Naeem Callaway

"Start by doing what's necessary; then do what's possible; and suddenly you are doing the impossible." - Francis of Assisi

"Start small. Every goal can be broken down into smaller steps. Commit to just one small step on the path and you're on your way to success." - The Sorites Principle

"Step by step and the thing is done." - Charles Atlas

"Step by step, stair by stair, be patient, believe, before long you'll be there." - Marc Erlbaum

"Success is no accident. It is hard work, perseverance, learning, studying, sacrifice and most of all, the love of what you are doing or learning to do." - Pele

"Success will never be a big step in the future, success is a small step taken just now." - Jonatan Mårtensson

"The first step toward getting somewhere is to decide that you are not going to stay where you are." - J.P. Morgan

"The journey of a thousand miles begins with a single step." - Lao Tzu

"The man who moves a mountain begins by carrying away small stones." - Confucius

"The road is long, but so long as I move forward, step by step, day by day, my success is a mathematical certainty." - The Sorites Principle

"The secret of getting ahead is getting started." - Mark Twain

"We can do anything we want so long as we stick to it long enough." - Hellen Keller

"When in doubt, just take the next small step." - Paulo Coelho

"You are never too old to set another goal or to dream a new dream." - C.S. Lewis

"You cannot expect miracles to happen overnight. Be patient, be loving, and little by little the change you seek will come." - Leon Brown

"Your destiny is determined by the choices you make. Choose now. Choose well." - Tony Robbins

# ■Bibliography

*Authentic Happiness* - Martin Seligman

*Bounce* - Matthew Syed

*Coaching for Performance* - Peter Whitmore

*Decisive* - Chip and Dan Heath

*First Things First* - Stephen R. Covey

*Getting Things Done* - David Allen

*Losing My Virginity* - Richard Branson

*Mindfulness* - Mark Williams and Dr. Danny Penman

*Mini Habits* - Stephen Guise

*Not Exactly* - Kees Van Deemter

*Outliers* - Malcolm Gladwell

*Spark!* – Dr. Peter J. Ratey

*Switch* - Chip and Dan Heath

*The Chimp Paradox* - Steve Peters

*The Happiness Hypothesis* - Jonathan Haidt

*The House at Pooh Corner* - A. A. Milne

*The One Thing* - Gary Keller and Jay Papasan

*The Power of Habit* - Charles Duhigg

*The Power of Others* - Michael Bond

*The Progress Principle* - Teresa Amabile and Steven Kramer

*The War of Art* - Steven Pressfield

*Willpower* - Roy F. Baumeister and John Tierney

*Your Brain At Work* - David Rock

# Biography

Productivity trainer, public speaker, life coach, business owner, company director, playwright and now author, Ian Gibbs was born in Sheffield, England where his family was convinced that due to his shy, retiring nature he would never venture far from home. After doing his degree in Theoretical Physics, Astronomy and Astrophysics at St. Andrews, Scotland and his Postgrad in Education in Cambridge, he decided he'd had enough of the crap weather and went to work in Barcelona for a year - or maybe two - to teach English. One day he woke up to realise he's now been there for 25 years, during which time he has set up one of Europe's leading educational Theatre-in-English companies: IPA Productions, he has written regular life-style columns for two Spanish magazines, was the guest blogger for the local business networking group. He now coaches the expat community and gives business training sessions on productivity and public speaking. When he is not training, coaching or speaking, he writes. He is the creator of 10 plays for children, 3 comic strips, 3 plays for adults, one bilingual story book, the USSB model for improving personal productivity and numerous personal development articles. The Sorites Principle is his first book.

He is married, has two children and a bouncy dog.

For more of our books, visit: www.guid-publications.com

29326231R00174

Printed in Great Britain
by Amazon